1995

University of St. Francis
GEN 809 S427

W9-BBI-851

Narrative and Culture

Edited by

Janice Carlisle and Daniel R. Schwarz

THE UNIVERSITY OF GEORGIA PRESS

Athens and London

LIBRARY
College of St. Francis
JOLIET, ILLINOIS

© 1994 by the University of Georgia Press
Athens, Georgia 30602
All rights reserved
Designed by Mary Mendell
Set in 10.5 on 13 Berkeley Medium by Tseng Information Systems
Printed and bound by Thomson-Shore
The paper in this book meets the guidelines for
permanence and durability of the Committee on
Production Guidelines for Book Longevity of the
Council on Library Resources.

Printed in the United States of America
98 97 96 95 94   C   5 4 3 2 1
98 97 96 95 94   P   5 4 3 2 1
Library of Congress Cataloging in Publication Data
Narrative and culture / edited by Janice Carlisle and Daniel R. Schwarz.
p.   cm.
Includes bibliographical references.
ISBN 0-8203-1572-9 (alk. paper). — ISBN 0-8203-1573-7 (pbk. : alk. paper)
1. Narration (Rhetoric)—Congresses.   2. Canon (Literature)—
Congresses.   3. Literature and society—Congresses.   4. Language
and culture—Congresses.   5. Motion pictures—Social aspects
—Congresses.   6. Motion pictures and literature—Congresses.
I. Carlisle, Janice.   II. Schwarz, Daniel R.
PN212.N373 1994
809—dc20   93-9953
British Library Cataloging in Publication Data available

809
S427

40.08

BVT $40.08

1-4-95

Contents

152, 700

Acknowledgments

We would like to thank, first and foremost, Karen Orchard of the University of Georgia Press: her support has been crucial to the completion of this project. Kelly Caudle exhibited great patience and care in shepherding the manuscript through copyediting and production. Janice Carlisle also thanks Evan DuVall for his diligent work on the bibliographical references and Sandra Haro for all the word processing she did and for the good cheer with which she did it. As always, Phillis Molock ably assisted Dan Schwarz, and she deserves more gratitude than he can express. Finally, we both thank the Society for the Study of Narrative Literature and the Department of English of Tulane University for providing the occasion on which earlier versions of these essays were presented.

Revised versions of the following essays appear by permission:

Nina Auerbach, "Revelations on Pages and Stages," *Victorian Literature and Culture* 21 (1993).

Jay Clayton, "The Narrative Turn in Minority Fiction," *American Literary History* 2 (1990): 375–93. By permission of Oxford University Press.

Vera Mark, "Cultural Pastiches: Intertextualities in the Moncrabeau Liars' Festival Narratives," *Cultural Anthropology* 6 (May 1991). By permission of the American Anthropological Association. Not for further reproduction.

Janice Carlisle

Introduction

The two terms that join to entitle this collection of essays, *narrative* and *culture,* seem to point to phenomena so ubiquitous and so inescapable that one need only conclude that, like language and consciousness, they are universal human conditions. The terms themselves have been used— and continue to be used—as if they apply everywhere and always in the same ways. In fact, however, they often mask the exclusionary tactics of those invoking them. In a recent attempt to define *culture,* Stephen Greenblatt complains that the term may be so "vague and encompass- ing" that it is scarcely "useful to students of literature," and the same may be said of *narrative,* which Fredric Jameson takes to be "the central func- tion or *instance* of the human mind." Yet this conventional generality of reference is misleading. J. Hillis Miller declares that "nothing seems more natural and universal to human beings than telling stories," and Raymond Williams may have used *culture* as a label for "all our common experience,"[1] but such claims to universality disguise the partiality and specificity of the often unacknowledged assumptions on which they are based. This collection of essays, emerging as it does from the occasion of the fifth annual Narrative Conference, participates in the critical trends that both question and, to some extent, validate global definitions of the terms that delimit its primary subject—the relation between the telling of tales and the engagement of their tellers and listeners in the practices of specific societies.

Organized in three categories, these essays chart the interpenetrations between narrative and culture in three distinct though interconnected areas of inquiry: canonical texts, visual narratives, and narrative reconstructions of earlier stories. The ways in which Daniel R. Schwarz and I have construed these categories reflect some of the more recent changes in our discipline. As Alan Nadel, the program chair of the 1993 Narrative Conference, confirmed, and as my own earlier experience in that role suggested, Toni Morrison has recently become the most canonical of authors if that title is accorded to writers whose works attract the attention of academic critics: for the conferences in both 1990 and 1993, her novels were the subject of more paper proposals than the works of any other author.[2] As a group, the essays in this collection also attest to one of the distinctive strengths of the conference at which they were first presented: its emphasis on interdisciplinary exchange and engagement. Even the essays that deal with more traditionally canonical literary texts epitomize that quality. Nina Auerbach, for example, discusses novels, theater, and painting; Mary Lou Emery treats sexological science and modern fiction as they engage issues of anthropological and ethnographic significance; and Daniel R. Schwarz places poetry in the context of painting. Classical fiction in this collection is featured along with postmodern media—photography, film, and television—just as the collection begins and ends with essays dealing with performances, those enacted on the British stage and those presented at a contemporary popular festival in southwestern France. Like many papers presented at the Narrative Conference, these essays cross national boundaries and historical periods almost as often as they move beyond disciplinary boundaries.

This interdisciplinary approach is, of course, one of the critical and theoretical trends that have encouraged the reconsideration of the traditional definitions of both *narrative* and *culture* as well as the formulation of new ones. Over the last several decades, the emergence of cultural studies as an alternative methodology and subject matter within departments of English, the move toward interdisciplinary programs across academic departments, and the "crisis" in the humanities in general have all provided opportunities for the reformulation of traditional values as well as for the questioning of their validity.[3] Daniel Schwarz's response to these trends appears in the introduction to his essay. I wish to argue here that while this collection of essays provides further instances of such a process, it reveals, more important, the need to focus on specific texts—literary and nonliterary—in order to avoid the partialities behind many of the generalizations that continue to dominate current critical debates.

According to the traditional definition of narrative, storytelling is marked by its achievement of the humanistic goals of coherence, progress, and rationality. As Daniel Schwarz puts it in *The Case for a Humanistic Poetics*:

> Narrative is both the representation of external events and the telling of those events. My interest in narrative derives from my belief that we make sense of our life by ordering it and giving it shape. The stories we tell ourselves provide continuity among the concatenation of diverse episodes in our lives, even if our stories inevitably distort and falsify. Each of us is continually writing and rewriting the text of our life, revising our memories and hopes, proposing plans, filtering disappointments through our defences and rationalizations, making adjustments in the way we present ourselves to ourselves and others. To the degree that we are self-conscious, we live in our narratives—our discourse—about our actions, thoughts, and feelings. . . . To omit narrative is to de-emphasize the kind of ordering on which we depend to convey meaning.

Such a logocentric conception of narrative, in which reading is so preeminent that it becomes the test of the examined life, depends for its significance on a specific conception of plot. Narrative, as Schwarz explains, involves a "continuous" plot "with a beginning, middle, and end," and it is based on "essential principles by which [it is] teleologically organized into a necessary and probable process to generate a particular structure of effects." To "convey meaning," a story must proceed in a way that seems likely and, indeed, almost inevitable.[4]

The idea of an orderly linking of events into a meaningful sequence is so central to modern Western conceptions of how human experience is embodied in language that it is frequently assumed to be universal. Hayden White makes this point when he defines modernity's valuation of narrative:

> Far from being a problem, then, narrative might be considered a solution to a problem of general human concern, namely the problem of how to translate *knowing* into *telling,* the problem of fashioning human experience into a form assimilable to structures of meaning that are generally human rather than culture-specific. . . . Far from being one code among many that a culture may utilize for endowing experience with meaning, narrative is a metacode, a human universal on the basis of which transcultural messages about the nature of a shared reality can be transmitted.[5]

As White goes on to demonstrate, however, certain forms of recording events—in particular, annals and chronicles—fall outside such a notion of narrative because they do not conform to the modernist's conception of coherence, and they fail to do so precisely because they reflect earlier, culturally specific assumptions about reality.

One need go no farther than Nina Auerbach's "Revelations on Pages and Stages," the first essay of this collection, to confirm White's thesis about the cultural specificity of a humanistic conception of narrative, and it is precisely her focus on culture that provides such a confirmation. Feminist theory and cultural studies, separately or in conjunction, have demonstrated that what is labeled universal by one group of people may be a way of ignoring the concerns or interests, or even the existence, of other groups. If acts of narration exert their power by creating patterns of "order" and "shape," such power is often exerted only at great cost to those excluded from or deformed by the construction of such meanings. Auerbach counts that cost in her cogent analysis of the relation between literary conceptions of "an integral character defining itself in significant acts" and the emphasis on the volatility and mutability of character prominently enacted on the Victorian stage. In a discussion that ranges from *Middlemarch* and *Bleak House* to stagings of *Hamlet* and the careers of a Victorian impresario and his leading lady, Auerbach demonstrates in specific instances the force of Teresa de Lauretis's claim that certain forms of narrative serve as instruments of male dominance:[6] Esther Summerson, Ophelia, and Ellen Terry are all diminished in the characters they must become and by the plots they must enact. For Auerbach, an understanding of culture—here the self-contradictory Victorian culture that supported both novels and theaters with hard cash and lavish displays of enthusiasm—is central: it is the context in which are acted out the struggles between requirements for narrative coherence and a character's impulse to escape such constraints. As such, Auerbach's analysis both participates in and responds to the developments that have attended the rise to prominence of cultural studies.

Despite that prominence, the term *culture,* like *narrative,* still continues to suggest either a specific meaning that aspires to universality or a wider, more generalized meaning that makes sense only in relation to historically specific situations. As Roy Wagner points out in *The Invention of Culture, culture* "exists in a broad and a narrow, an 'unmarked' and a 'marked' sense." The narrow, or "marked," meaning, the "high"-cultural sense of the word, involves the artistic endeavors and tastes of a minority of the socially and intellectually elite; the broad, or "unmarked," sense, based originally in the discipline of anthropology, extends "the notion of human refinement and domestication from the individual to the collective" by focusing on social relations and social practices.[7] The context in which the term appears, of course, signals the sense that is meant by a particular use. In a contribution to *Reading Narrative,* a collection of essays from an earlier Narrative Conference, Gerald Graff uses the two meanings of *culture* in one sentence without having to worry that they will be confused: analyzing the commercial conditions that shape the process of reading in postmodern society, Graff explains, "What I call the unofficial interpretive *culture* [reviews, publicity, gossip, advertising hype] has never been considered a respectable topic, and it is still risky to mention the subject among people with pretensions to *culture*" (emphasis added).[8] Here, according to Graff, elite "marked" culture is served by keeping the mass culture of distribution and consumption as "unmarked" and unnoticed as possible.

Such a goal of mutual exclusion is typical of the conflicts that arise when the two meanings of the term *culture* vie with each other for predominance. When Raymond Williams was introducing his *Culture and Society 1780–1950* (1958), he could take almost for granted the narrower, Arnoldian definition of culture as the refinement of certain artistic and intellectual qualities in opposition to the practical demands and practical imperatives of everyday life. Williams's claim that *culture* should refer to "a whole way of life" may now seem less than revolutionary, but it is now also easier to see that the use of the term by some of the practitioners of cultural studies exhibits its own brand of partiality. John Fiske, for instance, counters the exclusionary tactics of the Arnoldian view by setting out the negations through which the project of cultural studies can be understood:

> The term "culture," used in the phrase "cultural studies," is neither aesthetic nor humanist in emphasis, but political. Culture is not conceived of as the aesthetic ideals of form and beauty to be found in great art, nor in more humanist terms as the voice of the "human spirit" that transcends the boundaries of time and nation to speak to a hypothetical universal man (the gender is deliberate—women play little or no role in this conception of culture). Culture is not, then, the aesthetic products of the human spirit acting as a bulwark against the tide of grubby industrial materialism and vulgarity, but

rather a way of living within an industrial society that encompasses all the meanings of that social experience.[9]

Here again, the apparently inclusive phrase "way of living" attempts to outdo the supposed universality of the narrow conception of an elite and aestheticized humanism, and once again it does so as a way of masking its own specific limitations. By "way of living" Fiske means, as his essay goes on to demonstrate, a conception of social relations that is delimited by its emphasis on the unequal accesses to power and the divisions among groups of people differentiated by race, class, and gender. In some hands such a conception may exclude as much as it includes.

If, as Cornell West cogently argues, "hegemonic Western discourses . . . invoke universality, scientificity, and objectivity in order to hide cultural plurality, conceal the power-laden play of differences, and preserve hierarchical . . . relations," the practice of cultural studies, as its proponents readily admit, construes culture to serve its own necessarily limited purposes. In a definition of the field more recent than Fiske's, however, the editors of the collection *Cultural Studies* argue that it "operates in the tension between its tendencies to embrace both a broad, anthropological and a more narrowly humanistic conception of culture": "Cultural studies is thus committed to the study of the entire range of a society's arts, beliefs, institutions, and communicative practices." Yet the need or impulse to make such an apparently universal claim can be resisted by following a tendency that cultural studies shares with other strains of poststructuralist thought: the rejection of totalizing methods in favor of what Clifford Geertz calls "local knowledge."[10] By focusing directly and intently on specific instances of the interplay between narrative and culture, the essays in this volume demonstrate the value of dismissing universalizing definitions in order to try to recognize the "local" conditions that determine the effects of this interplay.

In the following essays narrative often emerges as a power that controls and represses. Thomas Byers rereads *The Last of the Mohicans* to locate the "extreme repressive violence" exerted by the binary oppositions that structure Cooper's storytelling. While Auerbach sees Esther Summerson's scars as the marks of deformation exacted by the demand for coherent characters, Byers sees Magua's scars as the inscription of white culture on his body. Similarly, Mary Lou Emery explores the "exchanges, reversals, and retrievals of narrative possibilities" as they are enacted in plots of evolutionary development in novels by May Sinclair and D. H. Lawrence. As Emery explains, "early twentieth-century traffic in plots of female subjectivity and sexuality"—like the earlier traffic in women analyzed by Gayle Rubin[11]—exerts a "violent coercion" that brings women "'home' to a (reformed) marriage plot." In a bold move that identifies male novelists and female critics, Colleen Kennedy examines the "narrative control" inscribed in novels and applauded by critics, a control that ultimately erases its female subjects so that Lolita becomes a "symbol of the vulgar" and the female reader disappears in her identification of herself as a male reader delighting in art as "surplus pleasure." The final essay of part 2, which deals with visual narratives, makes such a point even more forcefully. According to Paul Morrison, narrative presents itself as a form of the "revenge" enacted by a homophobic culture "on gayness," so that the "sickness of uncompleted narratives" (gay desire) becomes a completed "narrative of sickness" (AIDS as a punishment for gayness). Examining material as diverse as Freud's theories, Mapplethorpe's art, and Sontag's criticism, Morrison argues that even a universal fact like death is "meaningless in isolation from its cultural distribution and regulation," both of which are disciplinary processes in which narrative plays a crucial role.

Such essays challenge the humanistic notion of narrative as a liberal and liberating source of meaning and value, but they also refuse to accept any simplistic conception of narrative as the dumb instrument of a culture's control over helpless individuals or even over its oppressed minorities. In this sense, the present collection has its own story to tell. As one moves from readings of nineteenth-century fiction in the first part of the volume to essays on contemporary fiction, an emphasis on the re-creative power of narrative also becomes evident. Felipe Smith analyzes the stories embedded in images of African-American women as mammies and madonnas and of white women as witches, and he argues that these images are used against women as instruments of male—"black male/ white male"—oppression. According to Smith, however, Toni Morrison employs these images "to critique oppressive patriarchal formations extant in both Western economic imperialism and the rhetoric of black nationalism." Morrison therefore "reclaims" those images from the "pervasive cultural distrust" from which they have issued. The only faintly optimistic conclusion reached by Morrison and analyzed by Smith is cast in a larger and more hopeful context in Jay Clayton's consideration of the "narrative turn" in works by such writers as Morrison and Louise Erdrich. The claim that is implicit in Smith's essay becomes explicit in Clayton's: narrative can empower and liberate; it can even heal and save. Although such an assertion is reminiscent of nineteenth-century conceptions of art—for instance, George Eliot's insistence on novelists' ability to liberate their readers from the moral confines of their particular personal concerns—Clayton invokes postmodernist theory to locate this process in the context of "local political struggles." Clayton applies Lyotard's conception of the ways in which "grand metanarratives" of "scientific progress and political freedom" have yielded to "micronarratives" that legitimate "diverse, often conflicting enterprises and groups." Storytelling therefore draws its power both from the oral traditions of the past and from the contemporary social conditions that give new relevance to such traditions. By pointing to the "pragmatic dimension of narrative," Clayton argues that "there is nothing mystified about the claim that telling stories creates community." Such a claim, however, is valid only in relation to a particlar, "local" group.

This conclusion seems far removed, indeed, from the analysis of narrative offered by Auerbach, Byers, Emery, and Kennedy. Yet such a conception of the re-creative potential of narrative reappears in the second section of this collection. John Carlos Rowe discusses television shows that "spin off" from earlier series and argues that the medium uses repetition and recitation—characteristics that typify storytelling in oral cultures— to create a "social consensus." Despite claims by Jameson and Lyotard that consumer capitalism destroys the capacity of narrative to connect past and present or to confront the present, Rowe sees the spin-off epitomizing the ways in which TV creates a narrative of its own history in order to legitimate its status and authority. Although he is not particularly sanguine about the effects of such a process, Rowe does remind his readers that they must be attentive to the ways that TV, like traditional narrative, operates to construct experience and the extent to which it depends on the active engagement of its audience. Daniel R. Schwarz's reading of a poem by Wallace Stevens similarly focuses on the tendency of even the abstract style of imagist description to encourage readers to "recuperate . . . experience in language," to create and to elaborate on the stories that the images suggest. In fact, if one looks back to part 1 of this collection, the revelatory potential of narrative emerges even in the essays that examine its power to repress or oppress. In *The Last of the Mohicans,* for instance, Byers identifies a "*narrative* logic—really an illogic or ideologic"—that itself exposes the "violence of its repressions" and the "fragility" of its oppositions.

The final section of this collection, which treats both visual and verbal stories as they are retold in new contexts and in different media, again emphasizes the re-creative and recuperative capacities of narrative. Whereas the one essay on film in part 2—Ingeborg Majer O'Sickey's analysis of Wenders's *Der Himmel über Berlin*—treats the unified male subjectivity of classical narrative as both the goal and the motive force of the story told by the film, Caroline McCracken-Flesher analyzes cinematic versions of *Dr. Jekyll and Mr. Hyde*—or, to use her term, directoral readings of Stevenson's plot—to define the interactions between a story and its cultural context: "culture constructs narrative through the act of reading," and the "text's narrative matrix simultaneously restructures the intersecting culture." She demonstrates how the retelling of Stevenson's tale of possession and self-division allows twentieth-century directors to fend off contemporary threats, be they threats posed by drink, war, or feminists. Narrative, in this case, is a method of self-defense rather than an instrument of oppression.

Marcel Cornis-Pope takes this recuperative project even further. Responding to criticisms of postmodern fiction that demonstrate their own "nostalgic concept of narration as an effective totalizing machine," he examines how such fiction invalidates the "grand narratives" of classic realism even as it develops a new, if tentative, "re-creative rapport with reality." While surfiction and the systems novel challenge cultural authority and the "will to mastery" inherent in "all narrative structures," they also attempt to "reformulate the mastering systems they live with" through a doubled process of "disarticulation and re-creation." Such reformulations also characterize for Carol Siegel the translation of an epistolary novel into cinematic form. Locating the dynamics of two versions of *Dangerous Liaisons* in the historical specificity of their different cultures, Siegel concludes by noting that even such differences achieve a similar aim by allowing their spectators "the subsversive pleasures of a thorough enjoyment" of what each culture "calls evil." In the concluding essay, Vera Mark examines a contemporary cultural performance, the Moncrabeau Liars' Festival. She sees storytelling as a form of postmodern accommodation wherein, for example, the threat of being colonized by institutions of international commercialism can be treated as if it provided opportunities for a sound business venture voluntarily pursued by local businesspeople. The tall tales of the Liars' Festival reformulate problems as sources of amusement, and they speak for the "reimagined" values of community in response to the "transnational realities of the postmodern era." If at points in this collection it seems that narrative is an instrument of the powerful ideologies played out in cultural practices, it also becomes increasingly clear, as both Vera Mark and Jay Clayton demonstrate, that narrative may also be an agent of resistance to such forces and a means of communal self-affirmation and identification.

Why this collection tells this story, why it questions and at least partially reauthorizes the humanistic view of narrative, is, of course, yet another story. Part of the answer to these questions lies, no doubt, in the nature of the essays selected for inclusion here. At this point in the development of the critical discourse, essays that address the conjuncture of issues like narrative and culture will necessarily also broach problems of subjectivity, subjection, agency, and accommodation. In part, however, this plot emerges here because the essays have been arranged to move, in general, from nineteenth-century subjects to those drawn from the contemporary world of late capitalism. In the arrangement of its parts, then, this volume enacts a muted version of the master narrative of progress in which the present emerges, if only fitfully and incompletely, from the benightedness of the past. As such, the story that this collection tells invites scrutiny, and the motivations for its telling are not far to seek. It is certainly more comforting to locate the repressive power of narrative in the canonical works of the last century than it is to recognize that contemporaneous culture exerts similarly effective forms of control. The critic's fictions of self-determination are less likely to be called into question if the present is defined as the arena of complex accommodations between conflicting ideologies, a give-and-take in which contradictory impulses are both empowered and constrained, while more one-sided forms of domination are identified as things of the past.

Yet each of the individual essays here tells a more productive story than this analysis of the collection as a whole might suggest. By focusing on the relations between specific narratives and specific cultures, by blending discussions of theoretical issues with practical analysis, the writers of these essays resist precisely those universalized, but exclusionary notions of narrative and culture that I cite at the beginning of this introduction. In the process, they repeatedly demonstrate the value of interrogating the local conditions and local functions of the stories that particular cultures tell and to which their members listen. At the very least—and in these days of contention within the academy and without, this may be very much—each of these essays helps to make it more difficult to mistake the particular for the universal.

Notes

1 Stephen Greenblatt, "Culture," in *Critical Terms for Literary Study,* ed. Frank Lentricchia and Thomas McLaughlin (Chicago: University of Chicago Press, 1990), 225; Fredric Jameson, *The Political Unconscious* (Ithaca: Cornell University Press, 1981), 13; J. Hillis Miller, "Narrative," in *Critical Terms for Literary Study,* 66; Raymond Williams, *Culture and Society 1780–1950* (New York: Harper and Row, 1958), xvi.

2 Alan Nadel has told me, in fact, that Morrison was "far and away" the most frequently proposed subject for papers at the 1993 conference and that African-American women were the best-represented group of writers, although works by African-American men were only rarely the subject of paper proposals. At this conference in a paper called "The 'Pet Negro' System: The Politics of Mainstreaming Women Writers of the Harlem Renaissance," Sivagami Subbaraman offered a persuasive and therefore troubling argument that such canonization of specific African-American writers or of specific works by them is itself a mechanism of their containment.

3 See Patrick Brantlinger's discussion of the interconnections between these developments in chapter 1 of *Crusoe's Footprints: Cultural Studies in Britain and America* (New York: Routledge, 1990).

4 Daniel R. Schwarz, *The Case for a Humanistic Poetics* (Philadelphia: University of Pennsylvania Press, 1991), 108, 110; see also his "The Ethics of Reading: The Case for Pluralistic and Transactional Reading," *Novel* 29 (1988): 197–218.

5 Hayden White, "The Value of Narrativity in the Representation of Reality," in *On Narrative,* ed. W. J. T. Mitchell (Chicago: University of Chicago Press, 1981), 1–2.

6 Teresa de Lauretis, *Alice Doesn't: Feminism, Semiotics, Cinema* (Bloomington: Indiana University Press, 1984), chap. 5, "Desire in Narrative." See also her revision of this position in "Strategies of Coherence: The Poetics of Film Narrative," in *Reading Narrative: Form, Ethics, Ideology,* ed. James Phelan (Columbus: Ohio State University Press, 1989), 186–206.

7 Roy Wagner, *The Invention of Culture,* rev. ed. (Chicago: University of Chicago Press, 1981), 22, 21.

8 Gerald Graff, "Narrative and the Unofficial Interpretive Culture," in *Reading Narrative,* ed. Phelan, 6.

9 Williams, *Culture and Society,* xvi; John Fiske, "British Cultural Studies and Television," in *Channels of Discourse: Television and Contemporary Criticism,* ed. Robert C. Allen (Chapel Hill: University of North Carolina Press, 1987), 254.

10 Cornell West, "Marxist Theory and the Specificity of Afro-American Oppression," in *Marxism and the Interpretation of Culture,* ed. Cary Nelson and Lawrence Grossberg (Urbana: University of Illinois Press, 1988), 18. Cary Nelson, Paula Treichler, and Lawrence Grossberg, "Cultural Studies: An Introduction," in *Cultural Studies,* ed. Grossberg, Nelson, and Treichler (New York: Routledge, 1992), 4. In a particularly cogent fashion, Bruce Robbins points out the exclusionary effects of the relatively recent critical emphasis on narrative, although he also explains that the term *narrative* has borne much of the burden of finding "a common ground between . . . literary criticism's 'high culture' and anthropology's 'ordinary' culture"; see Robbins, "Death and Vocation: Narrativizing Narrative Theory," *PMLA* 107 (1992): 47. Also see Clifford Geertz, *Local Knowledge: Further Essays in Interpretive Anthropology* (New York:

Basic Books, 1983). Geertz is well known for his advocacy of what he calls the "thick description" of local cultural practices; see "Deep Play: Notes on the Balinese Cockfight," in *The Interpretation of Cultures* (New York: Basic Books, 1973), 412–53.

11 Gayle Rubin, "The Traffic in Women: Notes on the 'Political Economy' of Sex," in *Toward an Anthropology of Women,* ed. Rayna Reiter (New York: Monthly Review Press, 1975), 157–210.

Part One

The

Culture

of the

Canon

Nina Auerbach

Revelations on Pages and Stages

A French actress makes a cameo intrusion into the ordinariness of *Middlemarch* to stab her husband onstage. The murder is not important; British domesticity is filled with murders, if usually less conspicuous ones. What matters in *Middlemarch,* that exactingly scientific anatomy of character, is the theatrical meaning of the murderer. Laure does her best to explain herself to the worthy British doctor who offers to marry her into salvation, but she does so by eluding all the explanations that novels customarily offer.

> "I will tell you something," she said, in her cooing way, keeping her arms folded. "My foot really slipped."
>
> "I know, I know," said Lydgate deprecatingly. "It was a fatal accident—a dreadful stroke of calamity that bound me to you the more."
>
> Again Laure paused a little and then said, slowly, "*I meant to do it.*"
>
> Lydgate, strong man as he was, turned pale and trembled: moments seemed to pass before he rose and stood at a distance from her.
>
> "There was a secret, then," he said at last, even vehement. "He was brutal to you; you hated him."
>
> "No! he wearied me; he was too fond: he would live in Paris, and not in my country; that was not agreeable to me."
>
> "Great God!" said Lydgate, in a groan of horror. "And you planned to murder him?"
>
> "I did not plan; it came to me in the play—*I meant to do it.*"[1]

The four main plots of *Middlemarch* linger over their slow self-formation through the gradual accretion of causes and consequences, but no planning or plotting explains this actress's eruption. Laure has no secret motive. She is as far from being an intelligible character as Rachel, "the panther of the stage," is from recognizable humanity in George Henry Lewes's description of her: "with a panther's terrible beauty and undulating grace she moved and stood, glared and sprang. There always seemed something not human about her."[2] Laure too defines herself in unfathomable motion. Melodramatic stage directions punctuate her story without explaining it: she coos, poses, and pauses, prompting Lydgate to turn pale, tremble, even groan. Character in *Middlemarch* is constructed as "a process and an unfolding" (102), but Laure's performance unfolds out of nothing and leads nowhere. It "means" the intensity of its moment.

Laure's "*I meant to do it*" is purely theatrical, and thus, in a realistic novel, deeply chilling. Even comically conventional inhabitants of Middlemarch are made of intricate causal patterns; "metaphorically speaking, a strong lens applied to Mrs. Cadwallader's match-making will show a play of minute causes producing what may be called thought and speech vortices to bring her the sort of food she needed" (39); but no microscope, not even Lydgate's, can penetrate Laure's play. Stage meanings lack the developmental logic of novelistic motivations; with the randomness of lightning, they illuminate the disruptions and inconsistencies of character. A stage murder can be simultaneously accidental and deliberate, motivated and gratuitous. The horrified Lydgate is quick to relegate Laure to "the throng of stupid criminals," but her crime's incongruities allow her to stand alone. "I do not like husbands," she explains cryptically, refusing to shape her taste into a coherent, categorizable protest. George Eliot's contrapuntal case histories of the Casaubon, Lydgate, and Bulstrode marriages scrutinize the "play of minute causes" that can turn wifely organisms toward murder, but this wife has no discernible cause; she simply performs.

From a nineteenth-century medical perspective, the abruptness of Laure's obscurely motivated act is a symptom of monomania, "a localized but profound break in the unity of the psyche."[3] To act out of character is, in this definition, to be insane, but Victorian theatrical characters take their lives from such localized, profound breaks. Galvanized by ontological eruptions that clinicians of the time called insanity, they hold audiences by refusing to make sense.

George Eliot's lulling narrative voice tempts readers to respond to the murder (if it is one) as Lydgate does, resisting Laure's performance by categorizing her; it is easier to label than to confront the rifts performers expose in one's own character. Laure, however, ruptures Lydgate's own seeming consistency, exposing him as "incongruous" and therefore, according to his own profession's definition, mad:

> He knew that this was like the sudden impulse of a madman—incongruous even with his habitual foibles. No matter! [Marrying Laure] was the one thing which he was resolved to do. He had two selves within him apparently, and they must learn to accommodate each other and bear reciprocal impediments. Strange, that some of us, with quick alternate vision, see beyond our infatuations, and even while we rave on the heights, behold the wide plain where our habitual self pauses and awaits us. (104)

But which self is Lydgate's real—or at least habitual—one? The man we know in the novel is the infatuated one, not the calm gazer on the wide plain. The Lydgate we live with is a monomaniac consumed by a single role, that of helpless consort to Rosamond, another, but more refined, killer of husbands. The scientific assurance of *Middlemarch*'s narrator, the firmness with which she leads us into universalizing generalizations that ascend from "he" to "some of us" to the inclusive "we" and "us," distract the reader from Lydgate's chronic separation from his "habitual self." The intact observer on the wide plain gazes remotely at a histrionic double who rarely acknowledges the true man.

Laure's melodramatic intrusion into the even rhythms of *Middlemarch* introduces a prospect more threatening even than the marital murder that will dominate the novel: the actress's volatility evokes an answering volatility in one of George Eliot's most apparently stable characters. Confronting Laure, Lydgate lives in melodramatic stage directions, leaping and climbing onto the stage (104), turning pale, trembling, and groaning in horror. Laure shows us a good doctor who might have a Mr. Hyde capering within him, who might even *be* this capering Hyde, and not the good doctor at all. The advent of the actress dislodges the intricate web of provincial life, exposing fissures in the integrity of character and the meaning of acts. Choices in *Middlemarch* are fraught with portentous, inevitable, and often tragic consequences, but Laure gives her key line, "*I meant to do it,*" all the arbitrary shock of a stage death. The randomness, the contingency, of the murder and its affinity with theatrical improvisation rather than tragic inevitability call into question the very existence of an integral character defining itself in significant acts. The "habitual self" who "pauses and awaits us" on a "wide plain" becomes, like Beckett's Godot, a self who may never have been.

The energy of Victorian fiction comes from its compulsion to make sense of its own amplitude. *Middlemarch,* with its universalizing commentary and scientific claims, epitomized the ambition of a form that aimed to rise above its ephemeral journalistic origins, struggling to transcend the part issue's episodic clutter to rest on the stationary heights of an Arnoldian criticism of life. Like her characters, the narrator of *Middlemarch* experiments on her material to consolidate it, peering through microscopes, changing the lights for us, adding candles that turn random scratches into patterns, "unravelling certain human lots, and seeing how they were woven and interwoven" (96), in order to reveal their common sense. In 1871, with the novel poised on the verge of canonicity after decades of vulgar popularity, *Middlemarch* consolidated its genre's ambition to become literature by yearning, like its protagonists, toward "a binding theory which could . . . give the remotest sources of knowledge some bearing on [its] actions" (58).

But, as the sad self-knowledge of *Middlemarch* acknowledges, binding theories coerce as well as connect. The theatricality with which Laure unravels (if only for a page or two) the fabric of character woven into the assumptions that give *Middlemarch* its magnitude is, as George Eliot's narrator might put it, a parable. Laure's capacity to make Lydgate erupt out of the self he, and we, think is his own defines the danger the Victorian theater posed to the humanistic assumptions of its literature. The theater was an embarrassing inspiration to the Victorian novel, one whose centrality few literary scholars acknowledge even today; critics' own quests for self-enoblement through binding theories have led many to avoid acquaintance with that apparently primitive, scrappily documented, but culturally crucial institution, the Victorian theater.[4] In the same spirit, as Victorian novelists strove to mature, to be morally and psychologically complex, they regarded the theater with the sort of apologetic obsession Lydgate directs to the women in his life: an increasingly formidable rival, the theater seemed to lure novelists into childlike regression, intoxicating them with lovely surfaces, with sensuality, with silliness, with an expensive incoherence that underlay its supposed moral clarity.

The lure of this living theater has little to do with the theatricality that is so pronounced in Victorian novels: fictional theatricality is less a gesture toward the theater than it is a diminution of it into the florid, the overwrought, the meretricious. Such "theatrical" characters as Dickens's Quilp or *Middlemarch*'s Raffles are eccentric enough to die without touching us: by epitomizing the theater's extravagance, they enhance the novel's apparent reality. Even the theatricality of that supposed theater lover Dickens was fueled by competitive condescension, so that the two performances his novels represent—the antics of the Crummles company in *Nicholas Nickleby* and Wopsle's Hamlet in *Great Expectations*— are a truth-telling narrator's gleeful exposure of performing falsity.

Even critics who claim to relish the theater praise fictional theatricality in novelists' own condescending terms. J. B. Priestly, for example, celebrates the theatrical Dickens by relishing the exuberant excess of Wackford Squeers:

> Perhaps he is trying to make us, the readers, laugh. Perhaps . . . he is not really a horrible schoolmaster: *he is a superb comedian playing a horrible schoolmaster.* And as much might be said of many of the other characters, especially in the earlier novels. Perhaps other superb comedians are playing Sam Weller and his father, Dick Swiveller, Crummles, Mantalini, Pecksniff, and the rest. *They deliberately overdo their characters, making them more and more preposterous but more and more laughable, to entertain us.*[5]

For Priestly, and for many humanist writers still, to be theatrical is to be safely fake; the theatrical flares that Victorian novels send out are similar reassurances of preposterous exaggeration. But such reassuring signals appropriate the surface of theater while shunning its essence: a fluidity, an energy (like that of George Eliot's Laure) that can infect an audience or murder a mate without motive or consequences.

The art of theatrical character was concentrated in its murderers. From the ghoulish Sweeney Todd to the demure Lady Audley to the upright Mathias in *The Bells,* Victorian stage murderers seemed, on the face of it, more motivated than Laure; moreover, while they were always punished, she confesses and vanishes. But the ritual rewards and punishments of theatrical melodrama veiled an energy of violence that transcended motivation and made consequences irrelevant. "The frenzied nature of the homicide and the ensuing excess of the villain's retribution justify each other."[6] Sinful or retributive, theatrical murder was above all else a spectacle, one of the most popular exhibits in a medium whose essence was self-display. In *The Bells,* for instance, a respectable Burgomaster's guilty

memories of the murder he committed years before arouse all the resources of the stage: the domestic action opens out into an ornate dream
sequence involving snowy visions, mesmerism, a trial, and a hanging.
Murder is the cue for theatrical spectacle, while in novels it is generally a
guarantee of seriousness. Thackeray's Becky Sharp is an alluring mimic
until the novel damns her by hinting that she has not only mocked and
robbed her fat adorer; she may also have killed him. Authenticating her
perdition, Becky vanishes as a spectacle. Even in *Vanity Fair,* that most
mobile of Victorian novels, murder fixes the soul. It is too weighty an
activity for theatrical play.

Like twentieth-century films, the Victorian theater was memorable
less for the sort of self-mocking exaggeration J. B. Priestly praises in
Dickens than for intoxicating, surreally shifting images that often belied the rigid simplicity of the plays themselves: what was seen generally
overwhelmed what was said. The visual profligacy of pantomime, its
magic transformations, the fluidity of gender and genre, set the tone of
actual as opposed to fictional theatricality. "Late Victorian pantomime
was the most purely visual, pictorial, and lavish of nineteenth-century
theatrical arts and the most spectacular form of theatre in English stage
history," claims theater historian Michael R. Booth. "Spectacle existed for
its own sake more than in any other sort of theatre, feeding upon itself,
growing bigger and bigger, greedily consuming all the resources of technology, money, and manpower it was given. Yet pantomime spectacle
was a close relation of other kinds and other uses of spectacle," such as
Henry Irving's lofty production of *Faust* at the Lyceum in 1885.[7] Even
when it aspired to high culture, the theater lost itself in dizzying visual
play, overwhelming high seriousness with transformations, dreams, and
hypnotic nonsense.

Even a less aggressively sensuous theatricality can appear dangerous by definition. Jonas Barish's explication of Platonic antitheatricality
speaks for all those who endorse the integrity of a Lydgate in the face of
Laure's confusing and thus contaminating play:

> Mimesis, which can place new and unsettling thoughts in the mind,
> must be treated as a dangerous explosive. Except in rare moments,
> it works chiefly on the irrational side of us, giving license to our
> dreams and foul thoughts, to whatever in us is devious, intricate,
> and disordering. Theater being the quintessentially mimetic art, act-

ing being radically founded in multiplication of roles and transgression of boundaries, all that is urged in suspicion of poetry, music, recitation, and the other arts must apply here with a maximum of force and a minimum of regretful qualification.[8]

Just as Laure functions as a "dangerous explosive" to Lydgate's steady identity, so the theatrical institution disrupted the mighty claims of a literature founded on assumptions of integrity. In the spirit that led George Eliot to depict would-be heroes who are too noble for their trivializing age, Matthew Arnold exhorted to transcendence a literature whose mission was the preservation of our "best self" from dispersion into fragmented incoherence. But in the course of the nineteenth century, a literature committed to redeeming the best self from the tyranny of masks and petty roles confronted an increasingly successful rival: a theater that flaunted its mobility, aspiring to neither coherence nor transcendence. Even at its most artistic, when it "realized" supposedly timeless works of art—H. T. Craven's comedy *Meg's Diversion* (1866) contains the typical stage direction, "MEG *places her hand to her heart—Music—this realizes the picture of* [Philip Calderon's] *'Broken Vows'*"[9]—these deceptively frozen moments dissolved, unlike paintings on canvas, as soon as the viewer recognized them, mocking by their momentariness the supposed permanence of art.

This medium of gorgeous transformations brought fame to actors who, unlike literary characters, thrived on versatility. Not only were nineteenth-century actors expected to play a wide assortment of ages and generic types as they learned their trade in strenuous provincial tours; they were adept at blending into their gorgeous stage environments. Ideally, "a pictorial acting style perfectly suited a pictorial production style"; an accomplished actor could turn into a painting by any number of artists.[10] But even the greatest champions of actors relegated them to a place in the aesthetic hierarchy far below that of artists and authors. George Henry Lewes, one of the few literary men to commemorate acting as an art, elevated performers in evocative prose portraits only to dismiss their importance: "He who can make a stage mob bend and sway with his eloquence, what could he do with a real mob, no poet by to prompt him?"[11] The actor, then, is a sham made real only by the author's words. To dispel the mistrust of a self-preserving culture, successful Victorian actors gradually learned to subordinate their many identities to the appearance of a best self, simulating the apparent consistency of fictional characters. These "devious, intricate, and disordering" beings, as Barish calls them, learned acceptable selves from novels.

The rise of the nineteenth-century theater, its ascent out of mid-century disreputability to a fin-de-siècle centrality and chic that eclipsed the increasingly self-reflexive novel, is a wry achievement for an age that wanted its success stories to illustrate moral truths. Lady Macbeth might have supplied the moral of the theater's metamorphosis: "To beguile the time, look like the time." Between 1861 and 1901 (the year Queen Victoria died and Henry Irving lost his regal position as actor-manager of the Lyceum), the theater normalized itself into respectability: it domesticated not only its settings but also its actors, purging itself of the disruptive mobility that threatened to become anything with no warning. The novel had by that time made the leap from subversive popularity to cultural authority; inadvertently, it showed its chief competitor how to win respect. The last half of the nineteenth century brought the theater cultural canonicity when it learned to simulate the integrity of a readerly and middle-class approach to literary character.

Much has been written of the Robertsonian revolution of the early 1860s, in which the Bancrofts' tasteful mounting of Tom Robertson's gentle domestic comedies imported middle-class realism into a phantasmagoric medium; Marie Bancroft's canny eye for new bourgeois norms turned the Prince of Wales Theater into a simulation of a cozy home.[12] Less has been written about the tempering effect on actors of the Bancrofts' seductively ordinary mise-en-scène. Like their theater, the most successful Victorian performers subdued the versatility that, for most of them, was the pride of their art, embracing a uniformity that limited their repertoire while endearing them to audiences for whom knowable characters were an article of faith.

The exemplary career of Henry Irving set the pattern of theatrical development: the knighthood Irving won in 1895 consolidated the respectability of the entire theatrical profession. Self-transformed from the obscure John Brodribb, Irving assumed a multitude of characters before he became the hero that audiences saw as himself. During the long provincial apprenticeship that preceded his London success, Irving played roughly seven hundred roles, becoming everyone an eclectic theater made available, from ugly stepsisters to handsome heroes, from comic villains to glowing martyrs. His career reached its turning point in 1871, only a few weeks before the serialization of *Middlemarch* began, when he won acclaim for his portrayal of the guilt-stricken murderer Mathias in Leopold Lewis's *The Bells*. Audiences soon identified him solely with anguished repentance, choosing to forget that Mathias was initially only one act in an evening designed to display the performer's versatility, not his integrity: *The Bells* was originally paired with *Jingle*, an adaptation of Dickens's *Pickwick Papers* in which Irving played an irrepressible con man whose deceitful brio subverted Mathias's cathartic contrition. When he understood the nature of his own success, Irving pared the diabolical comedy from his performances, forcing his beloved partner, Ellen Terry, to do the same in a bereavement from which she never recovered.[13]

As he became more eminent and his Lyceum encased itself in high seriousness, Irving became more marmoreally Irvingesque, until even admirers like Arthur Symons complained that he was no longer able to sink himself into a part: "Mr. Irving, who is a man of genius, may be justly blamed, from a certain standpoint for the brilliant obtrusion of personality into all the characters which he represents."[14] Symons blamed Irving for his consummate histrionic achievement: the creation of a personality that destroyed his potential to be many people, turning himself from a player into a character as his age longed to believe in the term.

This amputation of superfluous selves was one of Victorian culture's most adept artistic compromises, one that elevated the novel and made theatricality officially acceptable. Its legacy clings to performers today. The spurious intimacy of movies and television, whose gigantic close-ups allow us to mistake actors' moles and pores for their souls, and the pseudo–truth telling imposed by typecasting, talk shows, confessional interviews, and memoirs, force generations of actors to bear witness to their sincerity before the public will accept them as performers. In a recent tribute to Cary Grant, Garson Kanin praised Grant's persona for its very monotony: "If an actor or an actress tries to create a different person, a different personality, for every single role, then the audience doesn't have anything to latch onto *except* the creative talent of that player. . . . They do not want a movie star to be anything but his own or her own self that they have come to admire and to love."[15] Audiences shy away from the "creative talent" that makes a performer many people; an actor is multiple, but a star must be familiar. Our cultural unease with actors *as* actors is a story at least as old as nineteenth-century novelists' quests for binding theories and Henry Irving's obliging suppression of his own and Ellen Terry's metamorphic play in deference to audiences looking for their souls.

Irving's canny transformation into a man one could claim to know was more than a theatrical trick; it affected future actors and even, perhaps, the invention of the new, more apparently intimate theatrical technology of film and television. Irving's self-making was informed by an ideology that determined not only the politics of his profession but also literary assumptions about the integrity and significance of character: to be great was to be legible, even translucent, to suppress discontinuity and surprise. Heroes worthy of commemoration contract into their own best selves. In a sense Irving performed in his person one central compromise of the Victorian novel, whose domestication of performer into character made possible the quasi-religious ardor with which all classes of readers absorbed novels at their peak of cultural authority. Esther Summerson's fluctuating scars in *Bleak House* are a paradigm of the ineffable, ultimately banished theatricality of Victorian literary characters because, like actors' multiple selves, these scars can be neither fully seen nor fully forgotten.

Esther Summerson carries half the narrative burden of Dickens's account of confusions, obfuscation, and tangled identities. The novel casts her in a healing role: her autobiographical narrative exemplifies the humane virtues of modesty, domestic duty, and kindness—"natural" attributes threatened with extinction by the stunting urban professionalism that infects the rest of *Bleak House*. Esther defines her purity of being by telling us about herself with compulsive precision: "I had always rather a noticing way—not a quick way, O no!—a silent way of noticing what passed before me, and thinking I should like to understand it better."[16] Too modest to tell us how good she is, she is a scrupulous if blushing recorder of others' praise: "Well! It was only their dear love for me, I know very well, and it is a long time ago. I must write it, even if I write it out again, because it gave me so much pleasure. They said there could be no East wind where Somebody was; they said that wherever Dame Durden went, there was sunshine and summer air" (482). Writing herself and writing herself out at the same time, Esther rehearses and revises her character continually, collaborating with her adoring audience to shape the formless Somebody into the adorable Dame Durden.

Everything in *Bleak House* is a mystery except—ostensibly—Esther. Few characters in any novel are so incessantly and authoritatively talked about. But Esther radiates a subterranean fascination because she cannot be so easily labeled, even by her allegorical name: her visual life evades that sunny, summery designation. For one thing, she so uncannily resembles the proud Lady Dedlock, whose illegitimate daughter she will discover she is, as to take on the identity of an avenging ghost. Even to herself, she becomes alien and spectral. Describing her first sight of Lady Dedlock, Esther sees herself erupt out of her narrative: "I—I, little Esther Summerson, the child who lived a life apart, and on whose birthday there was no rejoicing—seemed to arise before my own eyes, evoked out of the past by some power in this fashionable lady" (305). Her specter overwhelms her defining name; the Esther who rises before her own eyes obscures the reassuring Esther in whom the rhetoric of the novel tells us to believe.

Smallpox intensifies this undefined visual intensity. Delirious, she dreams transformations—"Dare I hint at that worse time when, strung together somewhere in great black space, there was a flaming necklace, or ring, or starry circle of some kind, of which *I* was one of the beads!" (544)—that are harbingers of her transformation once she is healed. The scars that destroy her youth and beauty turn her into the motherly, sexless Dame Durden she has struggled to construct. Esther's visual mutability forces her to become her own persona, obstructing her control over her future—she is less marriageable scarred—while giving her implicit power to question her apparently fixed identity. If her scarred self makes her the Dame Durden those who loved her had always called her, was the loving appellation itself a scar? And if Dame Durden is a mutilation of her true self, who was that authentic Esther *before* she was scarred? Or before she became Esther Summerson?

"Esther Summerson" is itself an assumed name like "Dame Durden" or "Henry Irving": Esther's mother's maiden name is Barbary, and her father is—ominously—Nemo. Names in *Bleak House* are sinister; their abundance carries the hovering suggestion that Esther is no one. Visually, though, there are more Esthers than names can encompass. A novel of preternatural visionary acuteness encourages us to look at Esther incessantly, but since her scars are evoked rather than described, we can never quite see her: she acquires the tantalizing indistinctness of a leading actress in a large nineteenth-century theater, a dominant presence never quite in focus. As with Victorian actresses, who turned themselves into enigmatic visual semaphores, each creating "her own sign conven-

152,700

LIBRARY
College of St. Francis
JOLIET, ILLINOIS

tions through which audiences perceived her,"[17] Esther's haunting, half-visualized image suggests multiple possibilities of being.

At the very end of her story, we learn that there may be no scars; perhaps there never were? Her husband looks lovingly at an Esther beyond the reader's line of sight:

> "I have been thinking about my old looks—such as they were. . . .
> I have been thinking, that I thought it was impossible that you *could*
> have loved me any better, even if I had retained them."
> " 'Such as they were'?" said Allan, laughing.
> "Such as they were, of course."
> "My dear Dame Durden," said Allan, drawing my arm through
> his, "do you ever look in the glass?" (935)

Since the reader cannot look in Esther's glass, the novel gives no answer to this tender question. Its trick is to make us wonder how many faces that glass might reflect and to sense the inadequacy of verbal labels and even loving names before a play of visual identities whose elusive potential is richer than words.[18]

Within our dear, knowable Esther hover a multitude of possible Esthers, all of them darker, some more sinister, than the official redeemer of *Bleak House*. In typical Victorian fashion, though, *Bleak House* curtails by its language and plot the multiple possibilities it allows its reader to glimpse. As Esther's genealogy and her illness combine to scatter her into myriad apparitions, her plot circumscribes her utterly. She begins by claiming that her story is "a progress": solitary and abused, she makes a new life, striving "to be industrious, contented, and kindhearted, and to do some good to some one, and win some love to myself if I could" (65). But by the end, her progress is taken out of her hands: her narrative is resolved when she becomes a pawn in others' plots. Inspector Bucket untangles her genealogical narrative by whirling her off on a surreal midnight chase through the labyrinth of London; his helpless passenger is so bemused that she loses the threads, the characters, the settings, of her own story. The philanthropic John Jarndyce resolves her love story in his magnanimous present of her to Woodcourt, along with a new Bleak House that the domestic virtuoso Esther is not even allowed to furnish. As Esther's fluid identities threaten to escape narrative definition, Dickens locks her inside a plot that deprives her of narrative agency. Her destiny and identity are determined and defined by authorizing men. The many Esthers we cannot see in the mirror are overwhelmed by an Esther whose story is so consummately finished that we forget the stories she might have told.

At the end, singleness of being encases Esther and dissipates her scars; her tender doctor assures us that she is, after all, the "dear Dame Durden" we always knew. A scarred stage heroine, Isabel Vane in T. A. Palmer's dramatization of Ellen Wood's *East Lynne,* is less easily restored. This runaway wife returns to East Lynne, her former home, maimed by suffering and a railroad accident. She claims to be Madame Vine, her own children's governess. Her husband and children accept her as Madame Vine, though marginal household figures—a servant, a dependent comic spinster—recognize Isabel to no avail. Weeping hungrily at her son's deathbed, Isabel Vane/Madame Vine remains impenetrable to those she loves. Dying little William longs to meet his "very own mama" in Heaven but senses that knowledge is impossible even there: "Do you think we shall know everybody there, or only our own relations? . . . And shall I know her, I have quite forgotten what she was like; shall I know her?"[19]

Since Heaven was far from the Victorian stage, Willie dies unknowing, cuing his mother's celebrated curtain line, one of Victorian England's most famous and resonant laments: "Oh, Willie, my child dead, dead, dead! and *he never knew me,* never called me mother!" (390; emphasis added). The transforming power of Isabel's scars is the climax of her theatrical fate; stage convention allows her to metamorphose out of domestic familiarity forever. No diagnosing husband overlooks Isabel's scars to tell her who she is. Mystery, opacity, and discontinuity determine the action even of this most moralistic of popular melodramas.

Ellen Wood's original novel gave the play its plot, but the novel dwells on the known and knowable, muffling the shock of Isabel's transformation just as *Bleak House* does Esther's. Wood makes of transformation a universal principle by philosophizing windily about change; she hints at the domestic apathy of Isabel's noble husband and his second wife, Barbara; she enumerates in clinical detail the injuries that make Isabel's transformation appear plausible; she connects wife and governess by focusing on Isabel's agony, her perpetual condition in the novel. Above all, Wood uses East Lynne itself as a principle of permanence that heals the breach between Isabel Vane and Madame Vine: "Mr. Carlyle was in the room, this very room, and he had soothed her sorrow, her almost childish sorrow, with kisses sweet. Ah me! poor thing! I think our hands would have shaken as hers did. The ornament and the kisses were Barbara's now."[20] Ellen Wood does her best to consolidate Isabel

Vane's scarred identity around the omnipresence of the house that holds her memories, while the stage Isabel Vane undergoes a metamorphosis no home can heal.

These scarred heroines, all more or less successfully transported out of their lovable selves, embody Victorian character at its most potent and potentially disruptive. Even the characters who consolidate such apparently seamless masterpieces as *Middlemarch* are prone to fissures and discontinuities that trouble omniscient authorities, for the life of all Victorian characters springs from an amorphous energy that goes beyond defining boundaries to share the performer's immeasurable suggestiveness. The metamorphic intensity of the Victorian theater threatens to swamp the redemptive moral coherence that justifies the existence of characters in novels.

In the second half of the twentieth century, academic critics have taken Victorian novels at their own monolithic valuation, stressing the unity, even uniformity, within their surface abundance. Mid-century formalist critics appreciated not amplitude but image patterns.[21] A later critical generation finds confusion more alluring; its leaders—George Levine, for example—find heroism in insistent sense making: "The Victorians, surely, did write with the awareness of indeterminate meaning and of solipsism, but they wrote *against* the very indeterminacy they tended to reveal. Their narratives reconstruct a world out of a world deconstructing, like modernist texts, all around them."[22]

Even critics who make a profession of resistance assume the single-mindedness of Victorian fiction. Feminist revisions like *The Madwoman in the Attic* and its progeny find within the variety and versatility of novels by women a single story, retold obsessively. Foucauldian critics try to fight free of the uniformity they assume is Victorian, accusing the novel of policing itself virtually out of existence in its adherence to "a linear, cumulative time of evolution" that "secures duration against the dispersive tendencies that are literally 'brought into line' by it. Once on this line, character or event may be successively placed and coherently evaluated."[23]

But this "line" is always about to be broken by the many things coherence cannot contain. Such readings of fiction suffer from the cultural parochialism they set out to expose, ignoring the disparate, half-acknowledged ideologies and genres that compose apparent hegemony. Victorian character is irresistibly dynamic because it is the site of an incessant struggle between the theatrical and the literary, the impulse to spill over boundaries and the will to confine. If we understand the values of a rival art form, the Victorian theater, we may appreciate the dynamic turbulence that keeps Victorian novels alive.

George Henry Lewes, who bridged, ambivalently, the worlds of page and stage, defined this turbulence in his powerful appreciations of the Romantic actor Edmund Kean. Kean was spotty and unpredictable, but his intensity made him the archetypal performing genius of Lewes's pantheon. Lewes commemorated Kean's greatness by repeating Coleridge's evocative tribute: "Seeing Kean act was reading Shakespeare by flashes of lightning."[24]

This paradoxical activity defines the mixed nature of Victorian performance. To Victorian bardolators, Shakespeare was so elevated a hero that he was virtually immobile. Serene and still, "out-topping knowledge" in Matthew Arnold's reverent sonnet, England's literary emblem of greatness was nothing if not consistent.[25] But lightning brings mystery, mobility, and discontinuity, fracturing the Bard's wisdom into a message no longer entirely comprehensible, turning the placid receptiveness of reading into struggle and uncertainty. Shakespeare on the page is an untroubled seer whom the stage can electrify into shapes as strange as those of another creature: Frankenstein's, who is also animated by lightning. The divided lives of Shakespearean characters in the nineteenth century embody the discordant vitality of constructions of character itself.

Ophelia is neither a monumental actor like Henry Irving nor a fictional narrator like Esther Summerson: she is somewhere between them, at once narrative cipher and visual icon. In the nineteenth century her potential for autonomous existence took on the authority of myth. Ophelia began her undefined life in Shakespeare's *Hamlet,* but her nineteenth-century incarnations in various narrative genres made her a site of the age's tension between mobility and domestication.[26] Fully at home neither in novels nor onstage; haunting both but hinting at stories foreign to both, Ophelia is the nebulous essence of Victorian character.

She is a cipher in Shakespeare. Ellen Terry, whose Ophelia made her the poignant darling of late Victorian audiences, scrawled impatiently in one of her *Hamlet* scripts that Ophelia is "Nothing on a stick!" Her sparse lines, her lack of poetry or initiative, and her indeterminate motivation place Ophelia among Shakespeare's most vacuous women. But visually, in the nineteenth century, she alone in *Hamlet* claimed the canvas; whereas Hamlet, in his few representations, emerged monotonously as the same dark-clad brooder, Ophelia's drowning and death animated a medley of powerful, preternatural female figures.[27]

As a living painting, Ophelia transcended the sketchiness of her role in the text. Her visual presence was so potent that it galvanized theatrical representation. Indelibly identified with Ophelia, Ellen Terry became the prisoner of her own pictorial plenitude. Michael R. Booth describes her power over artists and theirs over her performance:

> Her Ophelia created a pictorial as well as a theatrical stir. The Pre-Raphaelite qualities of her portrait of the character are evident in Henry James's description of "a somewhat angular maiden of the Gothic ages," and Hiatt's comparison with a Pre-Raphaelite saint or a madonna by Giovanni Bellini—a clear pictorialization of the innocence and purity in Ophelia. George Bernard Shaw took the view that a picture had come to life; the actress had added what she learnt in the studio [in her year as G. F. Watts's wife and model] to what she learnt on the stage so successfully that "it was exactly as if the powers of a beautiful picture of Ophelia had been extended to speaking and singing."[28]

This Ophelia is the creature of so many disparate artists that she becomes, it seems, *any* picture. Her visual authority infiltrated even the majestic objectivity of Victorian science: Ophelia engravings illustrated medical types of female insanity, allowing doctors to "explain" their patients by dressing them up to be photographed in the conventional Ophelia garb of garlands, weeds, and white draperies.[29] The escape of character from character's confines could go no further. As spectacle, Ophelia gained an authority—aesthetic, religious, political, and scientific—utterly foreign to her literary role. No words on a page can encompass all the Ophelias spectators saw.

In literature, though, Ophelia's parallel story is one of overdetermination and constraint. The literary appropriation of Shakespeare begun by the Shakespearean narratives of Coleridge, Lamb, and Hazlitt and extending into our own century was at odds with the multiple suggestiveness of visual imagery and with the speaking silences possible in the theater. Coleridge, for example, re-creates Ophelia as absence, expatiating on Hamlet's reference in the nunnery scene to "the faults of the sex from which Ophelia is so characteristically free that the freedom therefrom constitutes her character. Here again Shakespeare's charm of

constituting female character by absence of characters, [of] outjuttings."
Coleridge's approval relegates Ophelia from multiplicity to negation; she
is what she is not: "The soliloquy of Ophelia is the perfection of love!—
so exquisitely unselfish!" "This antitheatrical understanding of Shakespeare," as Jonathan Arac calls it, commemorated a version of character
that was coherent, consistent, and, above all, explicable in words and
reducible to them.[30] Its Ophelia modulates accordingly from a demi-
divinity exuding undefined powers to the suffering star of a case history
whose motives are translucent. Like Lydgate confronting the disruptive
surprises of Laure, literature classifies Ophelia when it considers her at
all, turning her into a type amenable to explication.

Ophelia makes cameo appearances in various novels, doubling at key
moments for such broken, maddened women as Maggie Tulliver and
Catherine Linton: at their grandest and most doomed, mid-Victorian
heroines take on the contours of painters' mad Ophelia icon. But her
most powerful and sustained appearance comes in a work that is now
unfairly derided: Mary Cowden Clarke's popular series of novelistic case
histories, *The Girlhood of Shakespeare's Heroines*. With great ingenuity,
Clarke "explains" each heroine by providing her with a minutely realized
and vivid childhood, forming her character and elaborating her motivations so carefully that her behavior in her play becomes a mere coda
to the drama of her girlhood. Clarke's *Girlhood* is the Victorian novel's
consummate and most compelling capture of the stage: Shakespeare's
sketchily realized heroines, who can be played in any number of ways,
are exhaustively interpreted in a series of novels of development. "The
Rose of Elsinore," Clarke's account of the successive traumas that form
Ophelia, locks the heroine into so harrowing a series of events that there
is no room in her character for disruptive ambiguities.

Clarke's Ophelia begins life as a vacancy: "The babe lay on the nurse's
knee. *Could any impression have been received* through those wide-
stretched eyes, that stared as wonderingly *as if* they were in fact beholding amazed the new existence upon which they had so lately opened,
the child *would have seen* that it lay in a spacious apartment, furnished
with all the tokens of wealth and magnificence, which those ruder ages
could command."[31] The babe has no character; her eyes are sightless.
Bringing nothing to her world, she grows up to take the shape of the terrible events that happen to her. These events are initiated by a group of
women who have no place in Shakespeare's kingdom.

Her loving mother, Auodra, must leave the child with her nurse to travel to Paris with the clownish Polonius—an ancillary figure in Clarke's revision. Ophelia's stay among peasants is a cadenza of sexual traumas. Jutha, her young companion and protector, is seduced by Eric, a careless and cruel aristocrat; she dies when he abandons her. Simultaneously, Ophelia is pursued by the bearlike simpleton Ulf, a personification of brutal male sexuality. Auodra returns in the nick of time, just as Ulf is about to molest the child, but the girl's return to her family and station—the happy ending that would bring closure to most Victorian novels—holds only further abuse: at Court, Ophelia's new friend Thyra is seduced and abandoned by the same Eric who betrayed Jutha. In consequence Thyra dies still more horribly than the peasant girl.

In the climax of this carnage among women, Auodra dies. On her deathbed she warns Ophelia—as if the preceding events were not warning enough—of the unknown Hamlet's capacity to betray her. Auodra is so authoritative and beloved that Polonius's later warning against Hamlet becomes superfluous, as, in fact, does all *Hamlet*'s ensuing violence. Ophelia's destiny and her madness are determined before the play begins. In case we doubt the power of one trauma to form her conclusively, the same trauma recurs with only slight variations. The heroine has no space for surprises. Under these circumstances, anyone would become Ophelia.

Even Ophelia's silence, that theatrical virtue of her defective role, is naturalized out of mystery: it is an inevitable consequence of her transplantation. "Among these rough cottage people, more and more did the child feel herself alone and apart. Her shyness and sparing speech grew upon her. She was not unhappy; but she became grave, strangely quiet and reserved for a little creature of her years, and so confirmed in her habit of silence, that she might almost have passed for dumb" (2:205). Everything is explained. Like Esther Summerson in the final chapters of *Bleak House,* Clarke's Ophelia is the consummate creature of events. She loses her variety to become her plot.

This discrepancy among Ophelias defines an age that could not stop telling stories while insisting on controlling the stories it told. The visual energy of Victorian performance fought with a narrative ideology avid to define, to place, to understand, to explain. This tension between what we see and what is said, between the theatrical and the diagnostic imaginations, accounts for the uncanny life of nineteenth-century characters. Generated from warring ideologies, haunting—as Ophelia does—

mighty opposites, they simultaneously played and evaded all the incompatible needs that cultural imperatives demanded they fulfill.

Notes

1 George Eliot, *Middlemarch,* ed. Bert G. Hornback (1871–73; New York: Norton, 1977), 105. Hereafter cited parenthetically in the text.

2 George Henry Lewes, *On Actors and the Art of Acting* (New York: Bretano's, 1875), 35.

3 Simon During, "The Strange Case of Monomania: Patriarchy in Literature, Murder in *Middlemarch,* Drowning in *Daniel Deronda,*" *Representations* 23 (1988): 86.

4 Some exceptions, to which this essay is greatly indebted, are Martin Meisel, *Realizations: Narrative, Pictorial, and Theatrical Arts in Nineteenth-Century England* (Princeton: Princeton University Press, 1983); Carl Woodring, *Nature into Art: Cultural Transformations in Nineteenth-Century Britain* (Cambridge: Harvard University Press, 1989); Edwin M. Eigner, *The Dickens Pantomime* (Berkeley: University of California Press, 1989); and Nina Auerbach, *Private Theatricals: The Lives of the Victorians* (Cambridge: Harvard University Press, 1990). These critics have begun to weave coherent cultural statements out of the apparently intractable empiricism of Victorian theater history.

   In order to dispel the vexed academic distinction between "drama" (plays studied as literary texts) and "theater" (attention to the elusive conditions within which plays are seen and heard), I quote a theater historian's stirring definition of his enterprise: "The miracle of theatre is that a community, an audience, has agreed to let drama happen" (J. L. Styan, *Drama, Stage and Audience* [Cambridge: Cambridge University Press, 1975], 3). This essay asks the reader to imagine the sketchy texts of Victorian drama "happening" before audiences whose senses were more responsive than their official ideology.

5 J. B. Priestly, "The Life of Dickens," in *Charles Dickens 1812–1870,* ed. E. W. F. Tomlin (New York: Simon and Schuster, 1969), 27. Second italics mine.

6 Beth Kalikoff, *Murder and Moral Decay in Victorian Popular Literature* (Ann Arbor: University of Michigan Research Press, 1986), 28.

7 Michael R. Booth, *Victorian Spectacular Theatre 1850–1910* (London: Routledge, 1981), 92.

8 Jonas Barish, *The Antitheatrical Prejudice* (Berkeley: University of California Press, 1981), 26.

9 Meisel, *Realizations,* 91–92.

10 Booth, *Spectacular Theatre,* 157.

11 Lewes, *Actors and the Art of Acting,* 58.

12 George Rowell, *The Victorian Theatre, 1792–1914,* 2d ed. (Cambridge: Cambridge University Press, 1978), 75–84. In 1898, Arthur Wing Pinero's nostalgic *Trelawney of the 'Wells'* celebrated the marriage between theatricality and middle-class respectability that the new domestic realism made possible, thus formulating a metatheatrical myth of a union that was in fact an unresolved, if fruitful, antagonism in the world beyond the stage.

13 Nina Auerbach, *Ellen Terry, Player in Her Time* (New York: Norton, 1987), 175–266.

14 "Arthur Roberts," *Star* (1893), quoted in John Stokes, *In the Nineties* (Chicago: University of Chicago Press, 1989), 91.

15 Garson Kanin, *Cary Grant: The Leading Man* (Documentary, PBS, October 23, 1989).

16 Charles Dickens, *Bleak House* (1853; Middlesex, England: Penguin Books, 1971), 62–63. Hereafter cited parenthetically in the text.

17 John Stokes, Michael R. Booth, and Susan Bassnett, *Bernhardt, Terry, Duse: The Actress in Her Time* (Cambridge: Cambridge University Press, 1988), 4.

18 Esther's scars forced a recent BBC serialization into laborious ingenuity. A doctor was dragged in to explain that smallpox scars sometimes faded; they did so accordingly, with predictable regularity from episode to episode, as the actress's face evolved from near-leprous disfigurement to perfect clarity in the end. In Dickens's novel, though, the mobile scars are emblems of a play conventional characterization forbids, making us see out of the corner of our eye a medley of Esthers beyond the boundaries of her official identity. The theatrical suggestiveness of *Bleak House* may be too delicately subversive for theatrical adaptation.

19 T. A. Palmer, *East Lynne* (1874), in *Nineteenth-Century British Drama*, ed. Leonard A. N. Ashley (Glenview, Ill.: Scott, Foresman, 1967), 389.

20 Ellen Wood, *East Lynne* (1861; New Brunswick, N.J.: Rutgers University Press, 1984), 464.

21 See, for instance, Barbara Hardy's influential account of George Eliot's covert coherence:

> The novel may be described in terms of the outline—the disposition of its trunk and limbs—but it must also be recognized as depending on the presence of a pattern in every unit, like the pattern within the pattern of a Chinese puzzle or of any bit of matter. . . . George Eliot's organization, like Shakespeare's, extends, for instance, to her imagery. Her irony, her continuity, and her presentation of change and collision, depend to some extent on repetitions, more or less prominent, of phrases and images which may make a casual first appearance. (*The Novels of George Eliot: A Study in Form* [1959; New York: Oxford, 1967], 8–9)

22 George Levine, *The Realistic Imagination: English Fiction from Frankenstein to Lady Chatterley* (Chicago: University of Chicago Press, 1981), 4.

23 D. A. Miller, *The Novel and the Police* (Berkeley: University of California Press, 1988), 26.

24 Lewes, *Actors and the Art of Acting*, 14.

25 Auerbach, *Private Theatricals*, 4–8.

26 Elaine Showalter, "Representing Ophelia: Women, Madness, and the Responsibilities of Feminist Criticism," in *Shakespeare and the Question of Theory*, ed. Patricia Parker and Geoffrey Hartman (New York: Methuen, 1985), 77–94. Like many accounts of Victorian constructions of Shakespeare, Elaine Showalter's sociologically suggestive survey of Ophelia's representational history says little about Ophelia's complex role in theatrical and antitheatrical narratives, or, indeed, in the theater.

27 Auerbach, *Ellen Terry*, 106–11, 240–47, analyzes the variety of Victorian Ophelia paintings.

28 Stokes, Booth, Bassnett, *Bernhardt, Terry, Duse*, 83–84.

29 Showalter, "Representing Ophelia," 80, 86.

30 Samuel Taylor Coleridge, *Shakespearian Criticism,* ed. T. M. Raysor, 2 vols. (London: Dent, 1960), 1:27; Jonathan Arac, "*Hamlet, Little Dorrit,* and the History of Character," *South Atlantic Quarterly* 87 (1988): 323.

31 Mary Cowden Clarke, *The Girlhood of Shakespeare's Heroines,* 3 vols. (1851; New York: AMS Press, 1974), 2:183; emphasis added. Hereafter cited parenthetically in the text.

Thomas B. Byers

The Difference Cooper Makes: The Cultural

Text of *The Last of the Mohicans*

The third paragraph of *The Last of the Mohicans* introduces the lake that is at the center of the plot. A dispute over the lake's name repeats, in small, the overlay of conflicts concerning title to the territory. The lake has been given different names by the French and the British, who are at war over it. But even in their difference the two European empires are, in an important regard, as one: "The two united to rob the untutored possessors of its wooded scenery of their native right to perpetuate its original appellation of 'Horican.'"[1] Cooper's text resists the imperial theft of the native right of right naming by insistently reiterating the supposedly original, appropriate name, not only in the voice of the heroic Hawk-eye but in that of the omniscient narrator as well. Using this name within this (political) frame is only one of Cooper's many ways of criticizing the behavior of his own race and expressing his sympathy with the disenfranchised and vanishing "Indians."[2]

There is, however, a fly in the onomastic ointment that Cooper would rub on (or in) the wounds of imperialism and genocide. The first (1826) edition of *Mohicans* has a beginning before the beginning, a head before the tale, in the form of a Preface. This is replaced in the 1831 Bentley Standard Novels Edition by a new Introduction, which, like its predecessor, is necessitated by the "obscurity in the Indian traditions, and . . . confusion in the Indian names,"[3] an obscurity that "the whites" have compounded "greatly . . . by their own manner of corrupting names" (1850, 6). Perhaps the most telling example of this white "manner" in *Mohicans* is one not revealed until the Putnam Edition of 1850, where a paragraph is added at the Introduction's tail end:

There is one point on which we would wish to say a word before closing this preface. Hawk-eye calls the *Lac du Saint Sacrement,* the "Horican." As we believe this to be an appropriation of the name that has its origin with ourselves, the time has arrived, perhaps, when the fact should be frankly admitted. While writing this book, fully a quarter of a century since, it occurred to us that the French name of this lake was too complicated, the American [originally English] too commonplace, and the Indian too unpronounceable, for either to be used familiarly in a work of fiction. Looking over an ancient map, it was ascertained that a tribe of Indians, called "Les Horicans" by the French, existed in the neighborhood of this beautiful sheet of water. As every word uttered by Natty Bumppo was not to be received as rigid truth, we took the liberty of putting the "Horican" into his mouth, as the substitute for "Lake George." The name has appeared to find favor, and all things considered, it may possibly be quite as well to let it stand. . . . We relieve our conscience by the confession, at all events, leaving it to exercise its authority as it may see fit. (8)

Thus the water's name is a Derridean's (wet) dream: the original appellation, given by native right of possession, turns out to be the last name, not the first—a supplement in fiction for what history lacks. It is an appropriation, moreover, not of a native name for the place but rather of a French name for some natives who never appear but remain lost in the prehistory of the narrative. The purportedly natural sign is unmasked as an arbitrary signifier, at several removes from both its signified and its ostensible founding subjects. It stands in for the one name—the actual name used by the actual Native Americans—that the text cannot or will not speak. The language of the colonized other remains "unpronounceable."

If the struggle over names repeats the struggle over the land, Cooper's role in the naming signifies his implication in the very dispossession of the Indians that he criticizes. He is merely the latest in a series of those who have appropriated the right to (name) the place. And like the name "Horican," his text as a whole becomes fiction's supplement for history's lack. Cooper notes the need for such supplementation when, in a passage that immediately follows (and implicitly justifies) his graphic description of the massacre at Fort William Henry, he faults history for its tendency, over time, to forget such horrors in an attempt to surround "its heroes," like Montcalm, "in an atmosphere of imaginary brightness" (180). Ultimately, of course, the issue of Montcalm's reputation is not central. The larger function of the massacre scene is part of a general mission in *Mohicans* that stands in opposition to the text's critique of white imperialism: the mission of supplementing history's lack of a sufficient rationale for the displacement and extermination of the Native Americans.

Many of the strategies of this supplementation, and many of the contradictions within and countertendencies to it, have been explored by other critics, from Roy Harvey Pearce and Donald Davie in the 1960s to Lora Romero and Forrest G. Robinson in 1991. Robinson offers a particularly fine analysis of Cooper's "patterns of virtually simultaneous address and denial, seeing and not seeing, with the[ir] clear implication that Cooper and his audience could neither confront directly nor fully repress their painful sense of moral responsibility for the destruction of the Native Americans."[4] The remainder of this essay will extend that analysis, particularly with regard to what Jane Tompkins has identified as Cooper's "thesis": "that the stability and integrity of a social order depend upon maintaining intact [the] traditional categories of sameness and difference" that give the order its identity and structure. In Tompkins's view this is why "an obsessive preoccupation with systems of classification—the insignia by which race is distinguished from race, nation from nation, tribe from tribe, human from animal, male from female—dominates every aspect of the novel."[5] The "cultural work" of *The Last of the Mohicans* is in large part the reiteration of the traditional categories, most notably the category of race, in the interest of defending, if not the rightness, then at least the "stability and integrity" of white hegemony. The work's supplement to history becomes (as supplementation often does) not an addition of something new but an obsessive repetition of terms that were already insufficient.

In a certain sense Tompkins herself simply repeats this repetition. For having identified the designs that the work has on us, she sees no gap between design and execution. She finds in Cooper "no ambiguities worth shaking a stick at," and she describes the world of his fiction as "morally secure forests, where good and evil were clearly known"—where the traditional categories and oppositions hold up.[6] As Cooper senses yet represses the gaps and contradictions in his culture's account of the "Indian problem" and thereby repeats them in the flaws and rips in his text's fabric, so Tompkins cites yet blinks at these flaws and rips. It is these that account for the *obsessive* quality of Cooper's preoccupation with categories and for the repetitive plots, the "grotesque concatenations of events," the "sensationalism and cliché," and other excesses of the prose, as he tries again and again to stitch together the ideas and emotions between which he is torn.[7] Cooper as cultural accountant is not so much Tompkins's mathematician, "solving or balancing . . . equations,"[8] as he is Natty Bumppo, who, in his fear of being misperceived as racially mixed, must declare over and over (about two dozen times) that he is "a man without a cross" of blood; he can only add, and can add only what he has already added.

The pressure behind Natty's, and Cooper's, insistence is precisely the pressure behind the novel: it is generally the "need for self-justification" and specifically the need to "establish the racial identity of Americans," as Tompkins suggests.[9] But it is more than that: it is the need to do these things in the face of an awareness on some level of the artificiality and flimsiness of the categories on which this identity and justification depend—an awareness that refuses, in Cooper's text, to go peacefully.[10] This is why, though Cooper's novel may be a New Critic's nightmare, it is a deconstructionist's dream: its structuring oppositions are in a state of continual collapse—a state that requires a continual, and ever more jury-rigged, shoring up. Such dualisms as civilization/wildness, culture/nature, purity/taint, innocence/guilt, and white/nonwhite can be sustained in the end only by the assertion of an extreme repressive violence. In Cooper's tale this is the narrative violence of the deaths of Uncas and Cora, which must occur so that the specter of miscegenation can be laid to rest. This inexorable violence in the name of preserving difference is the text's mark of the larger cultural work of eradicating the Indians.

Cooper's weaving of the pattern of racial differences is shot through with overdetermination and inconsistency. In some cases where his culture offers two competing systems of representation, he simply superimposes the two, with no apparent recognition of their contradictions. Thus he sees the Indians simultaneously as red devils and noble savages, both naturally evil and naturally good. He further confuses the issue by suggesting that the purest avatars of these two types, Magua and Uncas, respectively, are as they are partly because of their contacts with or similarities to whites—contacts or similarities that have diametrically opposed meanings in the two cases. Magua's tale of his encounter with white civilization is the story of a fall from Edenic innocence to barbarian (half-civilized) corruption and exile—a story in which the role of the satanic snake is played by demon rum (102–3). His hatred of the whites results not from natural difference or otherness but from a whipping that has inscribed their culture in scars on his back. The shirt he must wear to hide these scars is his version of Adam's fig leaf, the covering of his shame. It is also, as Tompkins points out, a sign of his loss of both racial and gender identity, and she rightly suggests that "he is bad" not by nature but "because his position in the social organization of the novel violates the boundaries that must be kept intact in order for social harmony to exist."[11]

Uncas presents a strikingly different case. At one point, when he and Duncan Heyward witness the tender reunion of the Munro sisters after their rescue from Magua, the men's reactions are extremely telling: "The manhood of Heyward felt no shame, in dropping tears over this spectacle of affectionate rapture; and Uncas stood, fresh and blood-stained from the combat, an unmoved looker-on, it is true, but with eyes that had already lost their fierceness, and were beaming with a sympathy, that elevated him far above the intelligence, and advanced him probably centuries before the practices of his nation" (115). Heyward, the civilized white man who in the end will be granted the right to define the future by propagating the species, openly weeps. Uncas does not go so far. But his eyes do reveal a level of emotional identification with the whites, and in this feeling he is seen as more highly evolved than others of his nation. The clear implication is that if they were to survive, the whole nation would evolve so—in the direction of white civilization.[12] Thus the story of the Indians is at once a story of a fall from plenitude toward whiteness as corruption and a story of progress from savagery toward whiteness as moral telos. Moreover, the difference in *Indian nature*—the difference between Uncas and Magua—is neither really natural nor really Indian. It is instead a repetition and even a product of differences *within white culture:* the difference between whites as the models and enforcers of civilized virtue and whites as the tempters who corrupt natural goodness.

While Cooper at times—as in the massacre scene—sees the Indians simply as brutal "raving savages" (207), at other times he exhibits a rather sophisticated awareness that the difference between red and white is between two cultures rather than between nature and culture. He allows both Cora and Munro to speak quite strongly against racial discrimination, and he even has moments of a more or less explicit anti-ethnocentrism. Nonetheless, he can only go so far. He reaches his limit, as Tompkins indicates, on the issue of miscegenation. To accept this would entail not only the surrender of the white man's control over the female body but the loss of race as a hegemonic category. Miscegenation is thus Cooper's fundamental taboo, standing to his opposition between whites and Indians as incest does to Lévi-Strauss's between culture and nature.[13] It is the very articulation of difference, and the very foundation of identity.

Cooper's stake in this taboo is, once again, overdetermined. It commingles the terms of individual psychology and social hegemony in a way that indicates how utterly mixed these inevitably are for the socially constructed subject. (Indeed, it is arguable that the commingling—one is tempted to say "the miscegenation"—of these terms in *Mohicans* contributes as much as anything to the text's enduring interest.) To the degree that, as Leslie Fiedler points out, people of color are to Caucasians a representation of the latter's unconscious,[14] miscegenation becomes the undoing of the primal repression of incestuous desire. This repression constitutes the difference between the conscious and the unconscious and grants entry to the symbolic order in which the individual has a sense of coherence; the author, a sense of authority; the social subject, an investment in the social order. It is, then, no more wonder that Cooper's Indians reject this taboo and actively seek to violate it than it is that the author himself feels compelled to sustain it. On a social level, the Indians are rebelling against the system of difference by which they are *oppressed;* on a psychic level, they represent the *repressed* that seeks to return. In this light, their reference to the white leaders whom they serve as their "fathers" is as latently subversive as it is overtly submissive.

Cooper's refusal to cross the racial-sexual boundary and his nagging sense of the arbitrariness of this taboo are both marked in the speech in which Tamenund, the Indian patriarch, points out the arrogance of the whites' refusal to consider racial mixing: "I know that the pale-faces are a proud and hungry race. I know that they claim, not only to have the earth, but that the meanest of their color is better than Sachems of the red man. The dogs and crows of their tribes . . . would bark and caw, before they would take a woman to their wigwams, whose blood was not of the color of snow." In response, Cora, who is herself of mixed blood, affirms both the taboo itself and a further taboo against interrogating its justification: "It is so. . . . But why—it is not permitted us to inquire" (305).[15] From this point on, the suppression of miscegenation gathers strength both in the plot—as all those who have suggested or implied or desired or defended it die—and in the discourse, as David Gamut (327), Hawk-eye (344, 347), and even Cora herself express an animus against it. When Tamenund tries to send Cora to Magua with the admonition, "A great warrior takes thee to wife. Go—thy race will not end," she replies, "Better, a thousand times, it should . . . than meet with such a degradation" (313). The language here makes it clear that the degradation is specifically racial, not merely individual.

As for Gamut, his opposition is framed by a biblical precedent; he compares Hawk-eye's war party in the final conflict with Magua and his tribe to "the children of Jacob going out to battle against the Shechemites, for wickedly aspiring to wedlock with a woman of a race that was favored of the Lord" (386–87).[16] Hawk-eye's opposition is put in analogies that suggest that miscegenation violates natural law (347). These rhetorical strategies not only fit the two characters but also invoke the two most important normative discourses of the time in defense against the threat of race mixing.

The climax of authoritative opposition to this threat comes when the death of Cora is sanctioned by God as preferable to the "fate worse than death" of racial mixing. Presented by the villainous Magua with a choice between his wigwam and his knife, Cora "regarded him not, but dropping on her knees, she raised her eyes and stretched her arms toward heaven, saying in a meek and yet confiding voice: 'I am thine! Do with me as thou seest best!'" (399). Two paragraphs later, surely in answer to her prayer, she dies. Yet even here the coherence of the book's vision is subverted, as the overdetermination of Cora's death reveals the desperation of Cooper's design. For the crossing that Cora must avoid has already occurred; she is already stained by the sin not only of her own parents but of an unnamed, remote ancestor from whom her mother inherited mixed blood. The cultural work of her death is to "solve" two equations that are both self-contradictory and irreconcilable: she dies at once to preserve a racial "purity" she does not possess and to expiate a sexual "sin" she did not commit.

Tompkins's reading of Cora's death is one of the moments where the critic repeats, rather than recognizing, the confusion of Cooper's text. Earlier, she noted that "Cooper's focus in constructing his character is on the mixture of nationalities and races that Cora represents and on the social problems that this mixture will pose."[17] But when Cora's mixed blood suggests an unresolved tension, as it does in its overdetermination of her death scene, Tompkins simply homogenizes it: "When Cora faces Magua on *their* clifftop, the situation admits of no compromise because Magua is a red man and Cora is white: there is no choice to be made between the wigwam and the knife of Le Subtil because the Anglo-

Saxon tradition of racial purity would not permit it."[18] What ultimately emerges from Cora's sudden whitewashing is that the category of race is, in her case, *both* biological and cultural. She is excluded from marriage to a white man by a cultural rule concerning her blood's genetic, hence "natural" taint; her upbringing is of no consequence here. But she is prohibited from marriage to a red man by her need to support, as a norm of the white culture in which she has been raised and educated, the very system of racial purity that ultimately excludes her.

Here again Cooper's miscegenation taboo curiously parallels Lévi-Strauss's account of the incest taboo. The latter is, in Derrida's analysis of it, at once what *marks off* human culture from animal nature and the one thing that *crosses the line,* since the taboo is at once cultural (part of a cultural code) and natural (because universal across cultures).[19] Similarly, the miscegenation taboo, which marks off racial difference and the difference between "primitive" (natural) and "civilized" (cultured) humanity, is also at once natural and cultural—based on Cora's biology (and hence absolute, beyond inquiry) when it prevents Heyward's acceptance of a match with Cora, but based only on her nurture (and hence only customary) when it prevents Cora's acceptance of a match with Magua. Hence with both taboos the foundation of the system of differences itself deconstructs those differences; that which separates nature and culture, "primitive" and "civilized" into either/or terms is itself both the one and the other.

Ultimately, *The Last of the Mohicans* fails to add anything significantly new to the defense of white hegemony; rather, it simply reiterates the arbitrary terms of that defense in a way that comes dangerously close to exposing the hollowness of its repetition and revealing the collapse of its logic. Nonetheless it does manage, by an insistent *narrative* logic— really an illogic or an ideologic—to offer what Tompkins calls a " 'fit' with the features of its immediate context."[20] It addresses that context's need "somehow to express guilt and to repress it at the same time,"[21] so as to recertify emotionally, as both natural and virtuous, its arbitrary discriminations of difference. But to read the text uncritically, as Tompkins recommends, is merely to identify its project as a "blueprint for [white] survival."[22] It must be read instead with a difference, in a way that will specify both the violence of its repressions and the fragility of the structures of opposition erected upon them. Such a reading attempts to disclose the textual consequences of insisting on unfounded distinctions.

To do so is, in this case, also to point toward the cultural consequences of this insistence—to suggest whose survival is in the blueprint, and whose is not. It is to read Cooper's cultural work not only as a design (on and for the whites) but as an execution (of the Indians).

Notes

1 James Fenimore Cooper, *The Last of the Mohicans: A Narrative of 1757* (1850; Albany: State University of New York Press, 1983), 12. Hereafter cited parenthetically in the text. Cooper glosses this name as "the tail of the Lake." Geographically, the lake is (ostensibly) named as the tail of another lake (Champlain). Textually, however, the name of the lake is, in small, the tale of the lake it names—the tale of a struggle over names. The other name for this tale, of course, is *The Last of the Mohicans.*

2 This alien misnomer seems ironically appropriate in this context, depending, as it does, on a white man's misapprehension of place. It is in any case Cooper's word throughout his text, and I have chosen to use it here partly as a reminder of the distinction between his fictional Indians and the actual Native Americans of whom they are at once a representation and a repression.

3 Cooper, *The Last of the Mohicans,* Bentley Standard Novels (London, 1831), 5.

4 Forrest G. Robinson, "Uncertain Borders: Race, Sex, and Civilization in *The Last of the Mohicans,*" *Arizona Quarterly* 47 (1991): 20–21; Roy Harvey Pearce, *The Savages of America: A Study of the Indian and the Idea of Civilization,* rev. ed. (Baltimore: Johns Hopkins University Press, 1965); Donald Davie, *The Heyday of Sir Walter Scott* (New York: Barnes and Noble, 1961); Lora Romero, "Vanishing Indians: Gender, Empire, and New Historicism," *American Literature* 63 (1991): 385–404.

5 Jane Tompkins, *Sensational Designs: The Cultural Work of American Fiction, 1790–1860* (New York: Oxford University Press, 1985), 118, 105.

6 Tompkins, *Sensational Designs,* 99.

7 Tompkins, *Sensational Designs,* 119, 95.

8 Tompkins, *Sensational Designs,* xvi.

9 Tompkins, *Sensational Designs,* 110, 111.

10 A parallel need to justify both Cooper and herself, and a curiously parallel collapse of the grounds of her justification, mark Tompkins's text. Offering her work as a corrective to New Critical readings and canonizations of American literature, she claims that both her "aims and values," even "some of the tactics that I have used in interpreting the texts under discussion," are grounded in the "writings of structuralist and post-structuralist thinkers: Lévi-Strauss, Derrida, and Foucault; Stanley Fish, Edward Said, and Barbara Herrnstein Smith" (xv). Yet when she herself reads Cooper, she reinstates many of the New Critical values articulated by figures like Cleanth Brooks and Robert Penn Warren: unity of intention and effect, coherence of execution (Cleanth Brooks and Robert Penn Warren, eds., *Understanding Poetry: An Anthology for College Students* [New York: Henry Holt, 1938], 18–19), and balancing of tensions (Cleanth Brooks, *The Well-Wrought Urn: Studies in the Structure of Poetry* [1947; New York: Harvest-Harcourt, 1975], 203), though the tensions Tomp-

kins finds balanced in Cooper are cultural rather than aesthetic. She also repeats the New Critics' bracketing of political judgment in favor of sympathetic attention. All in all, Tompkins's attack on the New Critics stands in curious juxtaposition to her repetition of their values. Much of the time it is easier to find the Brooks in her text than it is to catch the Fish.

11   Tompkins, *Sensational Designs*, 119.

12   For a further analysis and complication of the evolutionary motif, see Lora Romero's valuable "Vanishing Indians."

13   See Jacques Derrida, *Writing and Difference*, trans. Alan Bass (Chicago: University of Chicago Press, 1978), 283–84.

14   Leslie Fiedler, *Love and Death in the American Novel* (1960; New York: Laurel, Dell, 1969), 168, 175.

15   As Michele Frank has pointed out to me, Tamenund's speech itself represses the historical facts of miscegenation. White men did, in fact, have sex with and even sometimes marry Native American women (Whitman tells of such a marriage in "Song of Myself"). The social taboo against miscegenation was absolute for the whites only when it involved a white woman and a man of color. The cultural logic of this is obvious enough: if women are objects of exchange among men, the capacity enjoyed by one group of men both to maintain and to cross racial boundaries in controlling these objects is an assertion of dominance over the opposing group. Precisely the same logic, but with an even more extreme use of rape as an instrument of domination, governed the relations of white masters to their slaves in the antebellum South.

16   The passage to which he refers is Genesis 34. Ironically, Gamut seems to misread the passage, and he also ignores Genesis 49.5–7, where Jacob curses the cruel wrath of the sons involved. Here as elsewhere the authority of the defense against racial mixing is subverted. Once again it seems that Cooper can neither countenance miscegenation nor successfully suppress the illogic of the taboo against it.

17   Tompkins, *Sensational Designs*, 103.

18   Tompkins, *Sensational Designs*, 109.

19   Derrida, *Writing and Difference*, 283–84.

20   Tompkins, *Sensational Designs*, xviii.

21   Robinson, "Uncertain Borders," 7.

22   Tompkins, *Sensational Designs*, xvii.

Colleen Kennedy

The White Man's Guest, or Why Aren't More

Feminists Rereading *Lolita?*

She must be a true woman and she must be truly dead to trigger the literary climax.
—Susanne Kappeler, *The Pornography of Representation*

To my knowledge, there is only one feminist critique of *Lolita,* and that one appeared only recently. It is a striking scarcity, given that this book in particular would seem to invite feminist opinions.[1] Yet that fine critique, Linda Kauffman's "Framing *Lolita:* Is There a Woman in the Text?" explains its singularity: John Ray, Jr.'s, foreword, an obvious parody of both the psychologistic and moralistic readings that Nabokov despised, places such readings "at the bottom of the class," along with those of "feminists who may murmur against the brutality of Lolita's treatment."[2] My own experiences teaching and being taught the book confirm Kauffman's analysis. A few students refuse to read beyond the first few chapters; these students, if they are bold enough to announce their refusal in class, become subject to the derision of their more "sophisticated" peers and frequently of their professors.

Kauffman identifies these "readers [who] will go to any length to avoid being identified with" Ray as male critics who rely on Humbert's reading of Lolita and so produce misogynist readings that "elide Lolita herself."[3] I suggest that feminist critics, too—reading books very different from *Lolita*—ironically follow too closely the reading strategies put forward in *Lolita*'s afterword, Nabokov's instruction manual for the reader. I argue that Elaine Showalter's now famous injunction against "the feminist critique" in "Feminist Criticism in the Wilderness" has ironically resulted in some feminists' compliance with Nabokov's instructions. As Showalter defines it, feminist critique offers "readings of texts which consider the images and stereotypes of women in literature, the omissions and misconceptions about women in criticism, and woman-as-sign in semiotic systems."[4] In place of such critiques, Showalter endorses what she calls "gynocriticism," whose central questions are "How can we constitute women as a distinct literary group? What is *the difference* of women's writing?"[5] However, the danger of abandoning feminist critique too soon is that we also stop examining the structures through which women remain oppressed, leaving us to repeat those same structures in the new tradition we establish. Not enough work has been done comparing the terms by which male writers establish narrative control with the terms through which female writers—and I am speaking especially of critics—establish theirs. The resemblances may be frightening.

Let me illustrate by turning to *Lolita*'s afterword. There, Nabokov carefully distinguishes between art and pornography, between *Lolita* and what some readers would make of the book. Following Susanne Kappeler's example in *The Pornography of Representation,* however, I will argue that *Lolita* functions in much the same way that pornography does and in ways that implicate not only traditional responses to narrative but also some feminist responses inadvertently following in that tradition. In her preamble Kappeler notes that "pornography is not a special case of sexuality; it is a form of representation."[6] Nabokov seems to concur with Kappeler when he remarks in the afterword that "'pornography' connotes . . . certain strict rules of narration."[7] For Nabokov, however, these rules help contrive a representation that seems transparent in the face of the "real": "style, structure, imagery should never distract the reader from his tepid lust" (284). Here Nabokov relies on *the* truism of modern aesthetics: art does not provoke interest or appetite. Pornography is not art because it is dedicated only to the stimulation of appetite, and thus it is connected directly to the degraded "real" world.

For Kappeler, however, artistic representations *do* manifest desire, specifically for self-containment. Hence the aesthete's consistent emphasis on unity: "Representation is not so much the means of representing an object through imitation . . . as a means of self-representation through authorship. . . . Culture, as we know it, is patriarchy's self-image."[8] Divorcing pornography from art, as Nabokov insists we must do, masks an appetite that the two have in common: a desire for control, for self-determination. This desire is masked particularly well in modern aesthetics and in "nonrealistic" literature, in which the writer and the reader conveniently disappear from the field of representation.[9] Consequently, Kappeler reminds us that "crucial factors of representation are the author and the perceiver: agents who are not like characters firmly placed within the representation as content. They are roles taken up by social beings in a context."[10] These roles are not as hidden in *Lolita* as they might be in other modern novels, especially to the extent that *Lolita* is a joke on bad readers (and as Kauffman indicates, feminists slip easily into this category).

The lesson for readers begins in the plot of *Lolita*. Narrator Humbert is a reader as well, and despite his "madness," a very proper reader who displays Nabokov's own distaste for popular culture.[11] Humbert justifies his desire for Lolita on aesthetic grounds, grounds she does not understand and cannot appreciate, thus warranting his paternalism. According to his own logic, Humbert is not violating a twelve-year-old girl; he is pursuing what Nabokov, in the afterword, will call "aesthetic bliss." Early in his narrative, Humbert insists that what he seeks—in his childhood romance with Annabel, in his physical pursuit of Lolita across the United States and back, and in his recounting of their "affair" in the narrative we read—is beyond the merely physical. His passion for Annabel could have been "assuaged," he says, "only by our actually imbibing and assimilating every particle of each other's soul and flesh" (14).

Lolita is never really a physical creature to Humbert—she is "a beloved face, a little ghost in natural colors" (14). Although physical descriptions of nymphets are rampant in the novel, Humbert nevertheless maintains that *the* essential property defining the nymphet is spiritual:

> I would have the reader see "nine" and "fourteen" as the boundaries—the mirrory beaches and rosy rocks—of an enchanted island haunted by those nymphets of mine and surrounded by a vast, misty sea. Between these age limits, are all girl-children nymphets? Of course not . . . and vulgarity, or at least what a given community terms so, does not necessarily impair certain mysterious characteristics, the fey grace, the elusive, shifty, soul-shattering insidious charm that separates the nymphet from such coevals of hers as are incomparably more dependent on the spatial world of synchronous phenomena than on that intangible island of entranced time where Lolita plays with her likes. (18)

Not only is the definitive characteristic of the nymphet something spiritual and elusive, but only the genius can see it: "You have to be an artist and a madman . . . in order to discern at once, by ineffable signs . . . the little deadly demon among the wholesome children; *she* stands unrecognized by them and unconscious herself of her fantastic power" (18–19). This power compels the man gifted enough to perceive, and yet at the same time threatens his self-control. It is power to be contained. Humbert, he would have us believe, is not motivated by physical lust so much as inspired by a demonic muse—his is the artist's calling.

Even in these early descriptions of the nymphet, however, we find the seeds of Humbert's disillusionment when he acknowledges Lolita's "vulgarity." In *The Resisting Reader,* Judith Fetterley claims that the American novel frequently aims to (re)discover America and (so) a properly American self: individual, self-determining, and most emphatically male. As she notes of *The Great Gatsby,* the American novel frequently manifests "the failure of America to live up to the expectations of the men who 'discovered' it."[12] The America of *Gatsby* is divided within: the "fresh green breast of the new world," the last thing on earth "commensurate to [man's] capacity to wonder," is also a kind of prostitute— her trees "[pander] in whispers to the last and greatest of all human dreams."[13] According to Fetterley, the transcendent American self is discovered precisely through conflict with and by achieving power over a female antagonist, who thus symbolically represents a vulgar, unrealized culture—the whore America—who at once threatens and so helps to reassert the autonomy of the male protagonist. This conflict has become aestheticized; its resolution has become a primary criterion defining a work of American literature as literature.

Significantly, Nabokov says that in writing *Lolita,* he was "faced by the task of inventing America." Borrowing a critic's formulation, he notes that the novel was the "record of my love affair with the . . . English language," a language he would "magically use to transcend the heritage in his own way" (283, 287). As it is in *Gatsby,* America—embodied in Lolita—is divided. The idealized construct Humbert imagines as Annabel incarnate (and to which the signifier "Lolita" more properly refers) is continually betrayed, threatened by Dolly Haze, the vulgar little girl who "seduces" Humbert and then leaves him. Recall the "fantastic power" that Lolita exerts, but unconsciously. This power Humbert assigns her is itself self-contradicting. On one hand, it is the vulgar; on the other, it is what must be distinguished and protected from the vulgar. To be literary, Lolita (*Lolita*) must be contrary as well, divided within. Consequently, despite Nabokov's own warning that he "detest[s] symbols and allegory," Lolita becomes at once representative of art (an "island of entranced time") and what threatens art (the vulgar).

Thus Nabokov represents Lolita, in stark contrast with Humbert, as a common reader and a conspicuous consumer: "she it was to whom ads were dedicated: the ideal consumer, the subject and object of every foul poster" (136). She prefers movie magazines to literature, ice cream sundaes to gourmet foods, and will do almost anything for money; during their brief affair, Humbert effectively prostitutes her. Humbert's knowledge of the beautiful, of the unconscious power she wields, allows him to justify to himself (and to us, the jury) what he does to her. Admittedly, he regrets it by the end; as he stands listening to children play, he says, "I knew that the hopelessly poignant thing was not Lolita's absence from my side, but the absence of her voice from that concord" (280). In fact, readers turn to this point in the novel to redeem Nabokov, who apparently condemns Humbert's actions not only through irony but also through Humbert's self-denigration.

Humbert, however, finally proposes to make things up to Lolita by granting her (really himself) the immortality of art; ostensibly, she will benefit from her own victimization. Here, asked to admire the beauty of Humbert's creation, we become complicit. In the closing lines of the novel, Humbert's voice joins with Nabokov's in an invocation to art: "And do not pity C. Q. One had to choose between him and H. H., and one wanted H. H. to exist at least a couple of months longer, so as to have him make you live in the minds of later generations. I am thinking of aurochs and angels, the secret of durable pigments, prophetic sonnets, the refuge of art. And this is the only immortality you and I may share, my Lolita" (281).

Nabokov's collusion with Humbert becomes even clearer in the afterword, as does the reader's collaboration with Nabokov in the institutional demands that the afterword defines and reflects. Proper readers— readers like Humbert—will see that the book is about art, not pedophilia; common readers, like Lolita, will read it expecting to consume pornography (or, like John Ray, Jr., morality). In fact, Nabokov suspects that the book was initially rejected by publishers precisely because it didn't fulfill their expectations of *pornography*: "Obscenity must be mated with banality because every kind of aesthetic enjoyment has to be entirely replaced by simple sexual stimulation" (284). Similarly, Nabokov asserts that "*Lolita* has no moral in tow," that he is "neither a reader nor a writer of didactic fiction" (286), because didactic fiction, too, depends on a kind of desire. Nevertheless, there is a lesson to be learned. The book teases the reader into reading for eroticism, or into reading like John Ray, Jr., only in order to correct that reading by the end of the book, when the author finally tells us what it means. The seduction of a twelve-year-old girl becomes the "reality" the reader must "overcome," in the same way that Humbert must overcome the vulgarity of Dolly; and this training of the reader becomes the means by which Nabokov may overcome the vulgarity of the culture.

Art must be read as art: the purpose of this book is to achieve for Nabokov, and for those few blessed (or cursed) readers, what Nabokov "shall bluntly call aesthetic bliss, that is a sense of being somehow, somewhere, connected with other states of being where art (curiosity, tenderness, kindness, ecstasy) is the norm" (286). Humbert's pursuit of Lolita is Nabokov's pursuit of *Lolita*. The book becomes a medium of exchange between Nabokov and the proper reader, who share, besides the joke, disdain for the culture Lolita represents, and who transcend it together at the novel's end. This sharing, however, requires what Fetterley calls an "immasculated" reader,[14] and, according to Kappeler, exposes the "disinterested" aesthetic as a power play.

To illustrate her point, Kappeler begins her book with the story of the torture and murder of a black South African man, Thomas Kasire, by his white employer. The employer was convicted only because of evidence he himself produced: a series of photographs documenting the employer's mastery through the worker's suffering and death. Kappeler notes that "the pictures are not documentary evidence, snapped by a journalist or observer by chance in the right place at the right time. The pictures are compositions, deliberate representations, conforming to a genre. The victim is forced to 'pose'; the perpetrator of the torture positions himself . . . with reference to the camera."[15] The white employer is both inside and out of the pictures of Thomas Kasire: in one picture, he confirms his power metonymically as he views his own arm tightening the chain around Kasire's neck; in another, Kasire stands alone, the "icon" of the power of the white man. Kappeler links these horrifying scenarios both to pornography and to the traditional literary positioning of author and reader:

> One white man, the host, is the [master of ceremony], also acting as torturer in the content of the picture, another white man, a guest, behind the camera, acting in the production of the picture. The two

look at each other. The one in the picture will come out of the picture and take the place of the man behind the camera, looking at the scene he has framed. . . .

The victim does not come out of the picture, the victim is dead. In this case literally, in the general sense of representation virtually, or functionally, as there is no designated role in the world, and in the continued existence of the representation, for the victim to take up.[16]

Joyce's Stephen Dedalus reminds us of the similarity between the employer's position and that of the modern artist: the employer, like the artist, remains "behind or beyond or above his handiwork, invisible, refined out of existence, indifferent, paring his fingernails."[17]

Recall the end of *Lolita,* the circumstance under which she might share immortality with Humbert: "I wish this memoir to be published," Humbert writes, "only when Lolita is no longer alive" (281). To be immortalized, Lolita—never really "living" to begin with, only an image of her stepfather's lust—must be dead. Pale, pregnant, and vulgar Dolly Schiller will die in childbirth. Humbert, however, *is* able to step out of the picture; he will transcend over Lolita's dead body. Both host and audience, he represents himself to himself in the rarefied reality of the confession. In turn, proper readers become the white man's guests, whom Nabokov invites at the close of the novel to share in the celebration of narrative mastery, of aesthetic power. Using his "baffling mirror," a camera of sorts, and shooting against "the black velvet backdrop" of his America construct, Nabokov, as we watch, "transcend[s] the heritage in his own way" (288).

That heritage is the "real," the degraded culture he cannot control. "Fiction," Kappeler says, "wants no part *in* reality, it is the Other to the real. It is the surplus of the real, it need have no function in the real, it need serve no purpose. . . . [Such] gratuitousness is the mark of the murderer's photography. It is for sheer surplus pleasure. . . . [I]t is a form of [the white man's] free expression of himself, an assertion of his subjectivity."[18] If he is to assert his self-possession, the artist's art cannot be contaminated by the real; it must kill the real to maintain its image as wholly separate. This is the argument Nabokov uses in the afterword to excuse the pornography of *Lolita.* However, as Fetterley points out, the artist must paradoxically include the real in order to enforce that separation, to declare his independence of the "objective" and the contingent.

But such independence needs to be legitimated by another subject.

Hence, Kappeler concludes, the need for guests: "In the structure of representation, the two subjects are the author and the spectator/reader, the white man and his guests. The woman is the object of exchange."[19] In this common narrative scenario, an other, a woman—in this case a young girl, and in many cases a "bad reader"—becomes an antagonist, a symbol of a decadent culture, something to be overcome. Her subordination and suffering are put on display for another proper reader—Kappeler's "white man's guest"—to enjoy as he vicariously experiences the transcendence of the narrative voice. The woman (the consumer, the corrupt reader) dies or disappears to effect the male writer's flight and control.

So it is not Lolita who shares in Humbert's/Nabokov's immortality but the proper reader, precisely as Lolita is exchanged, made the symbol of the vulgar. The pretense that art is "surplus pleasure" (an institutionalized pretense perpetuated by much literary criticism in this country) conceals the power at stake: literature's status as medium of exchange between two subjects, the white man and his guest. And, ironically, even as feminist critics repoliticize literature, we still repeat the very structure Kappeler exposes: "The role of producer has been abstracted to such an extent that the philosopher tells us it is gender-free, androgynous, democratically open to those talented enough, and that the role of receiver (spectator, reader) is equally neutral."[20]

Not only does *Lolita* continue to be read and enjoyed as art—not in spite of but *because* of its subject matter—but the same paradigm occurs in feminist readings of narratives by women, precisely because the roles of author and reader have been so long coded as "neutral," as a matter of talent rather than power. And indeed, to the extent that such roles have been exposed as belonging to a discourse of power, it should come as no surprise that women aspire to those roles. If, as Fetterley argues, the powerlessness of the woman reader "results from . . . the invocation to identify as male while being reminded that to be male—to be universal, to be American—is to be *not female*," then her conclusion is understandable: "Feminist criticism represents the discovery/recovery of a voice, a unique and uniquely powerful voice capable of *canceling out those other voices* . . . which spoke about us and to us and at us but never for us" (emphasis added).[21]

"Those other voices," however, still come through, and in the work of some of the most noted feminist critics writing in the United States. Women are understandably attracted to the power offered by these positions of producer and proper reader. The draw of the latter prevents many feminists from attacking the aesthetics that so often justify women's subordination. The draw of the former has an even stranger consequence: the voices canceled out (literally drowned out in two cases I will discuss) are those of women. As a polemical conclusion, let me call attention to a few passages from Elizabeth Abel's anthology *Writing and Sexual Difference,* in which Showalter's "Feminist Criticism in the Wilderness" appears as the first essay. In this volume, noted feminist critics—specifically Mary Jacobus, Margaret Homans, and Susan Gubar—celebrate the narrative voice freed through the suffering or death of a *female* character, an alter ego. Granted, the motives behind this criticism are different from the motive behind Nabokov's fiction: *Lolita* is largely a flexing of narrative muscle, and Jacobus, Homans, and Gubar are attempting to make a place for women's writing in a tradition dominated by men. Nevertheless, the resemblances in the means they use may reveal something about the costs of establishing such a place, may cause feminists to wonder to what extent this developing feminist aesthetic is implicated in the one that permits *Lolita.*

In their separate readings of *The Mill on the Floss,* Jacobus and Homans place George Eliot in a position of mastery similar to Nabokov's; they assert Eliot's transcendence, not over "those other voices" to which Fetterley refers so much as over Maggie Tulliver's drowned body. In "The Question of Language: Men of Maxims and *The Mill on the Floss,*" Mary Jacobus examines the means by which Eliot "finds herself as woman writing," very explicitly by "kill[ing] off the woman engulfed by masculine logic and language."[22] It is precisely by drowning Maggie that Eliot "finds herself": "Maggie—unassimilable, incomprehensible, 'fallen'—is her text, a 'dead' language which thereby gives all the greater scope to authorial imaginings, making it possible for the writer to come into being."[23]

Margaret Homans makes a very similar argument in "Eliot, Wordsworth, and the Scenes of the Sisters' Instruction." She asserts that "the literal reading that for Maggie results in death issues for Eliot in the novelist's originality."[24] As Jacobus does, Homans allows that "other voice" —in this case, Wordsworth's—to speak through Maggie: "It is in fact Maggie's death that consolidates Eliot's vital independence from Wordsworth."[25] While Maggie may be destroyed by the effects of "those other voices," in both Jacobus's and Homans's readings, she is sacrificed more explicitly to "authorial imaginings," the writer's "being," "the novelist's originality," Eliot's "vital independence." It is *not* the destructive mascu-

line voices that receive attention in these essays but the liberated authorial voice, which Eliot achieves by killing off Maggie.

In Susan Gubar's " 'The Blank Page' and Female Creativity," the female
artist's death becomes her means of transcendence. Gubar analyzes an
Isak Dineson story about a museum, kept by nuns, in which hang sheets
from the marital beds of princesses. All but one of the sheets is stained,
and Gubar remarks: "Not an ejaculation of pleasure but a reaction to
rending, the blood on the royal marriage sheets seems to imply that
women's paint and ink are produced through a painful wounding, a literal influence of male authority."[26] The true artist, for Gubar, is the one
who is not "influenced," who acts independently and so purportedly
produces writing that is *not* the result of "painful wounding" (that is, a
writing not contingent on experience). The one unstained sheet in the
museum thus "becomes radically subversive, the result of one woman's
defiance *which must have cost either her life or her honor.* . . . The blank
page is a mysterious but potent act of resistance" (emphasis added).[27]
However, while Gubar goes on to praise this act of resistance at length,
this is the first and last time she mentions its cost. The sheet, the defiant princess's "self-expression" and "a sacred space consecrated to female
creativity," is worth the price of her death—a "painful wounding" Gubar
prefers to keep out of this picture.[28]

Such celebrations of female creativity do give *some* women *some* real
power. They give us access to a dominant discourse, access manifest in
articles in *Critical Inquiry* and professorships at prominent universities.
But we still gain such access by bracketing art from the real, a bracketing Kappeler calls into question. Let me end with an anecdote. I taught
Lolita recently (ironically, as it turns out, in conjunction with Kappeler's
book and in order to encourage students to write a feminist critique of
both Nabokov and the institution that would canonize him). Two days
into the discussion, a young woman—a "naive" reader who had taken
only one introductory literature course previously—asked to be excused
from class until we had finished discussing the novel. Sexually abused
as a child, she simply could not bear to hear the novel (not Humbert,
but the novel) defended by other students. Incapable of being a proper
reader in this circumstance, she achieved no sense of control; she felt
victimized yet again. And naive though she was by our standards, she
saw immediately that to endorse *Lolita* is to endorse its contents.

Showalter urges feminists away from the feminist critique because
"the feminist obsession with correcting, modifying, supplementing, re-

vising, humanizing or even attacking male critical theory keeps us dependent on it and retards our progress in solving our own theoretical problems."[29] But if reality is really a text, then texts really (re)produce reality. And feminist critics—indeed, all readers and writers—need to consider much more carefully what it is that we reproduce.

Notes

1   The debate about the book's "obscenity" have been well documented; see, for example, Phyllis A. Roth's Introduction to *Critical Essays on Vladimir Nabokov* (Boston: G. K. Hall, 1984), 9–10. And recent articles have reexamined the novel in terms of Humbert's pedophilia rather than in artistic terms; see, for example, Nomi Tamir-Ghez, "The Art of Persuasion in Nabokov's *Lolita*," *Poetics Today* 1 (1979): 65–83. Lance Olsen, in "A Janus-Text: Realism, Fantasy, and Nabokov's *Lolita*," *Modern Fiction Studies* 32 (Spring 1986): 115–26, treats *Lolita* as "a struggle for power," but a struggle "between two competing modes of discourse" (fantasy and reality). However, only Linda Kauffman's article (cited below) addresses the misogyny in the novel.

2   Linda Kauffman, "Framing *Lolita*: Is There a Woman in the Text?" in *Refiguring the Father: New Feminist Readings of Patriarchy,* ed. Patricia Yaeger and Beth Kowalski-Wallace (Carbondale: Southern Illinois University Press, 1989), 132.

3   Kauffman, "Framing *Lolita*," 133, 143.

4   Elaine Showalter, "Feminist Criticism in the Wilderness," in *Writing and Sexual Difference,* ed. Elizabeth Abel (Chicago: University of Chicago Press, 1982), 12.

5   Showalter, "Feminist Criticism," 15.

6   Susanne Kappeler, *The Pornography of Representation* (Minneapolis: University of Minnesota Press, 1986), 2.

7   Vladimir Nabokov, *Lolita* (New York: Berkeley, 1977), 284. Subsequent references are noted parenthetically in the text.

8   Kappeler, *Pornography,* 53.

9   I am thinking particularly of those manifestos of modernism and the New Criticism that ban personality from the artwork: for example, T. S. Eliot's "Tradition and the Individual Talent," or W. K. Wimsatt and Monroe C. Beardsley's "The Affective Fallacy" and "The Intentional Fallacy," in *Critical Theory since Plato,* rev. ed., ed. Hazard Adams (New York: Harcourt Brace Jovanovich, 1992), 761–63 and 945–59.

10   Kappeler, *Pornography,* 3.

11   In *Strong Opinions* (New York: McGraw-Hill, 1973), Nabokov notes that "there is an average reality, perceived by all of us, but that is not the true reality: it is only the reality of general ideas, conventional forms of humdrummery, current editorials" (19). This general disdain for convention is manifest in Nabokov's consistent diatribes against groups, movements, and especially critics whose writing Nabokov felt reflected only those "conventional forms of humdrummery."

12   Judith Fetterley, *The Resisting Reader: A Feminist Approach to American Fiction* (Bloomington: Indiana University Press, 1978), xiii.

13 F. Scott Fitzgerald, *The Great Gatsby* (1925; New York: Charles Scribner's Sons, 1953), 182.

14 As Fetterley defines it, immasculation is the process by which women "readers and teachers and scholars . . . are taught to think as men, to identify with a male point of view, and to accept as normal and legitimate a male system of values, one of whose central principles is misogyny" (*Resisting Reader,* xx).

15 Kappeler, *Pornography,* 6.

16 Kappeler, *Pornography,* 8–9.

17 James Joyce, *Portrait of the Artist as a Young Man: Text, Criticism, and Notes,* ed. Chester G. Anderson (New York: Viking Press, 1968), 215.

18 Kappeler, *Pornography,* 9–10.

19 Kappeler, *Pornography,* 51.

20 Kappeler, *Pornography,* 53.

21 Fetterley, *Resisting Reader,* xxiii–xxiv.

22 Mary Jacobus, "The Question of Language: Men of Maxims and *The Mill on the Floss,*" in *Writing and Sexual Difference,* ed. Abel, 52, 51.

23 Jacobus, "The Question of Language," 46.

24 Margaret Homans, "Eliot, Wordsworth, and the Scenes of the Sisters' Instruction," in *Writing and Sexual Difference,* ed. Abel, 59.

25 Homans, "Eliot, Wordsworth," 69.

26 Susan Gubar, "'The Blank Page' and Female Creativity," in *Writing and Sexual Difference,* ed. Abel, 86.

27 Gubar, "'The Blank Page,'" 89.

28 Gubar, "'The Blank Page,'" 89, 91.

29 Showalter, "Feminist Criticism," 13.

Jay Clayton

The Narrative Turn in Minority Fiction

In Louise Erdrich's novel *Tracks* (1988), an old Chippewa known as Nanapush tells of using stories to hold off his own death: "During the year of sickness, when I was the last one left, I saved myself by starting a story. . . . I got well by talking. Death could not get a word in edgewise, grew discouraged, and traveled on." Perhaps because he is the last of his people to follow the old ways, Nanapush is the only character in Erdrich's three interrelated novels to make explicit claims about the power of narrative. Later in the text he tells of saving his granddaughter, who has almost frozen to death, by telling her stories through an entire night: "Once I had you I did not dare break the string between us and kept on moving my lips, holding you motionless with talking."[1]

Only Nanapush dwells on the power of stories, but all of Erdrich's novels rely on this strength, rely on the sinuous thread of narrative to weave the lives of her people into one seamless fabric. Part of the pleasure of reading *Love Medicine* (1984), her first published novel, is slowly piecing together how its many characters are related. *The Beet Queen* (1986) focuses on fewer people, but the theme of connections emerges even more insistently in the imagery that organizes the text. The figure of the web shows up repeatedly, in the "spider web of thick dead vines" that holds one character as in a hammock; in the silky nest a spider weaves in a baby's hair, a "complicated house" too beautiful to destroy; in the red maze a woman has knitted into a sweater, a "tangle of pathways" without an exit; and in the thread of flight, a thread that links three generations of people who have hardly known one another.[2] Consequently, when Nanapush talks about the mysterious patterns that stories reveal, we are prepared to understand: "There is a story to it the way there is a story to all, never visible while it is happening. Only after, when an old man sits dreaming and talking in his chair, the design springs clear."[3]

The theme of storytelling in Erdrich's fiction prompts me to think about the interest in narrative among writers of the last fifteen years, not only among minority writers but also among contemporary novelists generally.[4] Why has storytelling—particularly oral, folk, or traditional storytelling—become a prominent topic in current fiction? How does the *theme* of storytelling relate to the increased acceptability of the *technique* of narrative in today's writing? Since the mid-1970s, novelists have increasingly employed conventional narrative forms that seemed passé during the heyday of metafiction, language games, and self-reflexive experiments of the 1960s. One has only to name a few novels by well-known contemporary writers in which narrative figures not only as a primary technical resource but also as part of the theme—John Irving's *World According to Garp* (1978), John Gardner's *Freddy's Book* (1980), Anne Tyler's *Dinner at the Homesick Restaurant* (1982), Philip Roth's *Counterlife* (1986), Cynthia Ozick's *Messiah of Stockholm* (1987), John Barth's *Tidewater Tales* (1987), Paul Auster's *Moon Palace* (1989)—to see how widespread the phenomenon has become.[5] These novels, however, can hardly be called old-fashioned. Many novelists today insist on the importance of narrative even as they experiment with structure, style, and point of view. Like many postmodern texts, their novels call into question our usual assumptions about the difference between narrative and experimental works.

Leslie Marmon Silko's *Ceremony* (1977), for example, mixes accounts of Tayo, a "half-breed" living on a reservation in the years following World War II, with the poetry and myths of the Laguna Pueblo people; jumps back and forth among at least four different time periods; and combines powerful social criticism—of race relations, of white attitudes toward nature and technology, of nuclear arms—with traditional Indian beliefs. It engages in serious technical experimentation yet begins by instructing us in narrative's power:

> I will tell you something about stories,
> [he said]
> They aren't just entertainment.
> Don't be fooled.
> They are all we have, you see,

all we have to fight off
illness and death.[6]

Among works by Native Americans one can find examples of this combination in James Welch's myth-filled historical novel, *Fools Crow* (1986), which constitutes a profound opening to narrative revelations from the spare, lyrical techniques of his first novel, *Winter in the Blood* (1974); in Michael Dorris's *Yellow Raft in Blue Water* (1987), with its three generations of narrators; and in the legends of N. Scott Momaday's *Ancient Child* (1989). But Native American fiction represents only one aspect of the recent interest in storytelling among minority writers. One could equally point to the use of traditional oral tales—called *cuentos*—in the work of the Chicano novelist Rudolpho Anaya.[7] Or one could point to the flamboyant figure of the storyteller in Maxine Hong Kingston's *Tripmaster Monkey: His Fake Book* (1989), the alternating narrators of Amy Tan's *Joy Luck Club* (1989), and the "American Story" of Gish Jen's *Typical American* (1991). Some of the most direct treatments of the theme of storytelling in recent years, however, have taken place in novels by African Americans.[8]

Alice Walker's *Meridian* (1976) memorializes a slave named Louvinie, who had her tongue cut out as punishment for scaring a white child to death with her tales. She learned the gift of storytelling from her parents in Africa, who could discover the identity of murderers by entangling them in a detailed retelling of the crime. The contemporary heroine of Gayl Jones's *Corregidora* (1975) is haunted by the fierce imperative to "make generations" so that the story of her grandmother and great-grandmother's abuse by the same man will not go untold. David Bradley dedicates *The Chaneysville Incident* (1981) to the storytellers and historians in his life, and the novel climaxes in a night-long retelling of a historical narrative, the story of a group of escaped slaves driven to kill their children and themselves rather than be recaptured. At the beginning of the novel, the narrator's memory of an old man's stories is what sets him searching for the truth of the past; at the end, another old man's tale gives the slaves strength to commit suicide. More often, though, stories provide the strength to live. Both Toni Cade Bambara's *Salt Eaters* (1980) and Audre Lorde's *Zami* (1982) feature moments when telling stories literally keeps characters alive,[9] and John Edgar Wideman's *Reuben* (1987) focuses on an unlicensed lawyer who solves problems simply by listening to his clients tell their stories. Toni Morrison has often spoken of the importance of storytelling to her art and to the lives of the people she writes about: "People crave narration. . . . That's the way they learn things. That's the way human beings organize their human knowledge—fairy tales, myths. All narration."[10]

Despite the prominence of narrative in contemporary fiction of all kinds, I have chosen to focus on writers of color for several reasons. To begin with, the theme of storytelling is particularly visible in these writers because of the importance of traditional folk culture to their communities. This theme, in turn, helps to make explicit some of the special uses to which the technique of narrative is being put today. Finally, the narrative turn in fiction is related to the emphasis in postmodern society on local political struggles. The tactical value of narrative in politics is by no means restricted to minority writers or minority causes, but the comparatively insular nature of oppressed or marginal groups dramatizes the altered political function of narrative today.

The Politics of Contemporary Narrative

When the narrative turn among white establishment writers first began to attract the attention of literary critics, it was quickly dismissed as a symptom of political reaction paralleling the turn to the right among the United States electorate. Writing in 1982, Larry McCaffery noticed that "experimentalism *per se* . . . is not nearly as important to writers today as it was a decade ago" and attributed this trend to the "conservativism of our times."[11] Such diagnoses became a commonplace of book review sections and literary quarterlies during the 1980s. Many commentators could not resist drawing a parallel between what they saw as the complacent social attitudes of the Reagan and Bush eras and the turn to more accessible narrative conventions. The very success of recent narrative works in attracting a wider readership than the metafiction of the 1960s ever earned has been taken as evidence that some of our most serious novelists have made a compromise with the times. John Gardner's notorious call in 1978 for a return to "moral fiction" certainly reinforced the impression that interest in narrative went hand-in-hand with conservative social views.[12]

This impression, however, could not be further from the truth. The narrative turn does not represent a return to old-fashioned values or conventions. In fact, the very dichotomy between daring experiments and safe traditional works seems anachronistic, an opposition that more accurately describes the high-modernist rebellion against nineteenth-century literature at the beginning of this century than the flexible, ad hoc arrangements of contemporary writing. Far from seeming a secure prop of the establishment, narrative is often viewed by novelists today as an oppositional technique because of its association with unauthorized forms of knowledge, what Foucault has called "subjugated" and Morrison "discredited" knowledge. Scorned by official culture, narrative is one of the "naive knowledges, located low down on the hierarchy, beneath the required level of cognition or scientificity,"[13] and it can be all the more attractive to iconoclasts for that reason. Certainly, much of narrative's attraction for radicals in such fields as history, anthropology, psycho-analysis, and the law lies in the way it violates the discursive norms of their disciplines. In literature, narrative cannot have the same iconoclastic force, but its association with unauthorized knowledge can be and often is emphasized by drawing on oral forms (folktales, myths, legends, oral histories), by exploring less privileged written genres (diaries, letters, criminal confessions, slave narratives), by identifying the contemporary text with archaic symbolic modes (rituals, dreams, magic), and by writing about traditional activities (vernacular arts, recipes, folklore, quilting and other crafts, native music and dance).

Barbara Christian has written of the importance of these forms in black women's fiction: "This exploration of new forms based on the black woman's culture and her story has, from my perspective, revitalized the American novel and opened up new avenues of expression, indelibly altering our sense of the novelistic process."[14] From my perspective, too, the rich mixture of traditional narrative forms and contemporary political concerns—found not only in black women's writing but also in the fiction of black men and of other peoples of color, both male and female—represents the most important force transforming the North American novel of the 1980s and 1990s and has made this period and this place one of the most exciting for writing of the century.

Today the writing of social radicals often finds its best outlet in highly conventional forms. The difficulty of understanding this paradox is a source of confusion for one of the main characters in Walker's *Meridian*. The heroine, a young black activist, confesses to years of frustration with watching her mother's generation sublimate its anger through religion, singing the old hymns about salvation in Heaven instead of rising up to demand justice on earth. Meridian "had always thought of the black church as mainly a reactionary power." It is only when she witnesses a service on the anniversary of a young man's death by clubbing that she realizes that revolutionary sentiments can be stirred up by the most venerable observances. She suddenly could hear the congregation pleading: "let us weave your story and your son's life and death into what we already know—into the songs, the sermons. . . . [T]he music, the form of worship that has always sustained us, the kind of ritual you share with us, these are the ways to transformation that we know."[15]

I have emphasized the subversive uses of narrative in order to dispel a widespread assumption about the political complacency of contemporary fiction, but there is a more specific point to be made about the current revival of narrative. From both their practice and their explicit statements, one gathers that many novelists today believe that the act of telling a story can be empowering. This belief seems to be shared not only by the minority writers mentioned above but also by numerous white novelists. Minority writers and feminists have made the question of empowerment a major theme of their criticism—see Audre Lorde's "Uses of the Erotic: The Erotic as Power" for one example out of many— but that is no reason to deny that narrative can be empowering in other contexts as well.[16] Focusing on writers from oppressed or minority communities casts in greater relief the political dimension of narrative's capacity, but it is not meant to suggest that this capacity is unavailable or unexploited by writers from other segments of the population. In fact, the increased division of society into local communities, which is characteristic of advanced capitalism, makes this capacity more important to all groups, including economic and social elites that formerly may have relied on other forms of power. But that is another story.

Most minority writers acknowledge the reality of domination from above. From the nineteenth century onward, resistance to this domination has reflected a gamut of responses ranging from liberal advocacy of civil rights to violent rebellion. The first African-American narratives were addressed to a white ruling class and aimed to impress this readership with the humanity of African Americans, who were as deserving of freedom and respect as their readers. Although phrased in the pervasive American idiom of autonomy and often following the deeply individualistic pattern of spiritual conversion narratives, this literature sometimes had recourse to the language of civic republicanism when attempting to describe the benefits that would accrue to society at large if blacks were given the same rights as whites. In his *Narrative*, Frederick Douglass is careful to celebrate freedom's "responsibilities" as well as its "rights," and his break with the Garrisonians came in part because of his defense of the union and his support of electoral politics.[17] In the early twentieth century, the republican note was sounded more loudly by writers such as Booker T. Washington, who in *Up from Slavery* emphasizes his strong sense of public responsibility and civic virtue. This strain in African-American writing has received much criticism, but the dream of a just public realm that values the equal participation of all people, regardless of color, is a vision of power that will not go away.

William Andrews has argued that this vision, like other African-American models of a free society, is integrally related to narrative modes, to the development of what he calls "free storytelling." The ability to tell a free story is as empowering as any image of freedom contained within it. The contemporary novelist Charles Johnson would seem to agree, for in *Oxherding Tale* (1982), his extraordinarily free reworking of the slave narrative genre, he presents the liberation of his storytelling technique, "the manumission of first-person viewpoint," as just as important as the freeing of his main character. The vision of rebuilding and conserving a shared world that ends the novel depends on the narrator being able to pen the final words of his text: "This is my tale."[18]

More common in contemporary minority discourse is the use of narrative to exploit, in positive ways, what Foucault has called "disciplinary" modes of power. According to Foucault, power is not a hierarchical relationship, not something that those on the top hold over those below. Rather, everyone—the mighty as well as the humble—is positioned by networks of power that organize the social realm by shaping the way one thinks about the body, sexuality, kinship, the family, and all other contemporary modes of knowledge. In English his idea is fortuitously summed up by a pun: the fact that the word *discipline* means both "punishment" and "a specialized field of inquiry" indicates the way the organization of knowledge rules our lives.

Michel de Certeau has argued that Foucault's theory is too negative, that it neglects the way that everyday "practices" warp disciplines to their own ends: "If it is true that the grid of 'discipline' is everywhere becoming clearer and more extensive, it is all the more urgent to discover how an entire society resists being reduced to it, what popular procedures . . . manipulate the mechanisms of discipline and conform to them only in order to evade them."[19] He prefers to call these popular procedures "tactics" rather than "strategies" (the word used by Foucault), because the former seems to capture more effectively the provisional, opportunistic character of these responses. If strategic planning implies a general outline for an entire conflict, tactics suggests isolated and independent decisions, judgments made on the spot, under the pressure of engagement, often on foreign territory. De Certeau explores the tactical dimension in such everyday practices as talking, moving about, reading, shopping, and cooking, but he focuses on certain procedures that appear to highlight the devious creativity of the ordinary—games, gift giving, figurative language, and, perhaps most important of all, storytelling.

De Certeau identifies four ways that stories help people to escape disciplinary control. First, stories preserve the memory of successful tactics, ruses that can be used in daily life. They are "living museums of these tactics, the benchmarks of an apprenticeship," a less serious space, which nevertheless insinuates itself into official discourse—even into scientific writing—in the form of case histories, analogies, interviews, and so on.[20]

Second, stories preserve tactics not only in their content but also in their structure. The tricks and turns of narratives encode "moves"; they demonstrate native procedures that perhaps could not be taught directly. In thrall to a story's charm, we are moved in ways for which we cannot entirely account, made to practice procedures without being able to formulate exactly what we have learned. By showing rather than telling, narrative may escape the processes that recuperate or co-opt more explicit forms of knowledge. "Narration does indeed have a content, but it also belongs to the art of making a *coup*. . . . Its discourse is characterized more by a way of *exercising itself* than by the thing it indicates. And one must grasp a sense other than what is said. It produces effects, not objects."[21]

This aspect of stories—their trickiness, the canniness of a vernacular mode—is very important to minority literatures. Henry Louis Gates, Jr., has demonstrated the centrality, through more than three centuries, of trickster figures such as Esu-Elegbara and the "signifying monkey," which turn up in Africa as well as in all "New World African-informed cultures."[22] A similar trickster, the "tripmaster monkey," is the improvisational genius behind the manic narratives of Maxine Hong Kingston's latest work. Riddles, deceptive stories, and dreams that say more than the dreamer knows are common techniques of Coyote, the trickster figure in much Native American literature.

Third, the temporality of narrative offers an alternative to the spatializing procedures of most disciplines. Temporal devices, which are basic to narrative, make an impression of their own. As we move through a story, false leads, flashbacks, digressions, and reversals create effects that may be at odds with the official message that a work conveys. Whereas the meaning of a narrative can always be recovered by the organizing grids of disciplines, the process of reading or hearing narrative cannot be so easily systematized.

Finally, narrative possesses a performative dimension; it enacts as well as means. Just as the ritual process can have a transformative effect on its participants, so stories can change the person who becomes caught up in their charm. This transformative capacity is another aspect of narrative that figures prominently in writing by minorities. Silko organizes *Ceremony* entirely around this principle. African-American novelists frequently claim this power for their narratives: Walker dedicates a novel to the Spirit (*The Color Purple* [1982]); Morrison opens several texts with an allusion to ritual (*Sula* [1974] and *Song of Solomon* [1977]); other writers make healers, voodoo figures, or conjure women the presiding spirits of their novels (Bambara's *Salt Eater,* Ntozake Shange's *Sassafrass, Cypress and Indigo* [1982], Paule Marshall's *Praisesong for the Widow* [1983], and Gloria Naylor's *Mama Day* [1988]).

The conjunction between minority practice and some contemporary theories of power lends support to Gates's contention that the African-American tradition has developed its own version of many of the ideas now common in poststructuralism. It also helps us to understand why narrative is seen not as a prop of the status quo but as a source of empowerment for many oppressed or marginalized peoples. This conjunction, however, raises its own set of difficulties. How does a particular verbal structure possess power, either to raise up or to oppress? Is the power *in* a form of discourse or does it reside in the way that form is used? What relation, if any, exists between the kinds of power narrative possesses today and the organization of contemporary society?

Narrative Communities

Near the end of Toni Morrison's *Song of Solomon,* the protagonist, Milkman, travels to a small town in Pennsylvania where his father had lived as a boy. Milkman remains there for four days, during which he receives visits from every old man in the area who had known his forefathers, and from some who had only heard about them. They all speak of Milkman's family with awe and affection. For the first time, Milkman finds himself feeling some tenderness for the father he had always resented.

As the old men talk, Milkman begins to realize that there is something he can do for them, a service he can perform; he can continue the story: "That's why Milkman began to talk about his father, the boy they knew, the son of the fabulous Macon Dead. He bragged a little and they came alive. How many houses his father owned (they grinned); the new car every two years (they laughed); and when he told them how his father tried to buy the Erie Lackawanna (it sounded better that way), they hooted with joy."[23]

Storytelling works to educate Milkman in the virtues of community, in the importance of an organic link to the past and to the lives of those who surround him. It teaches him to respect the very people he had taken advantage of and abused—his family. A few pages later, Milkman will hear another story about his family's past, this time in a song chanted by children in a circle, and the experience will complete his transformation. Through the power of narrative he will have found his place in a community that he can call his own. It is a place for which he is willing to die.

According to Jean-François Lyotard, a defining feature of contemporary Western societies is the proliferation of such local narrative communities. In the course of the twentieth century, Lyotard argues in *The Postmodern Condition,* we have seen the decline of the grand metanarratives, especially the narratives of scientific progress and political freedom that have legitimated modernity since the time of the American and French revolutions. By means of these inspiring stories, modern science was able to establish itself as the reigning paradigm of truth and the modern state was able to achieve unity. But now the grand narrative, as a genre, has lost its credibility; we are suspicious of tales that claim to be true for everyone everywhere and at all times. In place of a few metanarratives there have arisen countless micronarratives, which offer "immediate legitimation" to diverse, often conflicting enterprises and groups.[24] Rather than promoting consensus, these micronarratives enable a splintering of the social world; rather than confirming a monological conception of truth (rational and scientific in its orientation), they offer an alternative model of knowledge.

This alternative, which Lyotard calls "narrative knowledge," is perfectly suited to the needs of contemporary postmodern society.[25] It includes not just verifiable statements about reality but also notions of competence, images of how to do things, how to live, how to care for one another, how to be happy. It must be judged not by the standards of truth or falsehood but by those of usefulness. Does it teach something that matters to one's existence in the particular historical conditions one inhabits? Does it convey some accepted belief, some habit or custom, some technical procedure or knack that one needs to know in order to succeed? This form of knowledge is local, contingent, and ephemeral; it is tolerant of "error," of everyday lore and old wives' tales, as long as the results are satisfactory.

As a description of "folk" ways of knowing, Lyotard's account of narrative knowledge puts into theoretical terms what African-American writers have known since the time of slavery.[26] Lyotard's contention that this kind of knowledge is peculiarly suited to the demands of living in a postmodern world, however, gives us another reason to look carefully at the relation between narrative and social empowerment. Lyotard's view of narrative practices parallels that of de Certeau in two respects. For both writers, narrative's temporality and its ability to record successful tactics are major reasons why it figures prominently in contemporary society. Lyotard's interest in legitimation prompts him to add two further reasons. First, stories, unlike scientific knowledge, lend themselves to a multiplicity of "language games." If "there are many different language games—a heterogeneity of elements," then monolithic institutions have trouble maintaining control over society. Micronarratives, distributed among discrete language games, only legitimate ad hoc arrangements, "only give rise to institutions in patches—local determinism." Second, stories position both speaker and listener within a pragmatics of communication or "speech act" situation.[27] In both cases, postmodern legitimation is oriented toward the local. The notion of multiple language games, adapted from Wittgenstein, preserves the integrity of differing perspectives, and the notion of "speech acts," adapted from Searle, locates the narrative subject and the addressee within a specific community of discourse.

Lyotard's localism fits in nicely with other accounts of contemporary society—with Foucault's "specific intellectual," engaged in local struggles, for example; or with the sociologist Daniel Bell's discussion of the "participation revolution," in which "many more groups now seek to establish their social rights—their claims on society—through the political order." Bell worries that this localism will lead to chaos because there will be no way to coordinate policy on the national level. One need endorse neither Bell's fears nor his proposed solutions to recognize the acuteness of his analysis. He discusses the multiplication of constituencies; the increasing primacy of the group, rather than the individual, as

a political unit; the changing networks of social relationships (from kinship to occupational and issue-oriented affiliations); the role of project
grants and mission orientation in dispersing the centralized power of
institutions and corporations; and the alteration of classic bureaucratic
structure by the growth of nonprofit organizations.[28] To these factors
we should add the rise in the 1980s of what are sometimes called the
"new social movements" and the "politics of identity." The orientation of
social movements today toward specific issues cuts across older ways of
organizing the social body (political party, class, etc.); and this fact applies to movements located along the entire spectrum of contemporary
values: environmentalism, the peace movement, pro choice, pro life, the
National Rifle Association, and religious fundamentalism. The same can
be said of the identity politics mobilizing many groups: women, people
of color, gay men and lesbians, people with disabilities, and the elderly.

Since this reorganization of the social body is often labeled fragmentation and treated as one of the most intractable problems confronting our
nation, it is worth taking a moment to look at some of the strengths of
this new dispensation. To begin with, identity politics, which derives its
power as much from a consumer economy as from a democratic policy,
may succeed in changing social attitudes—and hence altering everyday
practices—in patterns that are out of sync with legislative or judicial decisions from on high. The way women's roles have continued to change
despite the failure of the Equal Rights Amendment is one example;
the increase in visibility of lesbian and gay male life-styles despite the
Supreme Court's decision in *Bowers* v. *Hardwick* (and despite the enormous risks involved in such visibility) is another.[29] I am not suggesting
that misogyny and homophobia have disappeared—not when violence
toward women is as pervasive as ever and HIV infection is used as an excuse for new forms of discrimination, to say nothing of the persistence
of many old forms of prejudice—but I am arguing that local practices,
which are given power by an advanced capitalist economy, can offset
some of the effects of domination from above.

Not every aspect of Lyotard's thesis is as convincing as his treatment
of the connection between micronarratives and postmodern society. His
account of "postmodern science" oddly exalts a few areas of contemporary research—theories of fractals, catastrophes, and chaos—into an
account of all contemporary science and then uses it as proof that even
science "is theorizing its own evolution as discontinuous, catastrophic,
nonrectifiable, and paradoxical."[30] His faith in "paralogy," the pursuit of

instabilities and paradoxes in every realm, merely privileges the disruption of order for its own sake. We need to distinguish Lyotard's acute descriptions of advanced capitalist societies from what has been called the "anarchistic" and "irrationalist" strain in his thinking.[31]

Even if we restrict ourselves to the "sociological" vein in Lyotard, we are still confronted by the other questions posed earlier. How does a cultural form such as narrative possess power? The first point to be made is that nothing *in* narrative gives it a determined relation to a particular social order. This assertion goes against the conventional wisdom of much contemporary narrative theory. In its support, however, one should note that Lyotard nowhere distinguishes the formal properties of micronarratives from those of metanarratives. Although the two legitimize entirely different social orders, there is no difference in their structure. Both are characterized by all the common attributes of stories: a beginning, middle, and end; a hero who acts as the subject of the narrative; obstacles that impede the hero's progress; a mimetic or representational dimension; and a teleological organization of the whole.

If nothing in their formal character as narrative enables micronarratives and metanarratives to authorize conflicting forms of society, then perhaps the difference lies in how they are used, when and where they come into play, who is employing them, and for what ends. We began to get an inkling of this conclusion when we saw the way minority communities could turn conventional forms to their own uses. It goes against the grain of much twentieth-century thinking to assert that conditions outside a text—the conditions of its production and reception—should be considered in assessing a work of literature. But this idea in no way returns us to a nineteenth-century aesthetics of expression. For it is not the individual author and reader who count here but the social unit that these figures help to constitute. Lyotard implies as much when he draws an analogy between traditional oral storytelling and the pragmatics of micronarratives. In oral literature the narrative locates all relevant participants—the storyteller, the hero, and the listeners—within a community that the telling itself helps to bring into existence. A "collectivity that takes narrative as its key form of competence"—traditional communities and, I am arguing, many groups in advanced capitalism, particularly those that perceive themselves as oppressed or in the minority— "finds the raw material for its social bond not only in the meaning of the narratives it recounts, but also in the act of reciting them. . . . In a sense, the people are only that which actualizes the narratives."[32]

In *Just Gaming,* a work published the same year as *The Postmodern Condition,* Lyotard explains in more detail how traditional narratives achieve this effect. In oral societies the person who tells a story does not create it but passes it on; the narrator has heard the story being told and has been its recipient or addressee before becoming its speaker. As a result, the narrator is not an autonomous subject; the storyteller already is constituted by the relation between two poles, that of narrator and that of addressee. But there is a third position, that of referent, and every traditional storyteller implicitly occupies that position too, because the story always concerns the life of the tribe (its myths, legends, genealogy, achievements, and tragedies) from which the storyteller's identity is derived. Thus the pragmatics of traditional narrative creates interdependence, an intersubjectivity that exists not only among but also within every member of the community. Further, it obligates one to pass on what one has heard. Not to "relay" a story is to isolate oneself. Having heard a story, one "is bound to retell it, because, to refuse to retell it would mean that [one] does not want to share" in the life of the community; "as soon as I have been spoken to as well as spoken of (in the sense that I have a name, etc.) I have to speak."[33]

According to Lyotard, written narratives operate within the same pragmatics in a postmodern society, particularly in groups with a highly developed sense of shared concerns. This contemporary context, as much as the urge to recover a communal past, may explain the frequent references to oral storytelling in minority fiction. This is not to deny the existence of oral practices in contemporary life—in the tribalism that Silko describes or in the storytelling Morrison celebrates—rather, it is to assert that the power of these practices stems both from social conditions in the present and from the revival of a form from the past.

For both reasons, then, minority writers frequently make the pragmatics of traditional narrative a theme in their fiction. Silko describes a medicine man who speaks "as if nothing the old man said were his own but all had been said before and he was only there to repeat it."[34] By the end of *Ceremony* we understand that the protagonist's story is meant to have the same status—does, in fact, have that status for the tribal council that first hears it. The secularized hero of Kingston's *Tripmaster Monkey,* a graduate of Berkeley given to quoting Rilke, Yeats, and Whitman, still believes that passing on the traditional stories he has heard will have the same effect: "We make our place," the narrator proclaims. "We make theater, we make community."[35] The prologue to Gloria Naylor's *Mama Day* recounts a parable about a college-educated black man, doing ethnographical research on the island where he was born, who has forgotten how to listen and hence has no idea how to tell a story correctly. Morrison comments explicitly on the way the oral tradition affects her written works: "The point was to tell the same story again and again. . . . People who are listening comment on it and make it up, too, as it goes along. In the same way when a preacher delivers a sermon he really expects his congregation to listen, participate, approve, disapprove, and interject almost as much as he does." In her fiction, Morrison continues, "What you hear is what you remember. That oral quality is deliberate. . . . The open-ended quality that is sometimes a problematic in the novel form reminds me of the uses to which stories are put in the black community. The stories are constantly being retold, constantly being imagined within a framework."[36]

It would be easy to dismiss such sentiments as naive, as mere nostalgia for a primitive or non-Western sense of community, which has long since become impractical in contemporary America. Jürgen Habermas levels similar charges at postmodern thinking, including the ideas of Lyotard, because he perceives them as participating in a neoconservative attempt to escape modernity and undo the emancipatory project of the Enlightenment.[37] Does the interest of both minority writers and postmodern theorists in the intense communal bonds characteristic of traditional societies reveal them as mystified? Not at all. Those who reject this form of community as unrealistic tend to ignore the pragmatic dimension of narrative. They focus only on the magical or folkloric content of the narratives, and not on the act of storytelling itself. For better or for worse, there is nothing mystified about the claim that telling stories creates community.

Silko, Kingston, Naylor, Morrison, and numerous other minority writers are authorized as narrators in part by their prior status as listeners. This is another way of saying that they are able to speak of the black experience, say, because they are members of the black community. This notion is often phrased in negative terms as the assertion that white writers are incapable of capturing what it is like to be black. The distress that such statements produce among members of the dominant culture—and the protest that whites have written sensitive works about blacks—misses the point. The argument does not concern the capability (or incapability) of an individual but the dynamics of social bonds. It has nothing to do with sensitivity, imaginative power, negative capability, or the gift of empathizing with the other. It has to do with the pragmatic situation of the writer. Regardless of its content, a work by a white writer cannot function in the same way as a work by a black. It cannot create the same kind of community for African Americans because it does not issue from the same pragmatic situation. To speak from a position of marginality is to engage listeners in a different social relation from that of the dominant culture.

I hope this account of narrative's pragmatic role in forming communities has provided insight into one of the political uses of narrative today. It should be clear by now that narrative can assist in forging social bonds. Its power in this area is urgent and inescapable. We are exposed to it from earliest childhood, and it continues to work on us throughout our lives, helping to shape every community of which we are a part—families, professional associations, ethnic groups, social movements, regional identifications, national allegiances, and countless others. This motion of bonds returns us to one of the passages from Erdrich's *Tracks* with which I began: "Once I had you," Nanapush says to his granddaughter, "I did not dare break the string between us and kept on moving my lips."[38] The event he is remembering makes a claim about the power of words to heal. As part of the content of a novel, Nanapush's ability to keep his granddaughter from freezing to death by telling her stories can be assessed in physiological, psychological, or shamanistic terms—or perhaps in some combination of all three. But the content of this episode is not the only thing that matters. There is also the pragmatic dimension, the exchange between someone telling a story and someone listening to it. By speaking about their shared past, Nanapush forms a relationship in the present, a bond that had not existed prior to their exchange. More important than the event he recounts is the act of recounting itself. By moving his lips, Nanapush not only heals an individual; he creates a community.

Notes

1 Louise Erdrich, *Tracks* (New York: Henry Holt, 1988), 46, 167.
2 Erdrich, *Beet Queen* (New York: Henry Holt, 1986), 154, 176, 277, 335.
3 Erdrich, *Tracks,* 34.
4 The term *minority* is not meant to equate the social or cultural position of groups as various as African Americans, Hispanics, Asian Americans, and Native Americans, nor to submerge the differences between male and female experience within these groups. We need to keep in mind the different historical forms fascism has taken in each case, ranging from slavery to military conquest to genocide. Equally we need to

be aware of what the sociologist Deborah K. King has called the "multiple jeopardy" of women of color, who suffer "interactive oppressions" from race, gender, and class; see her "Multiple Jeopardy, Multiple Consciousness: The Context of a Black Feminist Ideology," *Signs* 14 (1988): 42–72. But *minority* does indicate the shared fact of difference—and, in many cases, exclusion—from the dominant culture.

5   The last example is drawn from an article by Michiko Kakutani ("Storytellers inside Stories Escape the Limits of Reality," *New York Times,* May 31, 1989; 15, 18) that remarks on this trend in the fiction of 1989. Like most commentators, she interprets this phenomenon as a conservative sign, a "nostalgia for the days when old-fashioned storytelling was possible, when stories and lives seemed to possess coherent beginnings, middles and ends" (18).

6   Leslie Marmon Silko, *Ceremony* (New York: Viking Press, 1977), 3.

7   For a definition of this form and a discussion of Anaya that compares his "crossgeneric" sense of form with that of Silko, see Reed Way Dasenbrock, "Forms of Biculturalism in Southwestern Literature: The Work of Rudolfo Anaya and Leslie Marmon Silko," *Genre* 21 (1988): 307–20. My understanding of Native American writing generally, and Silko in particular, has been helped by Paula Gunn Allen, *The Sacred Hoop: Recovering the Feminine in American Indian Traditions* (Boston: Beacon Press, 1986); Kenneth Lincoln, *Native American Renaissance* (Berkeley: University of California Press, 1983); and William Bevis, "Native American Novels: Homing In," in *Recovering the Word: Essays on Native American Literature,* ed. Brian Swann and Arnold Krupat (Berkeley: University of California Press, 1987), 580–620.

8   For discussions of the importance of storytelling in the African-American tradition, see Valerie Smith, *Self-Discovery and Authority in Afro-American Narrative* (Cambridge: Harvard University Press, 1987); Susan Willis, *Specifying: Black Women Writing the American Experience* (Madison: University of Wisconsin Press, 1987); and John F. Callahan, *In the African-American Grain: The Pursuit of Voice in Twentieth-Century Black Fiction* (Urbana: University of Illinois Press, 1988). Smith emphasizes the connection between narrative and community in the work of Toni Morrison, and Callahan stresses the oral character of African-American narrative, both of which are topics later in this essay.

9   See Audre Lorde, *Zami: A New Spelling of My Name* (Freedom, Calif.: Crossing Press, 1982), 22. Toni Cade Bambara's novel contains a scene set in a Japanese-American internment camp during World War II that presents an ironic reflection of Tayo's experiences as a Japanese POW in *Ceremony*. Bambara writes of the "stories keeping the people in the camps alive while the bill in Congress to sterilize the women of the camps got voted down by one vote" (*The Salt Eaters* [New York: Vintage Books, 1981], 222). Silko writes: "[Tayo] made a story for all of them, a story to give them strength. The words of the story poured out of his mouth as if they had substance, pebbles and stone extending to hold the corporal up, to keep his knees from buckling" (*Ceremony,* 11).

10 Toni Morrison, quoted in Theodore O. Mason, Jr., "The Novelist as Conservator: Stories and Comprehension in Toni Morrison's *Song of Solomon,*" *Contemporary Literature* 29 (1988): 565.

11 Larry McCaffery, *The Metafictional Muse: The Works of Robert Coover, Donald*

Barthelme, and William H. Gass (Pittsburgh: University of Pittsburgh Press, 1982), 261.

12   John Gardner, *On Moral Fiction* (New York: Basic Books, 1978).

13   Michel Foucault, *Power/Knowledge: Selected Interviews and Other Writings, 1972–1977,* trans. Colin Gordon et al., ed. Colin Gordon (New York: Pantheon Books, 1980), 82; Toni Morrison, "An Interview" (conducted by Nellie McKay), *Contemporary Literature* 24 (1983): 428.

14   Barbara Christian, *Black Feminist Criticism: Perspectives on Black Women Writers* (New York: Pergamon Press, 1985), 185.

15   Alice Walker, *Meridian* (New York: Pocket Books, 1976), 199–200.

16   Audre Lorde, "Uses of the Erotic: The Erotic as Power," in *Sister Outsider* (Freedom, Calif.: Crossing Press, 1984), 53–59.

17   See William L. Andrews, *To Tell a Free Story: The First Century of Afro-American Autobiography, 1760–1865* (Urbana: University of Illinois Press, 1986), 128, 214.

18   Charles Johnson, *Oxherding Tale* (Bloomington: Indiana University Press, 1982), 152, 176.

19   Michel de Certeau, *The Practice of Everyday Life* (Berkeley: University of California Press, 1984), xiv.

20   de Certeau, *Everyday Life,* 23.

21   de Certeau, *Everyday Life,* 79.

22   Henry Louis Gates, Jr., *The Signifying Monkey: A Theory of Afro-American Literary Criticism* (New York: Oxford University Press, 1988), 4.

23   Toni Morrison, *Song of Solomon* (New York: Knopf, 1977), 236.

24   Jean-François Lyotard, *The Postmodern Condition: A Report on Knowledge,* trans. Geoff Bennington and Brian Massumi (Minneapolis: University of Minnesota Press, 1984), 23.

25   Lyotard, *Postmodern Condition,* 18.

26   See Andrews, *To Tell a Free Story,* 265–91.

27   Lyotard, *Postmodern Condition,* 20, xxiv, 21.

28   Daniel Bell, *The Coming of Post-Industrial Society: A Venture in Social Forecasting* (New York: Basic Books, 1976), 365, 364.

29   For the increased risks involved for gay men and lesbians since the advent of AIDS, see Simon Watney, *Policing Desire: Pornography, AIDS, and the Media* (Minneapolis: University of Minnesota Press, 1987); and Douglas Crimp, ed., *AIDS: Cultural Analysis, Cultural Activism* (Cambridge: MIT Press, 1988). For documentation that social attitudes have not taken the same "right turn" made in national elections, see Thomas Ferguson and Joel Rogers, *Right Turn: The Decline of the Democrats and the Future of American Politics* (New York: Hill and Wang, 1986).

30   Lyotard, *Postmodern Condition,* 60.

31   The terms are Terry Eagleton's ("Capitalism, Modernism and Postmodernism," *New Left Review* 152 [1985]: 63, 70), but similar charges have been brought by others on the Left, notably Jürgen Habermas in *The Philosophical Discourse of Modernity,* trans. Frederick Lawrence (Cambridge: MIT Press, 1987), 4, as well as by liberals such as Eugene Goodheart and Richard Rorty. My criticism of Lyotard owes much to Rorty's essay "Habermas and Lyotard on Postmodernity," in *Habermas and Modernity,* ed.

Richard J. Bernstein (Cambridge: MIT Press, 1985), 163, 174, Rorty's desire to split the difference between the two thinkers captures my own sense of the need to discriminate between the sociologist and the anarchist in Lyotard (Lyotard himself acknowledges that *The Postmodern Condition* is "very strongly marked by sociology"; see "An Interview" [conducted by Willem van Reijen and Dick Veerman, trans. Roy Boyne], *Theory, Culture and Society* 5 [1988]: 277). Eagleton's essay, on the other hand, indiscriminately categorizes as "postmodernism" the irrationalist element in Lyotard and other theorists.

32 Lyotard, *Postmodern Condition,* 22–23.

33 Lyotard and Jean-Loup Thebaud, *Just Gaming,* trans. Wlad Godzich (Minneapolis: University of Minnesota Press, 1985), 35.

34 Silko, *Ceremony,* 35.

35 Maxine Hong Kingston, *Tripmaster Monkey: His Fake Book* (New York: Knopf, 1989), 261.

36 Morrison, "Interview," 421, 427.

37 See Habermas, "Modernity versus Postmodernity," trans. Seyla Ben-Habib, *New German Critique* 22 (1981): 3–14; and *The Philosophical Discourse of Modernity.* For good discussions of the debate between Habermas and Lyotard, see not only the Rorty essay mentioned above (n. 31) but also Martin Jay, "Habermas and Modernism," in *Habermas and Modernity,* ed. Bernstein, 125–39; and Andreas Huyssen, *After the Great Divide: Modernism, Mass Culture, Postmodernism* (Bloomington: Indiana University Press, 1986), 199–206.

38 Erdrich, *Tracks,* 167.

Felipe Smith

White Witch and Black Madonna: Reclamations of

the Feminine in Toni Morrison's *Tar Baby*

Toni Morrison's 1981 novel *Tar Baby* traces the breakdown in the relations of class, race, and gender on a fictional Caribbean island, Isle des
Chevaliers, by focusing on the household of Valerian Street, a retired
American candy manufacturer, and his wife, Margaret. Employing the
Street household as a microcosm of American sociopolitics, Morrison is
able to demonstrate convincingly how certain forms of oppression connect to Western capitalist and patriarchal values. But Morrison refuses
to resort to a blind Manichaeanism: rather than attributing all social evil
directly to the white male capitalist, Valerian, Morrison also shows an
interest both in the ways that victims of oppression contribute to each
other's suffering and in the ways that narrative conventions serve such
oppression.

For example, the novel's black male interloper, William Green, seems
at first glance to be a messiah figure, based on his nickname (Son) and on
his mysterious appearance at Christmastime at the suggestively named
Street estate, L'Arbe de la Croix. Son becomes the catalyst of a series
of events that expose long-suppressed family secrets and liberate the
estate's occupants of their guilt and grudges. But by the end of the novel,
Morrison has shown Son to be a man seemingly at war with domestic
tranquility. Having unintentionally killed his wife in a jealous rage years
before the novel's main action, Son has become a drifter who carefully
avoids romantic involvement. At the Street estate he meets and forms a
relationship with the fashion model Jadine Childs, the orphaned niece of
the black Philadelphians, Sidney and Ondine, who have worked for the
Streets all their adult lives. After numerous abusive episodes—including

once being held outside a high-rise apartment window by her wrists—
Jadine flees from Son, who threatens mayhem against anyone who tries
to keep them apart. In the final analysis, Son's impulsive physical violence against women is no more acceptable than Valerian's systematic
economic, ecological, and psychological violence against the island and
its inhabitants. Linked by a common need to dominate, the two men
gradually come to seem more alike than their ideological differences
would suggest, and whether it is describing Valerian's mastery of Isle des
Chevaliers or Son's attempt to control Jadine, the novel presents the masculine will to power as the chief obstacle to social justice and harmony.

Morrison frames the equation between forms of economic and gender oppression through her appropriation of a male-authored tradition
of feminine representation in African-American literature that I call the
white witch/black madonna dichotomy.[1] In this essay, I will show how
Morrison uses this motif, which arises out of an almost exclusively black
male/white male dialogue on the terms of American manhood, to critique oppressive patriarchal formations extant in both Western economic
imperialism and the rhetoric of black nationalism. Further, I will demonstrate that Morrison's use of the motif implicitly critiques the black
male-authored tradition itself through selective revisions. These revisions make clear that the textual struggle for dominance between black
and white males often takes place over the bodies of women inscribed
with narratives of their competing male desires, and Morrison's recla-
mation of those bodies marks her artistic intervention in that tradition.

The white witch and the black madonna as figures attached to specific
narrative traditions stem from the late nineteenth-century rhetoric that
dehumanized the black male into specific character types, prominent
among which was the brute rapist.[2] The myth of the black rapist was
invented by white males to justify the lynching of black men, who, according to this mythology, suffered from an uncontrollable lust for white
women and periodically sprang into spontaneous sexual violence if not
deterred by the fear of death and castration. Black men responded to the
myth of the black rapist with a counternarrative of the white seductress,
who, Siren-like, lures unwary black men to their death in her unending
search for human sacrificial victims on the altar of her vanity.

James Weldon Johnson's poem "The White Witch" is the first literary
work by a black American author that describes the white female seductress as a recognizable type. Published in Johnson's 1917 volume, *"Fifty
Years" and Other Poems*,[3] the poem warns black men to beware of white

women who would seduce them only to kill them. The historical justification for portraying white women as femmes fatales derives, no doubt, from the instances in which southern white women caught with black lovers would cry rape in order to save themselves from public censure.[4] The mass migration of blacks to the North that occurred in the early years of the twentieth century allowed for more frequent interracial liaisons upon which the image of the white seductress could be based; and in the North, a degree of freedom from the fear of reprisals allowed black men to charge white women openly with sexual duplicity. It is fairly certain that the white witch has an early twentieth-century origin, and as a literary motif it is probably Johnson's creation.[5]

Johnson's use of color to suggest a broader symbolism for the witch is a signal feature of the motif:

> Her lips are like carnations red,
> Her face like new-born lilies fair,
> Her eyes like ocean waters blue.

Her hair is described as "golden." While obviously rendering her as the Aryan ideal of feminine beauty, in his ironized "blazon" Johnson also encodes the witch with the colors of the American flag (red, white, and blue) and suggests through the color of her hair the object of the American Dream quest in its most elemental form—gold.[6] Beyond its application as a counternarrative to the myth of the black rapist, the white witch motif serves as a critique of the American promise of political freedom and economic opportunity by depicting the feminized embodiment of that ideal as a cruel destroyer of black men.[7]

Another poem collected in *"Fifty Years" and Other Poems*—printed four pages after "The White Witch," seemingly as an afterthought—is a poem Johnson titled "The Black Mammy." Like "The White Witch," it also first appeared in *Crisis,* five months after the poem about the seductress.[8] It envisions the alternate interracial fantasy—white male/black female—again from a black male perspective. Like the white witch, the black mammy presents an initially inviting figure, though in a maternal way. But her bosom is "pressed [to] / The golden head," not to the black one. Like the black male victim of the witch, the mammy succumbs to the lure of the golden hair, but the mammy's indiscretion is heightened by the narrator's feeling of betrayal. As the narrator's gentle questioning of the mammy's loyalty reveals, there is a hint of sexual jealousy in the complaint that the black male's prior claim to the mother's breast has been usurped by his adversary, the white male: "Came ne'er the thought to thee, swift like a stab, / That it some day might crush thy own black child?" Thus the female image that resonates throughout American culture as the sign of domesticity—the black mammy—qualifies, from a black male perspective, as an ambiguous signifier, an agent of familial and sexual treachery.

Implicitly, Johnson's mammy presents a contrasting ideal of black womanhood from the "All-mother" figures of W. E. B. Du Bois, who, as a scholar of the race and the editor of *Crisis,* had a great influence on Johnson. To Du Bois, the "All-mother" was an optimistic vision of uncompromised black womanhood as the fulfillment of the "race-idea" itself. This concept was "both the controlling metaphor of his vision of black womanhood, and also was central to his mystique of race," Patricia Morton explains.[9] What distinguishes the mammy from the idealized All-mother—"the black madonna"—is the topos of displacement. The black mammy, pictured with the white master's child on her knee, becomes a marker of black race colonization and of the usurpation of the black male's "rightful" seat of power. Her physical appearance serves as a reminder of this colonization: while the white master's wife may prolong a youthful appearance because she is relatively free of maternal duties, the black mammy projects physical bulk in correspondence to her increased domestic responsibility, and her lap is reserved for the interloper.[10] Wherever she appears in literature, the mammy undermines black male authority; her allegiance is to the white power structure whose domestic sphere she protects.

If the vampire image of the white witch has as its real-world referent the lore of the white seductress, the figurative colonization of the mammy can be traced to the legacy of slavery and also to the campaign of terror conducted against black households in the post-Reconstruction South. White lawlessness at that time featured both the increased lynching of black men under the guise of protecting white womanhood and also the widespread rape of black women by white men. This reassertion of the sexual mastery of white males over black women that occurred during slavery was primarily aimed at stifling black protest, but, accompanied by denials of the existence of any black hearth and home sufficient in sanctity to preclude "violation," it too had its symbolic aspect.[11] White men's exploitation of black women reflected the expectation that black men would do the same to white women if they came to power in a society that equated mastery with the domination of women.[12] From a black perspective, the child on the mammy's lap is a reminder of white-featured children born in the slave quarters. The colonized black female body—celebrated in iconography as fleshy, sensual, unresisting—made the black mammy into a sign of imperiled black domesticity. The "black madonna" remains, for the most part, an ideal—an intimation of a protective feminine power that the duplicitous mammy undermines.

Taken together, Johnson's poems reaffirm the pervasive cultural distrust of the feminine. The collective racial history of Klan violence and lynching, on the one hand, and the projected guilt and shame over black female concubinage during slavery, on the other, render the black male narrative voice paralyzed between opposed, threatening feminine ideations. Post-Reconstruction representations of the feminine in black male texts (especially in prose and drama) often conform to this misogynistic dualism, which usually contrasts the physically imposing black Earth Mother of the agrarian past to the seductive white witch of the urban, egalitarian future. And since both witch and mammy are duplicitous, working under the direction of the white male against black male interests, they intensify the sense of displacement and alienation that typifies the black male quest narratives of twentieth-century literature.

Contributors to this male-authored tradition include many notables in African-American literature: Jean Toomer, Claude McKay, Langston Hughes, Richard Wright, Chester Himes, James Baldwin, Amiri Baraka, Eldridge Cleaver, and Ishmael Reed, among others. Through the years, the witch/madonna motif has been used to articulate protests against the lynching epidemic (early phase), against black male invisibility in the urban North (middle phase), and against American cultural decadence (late period). In response to the excesses of this late period, black women writers have become more critical of characterizations of women that emphasize fickleness, shrewishness, treachery, and, in the case of the witch, demonic and monstrous power. Morrison, in particular, calls into question the counterhegemonic aims of such representations, which, if only on the symbolic level, seem trapped in the misogynistic terms of the original white racist discourse. Consider, for example, Calvin Hernton's observation that "any oppressed group, when obtaining power, tends to acquire the females of the group which has been the oppressor."[13] Whether the actual flesh-and-blood bodies of white women or simply their textual representations are involved, women's bodies are the battleground over which powerful male forces contend. In *Tar Baby,* Morrison indicates that such assumptions are as oppressive as the injustices they call attention to, and she lays claim to the witch/madonna motif to enable a variety of revisionary gestures.

In the first encounter between Son and Margaret Street, the archetypal meeting between the "black rapist" and the "white witch," the aging ex–beauty queen discovers Son hiding in her closet. Having cultivated an image that America associates with the prototypical black rapist, Son squats among Margaret's most precious possessions and, from her perspective, excretes his very racial essence: "Black. . . . In my things. . . . In all my things . . .": "In her things. Actually in her things. Probably jerking off. Black sperm was sticking in clots to her French jeans or down in the toe of her Anne Klein shoes. . . . She'd have the whole closet cleaned. Or better still, she'd throw them all out and buy everything new—from scratch."[14] Margaret, already discontented in Isle des Chevaliers, fears that by marking her belongings with his scent, Son has dispossessed her of what little sense of place she has there. But to Son, the space he occupies has already been "stolen" by the Streets; his presence merely reopens the issue of ownership to debate.

Later, Son meditates on the callousness of Valerian, who has fired two islanders—the yardman, Gideon, and the laundress, Marie Thérèse Foucault—on Christmas Eve. Despite Valerian's exploitation of the island "whose sugar and cocoa had allowed him to grow old in regal comfort," he feels justified in dismissing the servants who have stolen some of his apples. Jehovah-like, Valerian casts them out of his climate-controlled Eden because, according to Son, "they were thieves, and nobody knew thieves and thievery better than he did and he probably thought he was a law-abiding man, they all did, and they all always did." Son interprets the Western love of property and material objects as regressive anality: "They had not the dignity of wild animals who did not eat where they defecated but they could defecate over a whole people and come there and live and defecate some more by tearing up the land and that was why they loved property so, because they killed it and soiled it and defecated on it." To Son, "the Americans . . . were the worst because they were new at the business of defecation spent their whole lives bathing bathing bathing washing away the stench of cesspools as though pure soap had anything to do with purity" (174–75).

Both viewpoints rely on dehumanizing rhetoric to buttress territorial claims. On the one hand, Son's critique mocks the discourse of white race "purity," which enables the lynching of "black rapists" and other transgressors. On the other hand, Margaret's cry is sufficiently ambiguous to have raised a lynch mob in times past under the terms of what W. J. Cash has called "the Southern rape complex." According to Cash, post-Reconstruction southerners interpreted any act leading toward equality between the races as a collective rape of all white women because it would have the effect of putting the women into direct contact with their potential black male assailants.[15] Margaret's panic accepts the metaphor at face value; she treats her space and her possessions as an extension of her body, a body that must undergo ritual purification after Son has entered and defiled it. Being discovered in Margaret's closet earns Son not a lynch mob but an incredible invitation from Valerian to be his house guest. Yet Valerian's whimsical invitation puts the entire household into disarray by forcing everyone to rethink his or her degree of security in a domestic order subject to one man's arbitrary exercise of power.

But if Morrison suggests the irrelevance of the "Southern rape complex" in the post-1960s world of expanded racial contacts, Son's separatist philosophy places him as a romantic nationalist whose antagonism to white American culture has immunized him to the lure of the decadent white witch of American culture. "White folks and black folks should not sit down and eat together," says Son. "They should work together sometimes, but they should not eat together or live together or sleep together. Do any of those personal things in life" (181). On the lam as a fugitive after his wife's death, Son develops a critical stance toward America by learning to see it in terms of the international suffering caused by its official and unofficial policies. His transience signifies an unfulfilled quest for a transcendant black social order uncomplicated by the strife inherent in race, class, and gender.

As a first step in the establishment of this order, Son contests Valerian's mastery of L'Arbe de la Croix. When he questions Valerian's right to fire Gideon and Thérèse, Valerian orders him to leave, but he refuses. The tug-of-war is really over Jadine, whose Sorbonne education Valerian helped to finance. Valerian's sense of "owning" Jadine is unconscious, as is his feeling of ownership over all the others in his household, but Son takes Valerian's neofeudalism as a challenge. To Son, Jadine's Western values represent the hostile occupation of the collective black mind by the forces of Western cultural imperialism. In order to reconstitute a black domestic order safe from white male intrusion, he must purge Jadine of Valerian's value system and replace it with his own.

Morrison plays with the notion of the "land as woman" to accentuate the parallels between Valerian's environmental and Son's gender aggressions. Annette Kolodny has described "America's oldest and most cherished fantasy" as "an experience of the land as essentially feminine—that is, not simply the land as mother, but the land as woman, the total female principle of gratification—enclosing the individual in an environment of receptivity, repose, and painless and integral satisfaction."[16] Both Son and Valerian experience the places they call home as "essentially feminine." Valerian has imported technology that allows him to defy the tropical climate by growing plants native to his North American homeland. Appropriately, this favorite retreat is haunted by the ghost of his frigid first wife, who stubbornly (through abortion and other means) refused to yield him an heir and even in death mocks him with her barrenness.

In this greenhouse, Son shares trade secrets with Valerian just before they square off at the Christmas dinner. Responding to Valerian's hospitality, Son shows him how to make his hydrangea bloom: "I know all about plants. They like women, you have to jack them up every once in a while. Make 'em act nice, like they're supposed to" (127). Son succeeds in making the flowers bloom: "You should see the greenhouse now. . . . Black Magic," Valerian tells Margaret (163). Son's success reinforces the pervasive feminizing of the landscape by the narrative voice: the fog is "like the hair of maiden aunts," and an avocado like the breast of a young girl reaches itself into Son's hand.

But if the land-as-woman motif underscores the complementarity of masculine orientations to the landscape and to women, the witch/madonna motif reveals even more clearly the detrimental effects of male dominance. The story of the brokenhearted river that becomes transformed into a swamp when its path to the sea is blocked by man-made barriers is a parable on environmental exploitation. The island's inhabitants have named the swamp Sein de Vieilles (witch's tit), suggesting that the stream becomes a "witch" only after suffering from the masculinist aggression against the landscape sponsored by Valerian and his kind: "The men . . . folded the earth where there had been no fold and hollowed *her* where there had been no hollow" (7, emphasis added). It is a pointed little narrative that foreshadows the destructive impact of masculine manipulation and control over an essence perceived as feminine. It sheds light particularly on the evolution into "witchery" of the woman whose spirit, supplemented by the greenhouse ghost, holds sway over Valerian's estate—the white witch, Margaret Street.

Morrison equips Margaret with all the accoutrements of the white witch of black literary tradition: her hair is red; her skin is fair; her eyes are blue. The provisional nature of her eye color (instead of "baby blue" Morrison calls the color "blue-if-it's-a-boy-blue") encapsulates Margaret's marital history. She produced a male heir very early in the marriage to solidify her claim to Valerian, but upon realizing the trap that mother-hood represents, she began to direct her anger at the child in the form of abuse. If Margaret is the novel's "white witch," she is so largely because of her treatment of her own child, who becomes emotionally "orphaned" from his distant father and abusive mother. Still, Morrison wants us to see such abuse not as an outpouring of feminine evil but as a response to patriarchal forces embodied in Margaret's husband and son, against whose needs she rebels.

Like the pointy-nosed, long-nailed creatures of children's tales, Margaret has a nightly regimen that keeps "all her tips in shining order." Son Green immediately places the significance of her obsession with her "tips":

> Son thought . . . [t]hat inside [Margaret's] white smooth skin was liquid sugar, no bones, no cartilage—just liquid sugar, soft and a little pully. Quite unlike her tips, where all of her strength was. Direction, focus, aggression, tenacity—all that was tough and sur-vivalist in her lay in the tips of her fingers, the tips of her toes, her nose tip, her chin tip, and he suspected her breast tips were tiny brass knobs. . . .
>
> He was counting on the liquid sugar. Never mind the tips. (169)

The contemplation of the witch's physical form by the black male, a tra-ditional feature of the motif, reveals in this instance that Margaret's is a personality created in response to a hostile emotional environment so that all her hardness is on the exterior. If she is "liquid sugar" inside, that candy substance is the Margaret that Valerian Street, the Candy King, has constructed as a monument to his own vanity, a process begun the moment he first saw her on her float holding the paw of a polar bear, looking "all red and white, like the Valerians" (43).

If Margaret resembles the Valerians, the candies named in Valerian's honor when he was a boy, it is because Valerian has envisioned Mar-garet as the ideal object of his masculine enterprise: "his youth lay in her red whiteness, a snowy Valentine Valerian" (45–46). As Son sur-mises, the "essential" Margaret is soft and pliable. Her attempts to defy the aging process and her need to protect herself from Valerian's cutting criticisms have combined to shape her witchlike demeanor. Later, after Valerian has lost his control over her—when she is freed from his spell, as it were—Margaret is transformed into the woman she would have become without Valerian's manipulation: "Now he could see the lines the make-up had shielded brilliantly. . . . She looked real. Not like a piece of Valerian candy, but like a person on a bus, already formed, fleshed, thick with life which is not accessible to you" (206).

Through the analogy between Margaret and the red-and-white candies, Morrison connects Margaret as white witch to America, the land of broken promises. Like the sticky candy, America is a place of "redness" for Son:

> Since 1971 . . . the United States . . . [had] seemed sticky. Loud, red and sticky. Its fields spongy, its pavement slick with the blood of its best people. As soon as a man or a woman did something generous or said something bold, pictures of their funeral lines appeared in the foreign press. . . . When [Son] thought of America, he thought of the tongue that the Mexican drew in Uncle Sam's mouth: a map of the U.S. as an ill-shaped tongue ringed by teeth and crammed with the corpses of children. (143)

In this caricature of Margaret's child abuse, Morrison looks beyond the traditional complaint of America as a land of illusions and false hopes to describe it as a land where obsessions with self-actualization and perpetual youth cause parents "to grow vicious protecting" themselves from their own children, to think of their children as "predatory" if they require nourishment, and to see the deaths of children as a necessary evil to preserve the luxury and comfort of their own selfish lives.

Only by understanding Margaret's role as white witch do we get the full sense of Morrison's coordinate characterization of Jadine. Morrison uses the sensibilities of the emperor butterflies looking in through Jadine's window to connect witchlike activity—the murder of innocents—to Jadine:

> [The emperor butterflies] were clinging to the windows of [her] bedroom trying to see for themselves what the angel trumpets had described to them: the hides of ninety baby seals stitched together so nicely you could not tell what part had sheltered their cute little hearts and which had cushioned their skulls. . . . [A] few days ago a bunch of them had heard the woman called Jade telling the woman

called Margaret all about it. . . . Sure enough, there it was, swirling around the naked body of the woman called Jade. (74)

Once again it is through Son that Morrison establishes the significance of the image:

[To Son,] . . . the sealskin coat spread on her bed . . . looked more alive than seals themselves. He had seen them gliding like shadows in water off the coast of Greenland, moving like supple rocks on pebbly shores, and never had they looked so alive as they did now that their insides were gone: lambs, chickens, tuna, children—he had seen them all die by the ton. There was nothing like it in the world, except the slaughter of whole families in their sleep and [in Vietnam] he had seen that too. (112)

To the butterflies and to Son, the distinction between dead baby seals and dead human babies is inconsequential. Both are victims of a country whose reputation abroad is so ambiguously alluring and threatening that the washerwoman Thérèse could believe "that American women killed their babies with their fingernails" (128) and "took their children behind trees in the park and sold them to strangers" (130). Meanwhile, Thérèse's helper, Alma Estée, spends all her available cash on "a wig the color of dried blood" (257) so that she can look "American," presumably in imitation of the red-haired Margaret Street.

If Alma's wig ties her desire for the American standard of beauty to Margaret, ironically recapping Margaret's bloody personal history, the sealskin coat likewise links Jadine to Margaret. Margaret's path to becoming Mrs. Valerian Street began, after all, with her ride on a float during the Snow Carnival Parade, "holding on to a [polar bear's forefoot] like a bride" (13). This "Bride of Polar Bear" (46), as Valerian calls her, made "something inside him [kneel] down" the moment he saw her. Valerian's Circean conception of Margaret puts into sharper focus Jadine's fetishistic behavior with the fur coat: "She went to the bed where the skins of the ninety baby seals sprawled. She lay on top of them and ran her fingertips through the fur. . . . She pressed her thighs deep into its dark luxury. Then she lifted herself up and let her nipples brush the black hairs, back and forth, back and forth" (77–78). Later, Jadine licks the fur, finding it "fearful" and "seductive." That Jadine rules motherhood out of her future to preserve her girlish, moneymaking figure relates ironically to the onanistic pleasure she receives from giving her milkless nipples to the dead baby seals. Morrison details Jadine's autoeroticism on the coat to alert us to her narcissistic emotional investment in the materialistic death industry of Western culture, an obsession that finds expression in her "mink-colored eyes." Like the other childless and child-killing women in the novel, Jadine receives a personal gratification that derives from the slaughter of the innocents.

In imitation of Margaret's fealty to the beauty culture, Jadine has topped the former "principal beauty of Maine" by becoming internationally known in fashion circles as "the Copper Venus." But if Margaret has slight reason to fear Son's blackness seeping into "all [her] things" and contaminating her, the reasons for Jadine's paranoia in her later relationship with Son are all too clear. In the days before he is discovered in Margaret's closet, Son attempts to free Jadine from Margaret's spell—an enchantment he traces ultimately to Valerian's money and power—by going each night to stand over the sleeping Jadine, attempting to penetrate her dreams and insert into her unconscious mind a racialized narrative of feminine essence:

> [H]e had thought hard during those times in order to manipulate her dreams, to insert his own dreams into her so she would not wake or stir . . . but would lie still and dream steadily the dreams he wanted her to have about yellow houses with white doors which women opened and shouted Come on in, you honey you! and the fat black ladies in white dresses minding the pie table in the basement of the church and the white wet sheets flapping on a line and the sound of a six-string guitar plucked after supper while children scooped walnuts up off the ground and handed them to her. (102)

This text of domesticity and womanly essence has a more precise intent than merely to "unorphan" Jadine, to give her a "whole new childhood" and reverse the alienation from black culture that has resulted from her education under the Streets' supervision. The real purpose is to recolonize Jadine for the black nationalist enterprise by reading into her a racial history and folk literature: "Regarding her whole self as an ear, he whispered into every part of her stories of icecaps and singing fish, The Fox and the Stork, The Monkey and the Lion, The Spider Goes to Market" (194). But whereas the women in the doorways who welcome the weary traveler reveal Son's association of a reconstituted domestic refuge with the figure of the black madonna, we must keep in mind the fact that Son's exile from this utopian order stems directly from his homicidal violence against his unfaithful wife and the subsequent vigilance of his mother-in-law, which prevents his return.

Almost as if to mock Margaret's fears of his penetrating black essence, Son enacts the black rapist role with Jadine, again foretelling the violent turn that lies ahead in their relationship. Grabbing Jadine from behind during their first moment alone on the island, Son christens her—in effect—the "neo-white witch":

> "Rape? Why you little white girls always think somebody's try-ing to rape you?"
>
> "White?" She was startled out of fury, "I'm not . . . you know I'm not white!"
>
> "No? Then why don't you settle down and stop acting like it." (103)

For Son, Jadine's cultural whiteness makes her an accomplice to a cor-rupt civilization that he views as the scourge of the world. He thrusts his "loins as far as he [can] into the muted print of her Madeira skirt" (104) like an explorer planting a flag in newfound territory, but Jadine resists his imperial gesture: "if you think you can get away with telling me what a black woman is or ought to be . . ." (104).

As it turns out, Jadine's memories of being orphaned and her resul-tant fears of the emotional commitment that motherhood and daughter-hood imply make her particularly vulnerable to the criticism that she has abandoned the essence of black womanhood. She becomes a "cul-tural orphan," like the Streets' son, Michael. Her academic major in art history certifies her adherence to Western aesthetics, which Margaret embodies as white witch of American cultural decadence. The image of black womanhood that dominates Son's dreams is therefore an aesthetic nightmare to Jadine, and after her trip with Son to his hometown, she suffers another nocturnal episode of spatial intrusion (this time clearly hostile), which climaxes her attempt to conform to Son's expectations. The "ghosts" of all the black women she and Son have known collec-tively ("Rosa and Thérèse and Son's dead mother and Sally Sarah Sadie Brown and Ondine and Soldier's wife Ellen and Francine from the men-tal institution and her own dead mother and even the woman in yellow") come "crowding into the room, . . . spoiling her love-making, taking away her sex like succubi, but not his. . . . Pushing each other—nudging for space, they poured out of the dark like ants out of a hive" (222).

Morrison cleverly couples the moment of sexual penetration with

Jadine's paranoid fear of violation by Son's womanly ideal—indeed, the womanly ideal of all the black people she has known: "The women had looked awful to her: onion heels, potbellies, hair surrendered to rags and braids. And the breasts they thrust at her like weapons were soft loose bags closed at the tip with a brunette eye. . . . [P]art of the hurt was in having a vision at all—at being the helpless victim of a dream that chose you." But Jadine finds on later consideration that "most of the hurt was dread" that the "night women" were all "out to get her, tie her, bind her. Grab the person she had worked hard to become and choke it off with their soft loose tits" (225). Unleashed by Son into Jadine's private space through the window of access that her emotional commitment provides, these grotesque disembodied bodies attempt to force their formalized structurelessness onto Jadine much as Valerian's candied fantasy determines Margaret's adult self-ideation. What Son seeks is nothing less than a reversal of black familial history: in the isolated north Florida town whose absence of whites marks it as a racial space relatively free of fears of white intrusion, Son, the wanderer, dreams of an unviolated black female body that he can call home, not comprehending the intrusive nature of his own dreams of empire.

Son is not prepared to accept Jadine's rejection of his expectations of womanhood. From the perspective of his own emotional needs, only two possibilities exist: either black women accept and embody communal expectations, or they try to become "white." Inevitably, he reads Jadine's resistance as race treachery. Describing their volatile relationship through the vernacular context he prefers, Son constructs a version of the tar baby story that casts Valerian as the "farmer" out to subdue the unpredictable "rabbit" of black masculinity by using the artificial, feminine lure, a "superior managerial, administrative, clerk-in-a-fucking-loan-office . . . [g]atekeeper, advance bitch, house-bitch, welfare office torpedo, corporate cunt, tar baby side-of-the-road whore trap" (189) who can keep the black male claimant to his power from ever again violating his privileged space. "He made him a tar baby," Son screams at Jadine. "He made it, you hear me? He made it!" (233). What Son's outburst reveals to Jadine finally is that his attempt to conquer her is largely an indirect struggle with Valerian for the power to define and create utopia.

Predictably, when their relationship goes sour, Son sees Jadine no longer in terms of the black madonna he desires but as the deceitful house slave who has betrayed him to white male interests. He vents his anger at Jadine's engagement to the European lover who gave her the sealskin coat by describing her as a neo-black mammy:

> You sweep me under the rug and your children will cut your throat. That fucker in Europe, the one you were thinking about marrying? Go have his children. That should suit you. Then you can do exactly what you bitches have always done: take care of white folks' children. . . . So have that white man's baby, that's your job. You have been doing it for two hundred years, you can do it for two hundred more. (232)

The outburst confirms Jadine's suspicion that a fierce misogyny drives Son's idealization of black womanhood, and that acquiescence to its essentialism would bind her hopelessly to a cycle of masculine veneration and hatred. Jadine labels Son's fantasy of return to a male-centered domestic order a desire to feel "superior in a cradle," with her as his surrogate mammy. But to Son, Jadine's refusal to play the nurturing role on his behalf means that she has chosen to fulfill it on behalf of his enemies:

> If you have a white man's baby, you have *chosen* to be just another mammy only you are the *real* mammy 'cause you had it in your womb and you are still taking care of white folks' children. Fat or skinny, head rag or wig, cook or model, you take care of white folks' babies—that's what you do and when you don't have any white man's baby to take care of you make one—out of the babies black men give you. You turn little black babies into little white ones. (232)

Jadine emerges, in Son's interpretation, as the mediation of witch and mammy, akin to the child-destroyer Margaret, on the one hand, and to the childless Ondine, on the other, for enabling the physical and spiritual destruction of black babies.

The consequences of Son's attempts to control Jadine involve another important figure who dwells in the fluid boundaries between witch and madonna, Marie Thérèse Foucault. Thérèse serves as the Caribbean version of the black mammy supreme, her repute stemming from her "magical," ever-flowing breasts, which, though she is childless, have nursed hundreds of French babies. Though she is invisible to the Westerners, who unself-consciously refer to her as "one of the Marys," Son, in his motherlessness, is immediately attracted by her maternal deference to

him. Like Eva in Morrison's 1976 novel *Sula,* Thérèse must respond to
the problem of regressive, infantile behavior by a male. In *Sula,* Eva
characterizes her son Plum's general shiftlessness and drug dependency
as an attempt to "crawl back into her womb," and she sets him ablaze to
free him from his pain. Thérèse responds to Son's addiction to Jadine by
marooning him on the rocky far shore of Isle des Chevaliers.

The union of the childless mother and the motherless Son seems
the ideal conclusion to the novel's investigation of the black mammy-
cum-madonna as a cultural construct, but Morrison gives the pairing a
unique twist. In marooning Son in the wilderness of Isle des Chevaliers,
Thérèse, like the island's other ambiguous nonmothers, reacts spitefully
to the pressure created by another's overpowering need for security. For
what prompts her to volunteer to bring Son to the island in search of
news about Jadine is Son's lack of interest in her as an individual, specific woman. His inability to see her as more than a means of satisfying
his emotional addiction, though, ultimately causes the ruination of his
hopes for Jadine. Ironically, Son determines his own fate in having the
robust Thérèse, his image of the madonna come to life, impose exile
on him. When Thérèse merges into the fog, she becomes a disembodied
voice of the landscape itself. Like the "night women" of Jadine's fantasy,
she becomes the abstracted feminine ideal sitting in judgment on a trans-
gressor, and she forces Son to live under the conditions he has sought
to impose on Jadine. Far more than playing the island's "black witch"
to Margaret's white witch, Thérèse illustrates how such constructs trap
their makers: Son's "tar baby" is the tar baby of neopatriarchalism; the
"territory" he would colonize "possesses" him.

Morrison does not minimize Jadine's flaws in order to make clear Son's
culpability. Her flight from masculine companionship to avoid gender
dominance is extreme, and it does not portend well for the survival of
black families. But in contrast to Son's confinement on the rocky island,
Jadine's future may be read in her closing meditation on the queen ant, a
naturalistic narrative that Morrison uses to deconstruct, finally, the very
notion of an "essential female." The queen ant acts both to nurture and to
build without subordinating herself to a male. Morrison's recuperation
of the queen ant model from the "natural world" underscores the arbitrariness of "naturalizing" discourses based on patterns of social organization that originated in agricultural communities of centuries past.
By recovering the earlier, fearful analogy of the "night women" to "ants"

who pour into her claustrophobic relationship with Son, Jadine masters the threat of free-floating essentialisms as a preliminary step in the creation of her own self-possessed, maleless domestic regime—a "colony" of her own. It is a victory that helps to clarify Morrison's reappropriation and re-visioning of female bodies from the hostile narratives in which they had become trapped.

Notes

1   The origin of this dyadic construct in African-American literature and its development during the twentieth century are the subjects of a manuscript-in-progress, of which the present essay represents only a part.

2   See George M. Fredrickson, *The Black Image in the White Mind: The Debate on Afro-American Character and Destiny, 1867–1914* (New York: Harper and Row, 1971), 275-82, for a discussion of the development of this stereotype.

3   James Weldon Johnson, "The White Witch," reprinted in *Saint Peter Relates an Incident: Selected Poems* (New York: Viking Press, 1935), 34–36. Nonliterary descriptions of the white seductress go back at least as far as Ida B. Wells's *Southern Horrors* (1892). See Ida B. Wells-Barnett, *On Lynchings: Southern Horrors, A Red Record, and Mob Rule in New Orleans* (Salem, N.H.: Ayer, 1987), 7–12.

4   See, for example, Calvin Hernton, *Sex and Racism in America* (New York: Grove Press, 1965), 21–25.

5   In Johnson's 1912 novel, *The Autobiography of an Ex–Colored Man,* he creates the white femme fatale called the "widow," who strongly approaches but doesn't quite fulfill the role of the white witch. First, the competing male figure is another black man; second, it is not the black men who die but the "widow" herself. See *The Autobiography of an Ex–Colored Man* (New York: Penguin Books, 1990), 89–90. By 1915 Johnson had developed the "widow" type into the white witch. The poem "The White Witch" was published in the NAACP's magazine, *Crisis* 9 (March 1915): 239. Johnson claims in his (literal) autobiography, *Along This Way,* that the poem mystified some people at the time, but that he considered its meaning plain. See Johnson, *Along This Way: The Autobiography of James Weldon Johnson* (1933; New York: Viking Press, 1990), 306.

6   For a discussion of the origin and implications of the convention of the heraldric blazon in classical and Renaissance descriptions of women, see Nancy J. Vickers, "This Heraldry in Lucrece's Face," in *The Female Body in Western Culture: Contemporary Perspectives,* ed. Susan Rubin Suleiman (Cambridge: Harvard University Press, 1986), 209–21. Vickers asserts in her discussion of this convention that "the occasion, rhetoric and result [of male oratory in the blazon] are all informed by and thus inscribe, a battle between men that is figuratively fought out on the fields of woman's 'celebrated' body" (210). As I contend below, the patriotic blazon of the white witch motif similarly reinscribes this Western tradition in black male narratives while questioning its racial assumptions.

7   See Michael Fabre, "'Looking at the Naked Blonde—Closely' (or Scrutinizing Elli-son's Writing)," *Delta* 18 (April 1984): 127, for a similar reading of the dancer in Ellison's *Invisible Man*.

8   *Crisis* 10 (August 1915): 176.

9   See Eugene Levy, *James Weldon Johnson: Black Leader, Black Voice* (Chicago: University of Chicago Press, 1973), 104, 178–80; and Johnson, *Along This Way*, 203–4, for discussions of Johnson's relationship with Du Bois. See Joel Williamson, *The Crucible of Race: Black-White Relations in the American South since Emancipation* (New York: Oxford University Press, 1984), 399–413, for a discussion of Du Bois's race concepts. See Patricia Morton, *Disfigured Images: The Historical Assault on Afro-American Women* (New York: Praeger, 1991), 55–65, for an extensive discussion of Du Bois's "All-mother."

10 For the dichotomy in physical representation of the southern belle and the mammy, see Barbara Christian, *Black Women Novelists: The Development of a Tradition, 1892–1976* (Westport, Conn.: Greenwood Press, 1980), 8–12.

11 Angela Y. Davis, *Women, Race and Class* (New York: Vintage Books, 1981), 183-92.

12 See Hernton, *Sex and Racism in America*, 79.

13 Hernton, *Sex and Racism in America*, 79.

14 Toni Morrison, *Tar Baby* (New York: Knopf, 1981), 74, 73. All parenthetical references in the text refer to this source.

15 W. J. Cash, *The Mind of the South* (New York: Knopf, 1941), 119.

16 Annette Kolodny, *The Lay of the Land* (Chapel Hill: University of North Carolina Press, 1975), 4.

Part Two

The

Narrative

Eye

John Carlos Rowe

Spin-off: The Rhetoric of Television and

Postmodern Memory

But suddenly I am beginning not to trust my memory at all.—Paula (Ingrid Berg-
man) to Gregory (Charles Boyer) in *Gaslight*

In *Vineland*, Thomas Pynchon seems as hip as ever, especially as far
as the mass media are concerned. In 1973, in *Gravity's Rainbow*, Pynchon linked the film industry with technological and corporate systems
of control as the postmodern equivalents of more material imperialist
modes of domination. In *Vineland* (1990), Pynchon identifies the boob
tube as the next development in the "rewiring" of humans. It is part
of the historical narrative he began tracing in his first novel, *V*, in which
the entropic curve of history accelerates from the palpably human to
the inert parts of the machine. For Pynchon, television is the latest and
most refined mechanism for energetic dispersion and dehumanization.
At the Institute for Tubal Detoxification, patients have to "sing the house
hymn" every evening at supper:

> While you were sittin' there, starin' at "The
> Brady Bunch,"
> Big fat computer jus'
> Had you for lunch, now Th'
> Tube—
> It's plugged right in, to you! [1]

Characters hum themes from sitcoms and game shows, fantasize their
lives in the form of popular films, and spend "quality time" with their

kids watching such classic films on the Eight O'Clock Movie as Pee-wee Herman in *The Robert Musil Story*. Dialogue in the novel is full of verbal contractions and elisions—"Oh, w'll hell, why'n't you say so?"—that seem the equivalents in "non-Tubal reality" of the Tube's ineluctable destruction of clear speech and significant communication.

For all its faked countercultural charm, its hip appeal to the aging survivors of the New Left, *Vineland* is the literary equivalent of Allan Bloom's *Closing of the American Mind*. The boob tube is just another of the many narcotics in Pynchon's view of a hypocritical America zonked out on television, booze, cigarettes, and consumer culture while waging a righteous war on cocaine, heroin, marijuana, and "alternative" lifestyles. For Pynchon, it is the *rerun* that is the essence of television, and his assumption seems to be that the most insidious effect of television saturation is the loss of temporal and historical discrimination. In its relentless repetition, television reduces its "world" to an eternal present that utterly confounds fact and fiction. Pynchon's literary paranoia is perfectly understandable insofar as it empowers his own rather conventional claims for *literature's* powers of historical discrimination and interpretation. Literature's rhetoric—the power of metaphor—enables the reader to organize past and present, fiction and fact; television reduces everything to an indiscriminate *literality,* to postmodern *noise.*

This view of television as the principal medium of postmodern decadence is shared by culture critics from virtually every part of the political spectrum. Fredric Jameson interprets the postmodern, both as cultural symptom and as critical discourse, as characterized by "a commitment to surface and to the *superficial* in all senses of the word." In the case of postmodern architecture, music, literature, and deconstruction, such "superficiality" may be a critical strategy—Derrida's much-misunderstood "free-play" of signification, for example—that refuses the seriousness of monumental architecture, the formalism of classical music, the depth psychology of literary "realism," and so forth. But as a *symptom,* such superficiality manifests itself in a postmodern subjectivity that is merely the ruin of a more traditional self—the complex self celebrated in Freudian psychoanalysis and the James novel, for example—that has dissolved into "a host of networks and relations, of contradictory codes and interfering messages."[2] This is the "schizophrenic" subject of contemporary television's audience, it would appear, and in this Jameson seems essentially to agree with neoconservative educators from Bloom and William Bennett to Neal Postman that the Tube more than any other medium has done this to us.

In *Postmodernism or, The Cultural Logic of Late Capitalism,* Jameson still insists that "memory seems to play no role in television, commercial or otherwise," in contrast with the "afterimages" left by "the great moments of film," the latter still linked for Jameson with the possibility of modern art as critical of social reality. Jameson's relative neglect of postmodern "literature" in *Postmodernism* is understandable as a critical strategy designed to remind us that other media and cultural phenomena have rendered the literary avant-garde of Pynchon's youth a sort of inconsequential by-product of social transformation. But Jameson's omission of commercial television from his designedly monumental account of postmodernism is more difficult to justify, even though he tries to explain it in his chapter on experimental video by arguing: "Thinking anything adequate about commercial television may well involve ignoring it and thinking about something else; in this instance, experimental video (or alternatively, that new form or genre called MTV, which I cannot deal with here)."[3] Jameson complains that the inability of the cultural critic to find "critical distance" of the sort available in modernist films and art is clearly symptomatic of commercial television's loss of historical depth and thus narrative coherence.

This complaint—that the postmodern trivialization of the subject and its culture is accompanied by the destruction of *narrative*—is common in critical interpretations of postmodern culture. In *The Postmodern Condition,* Jean-François Lyotard distinguishes clearly between cultures founded on narrative practices—essentially precapitalist societies, such as that of the Cashinahua Indians—and the "performative efficiency" demanded in the language games of postindustrial capitalism. One of the chief values of mythic narratives for Lyotard is their ability to incorporate repetition as an integral part of their narrativity; in oral narratives, for example, recitation ensures the integration of past and present in the overall mythic narrative: "A collectivity that takes narrative as its key form of competence has no need to remember its past. It finds the raw material for its social bond not only in the meaning of the narratives it recounts, but also in the act of reciting them."[4] On the face of it, television would appear to meet these criteria, except for the powerful presumption (prejudice) among intellectuals that television is received passively and privately rather than *enacted* in a socially significant ritual of recitation. Yet, what else is meant by the humming and chanting we hear every day, from the family room to the streets, as the faint hosannahs of "Theme to 'The Brady Bunch'" or "Theme to the Love's Barbecue Commercial" ("When you're in Love's, the whole world's delicious") mark time for us? Above all, unlike the founding mythic narratives of precapitalist cultures, television has no identifiable "narrative," despite its reliance on a limited number of narratological devices and styles.

Jameson has identified *pastiche* as one of the key stylistic features of postmodernism, in part to distinguish postmodern combinatory forms from high-modern *montage* and *collage,* both of which have assumed a certain aesthetic seriousness in the course of modernism's legitimation. Jameson specifically associates pastiche with the "nostalgia film" and more generally with the "nostalgia crazes" and "retro" styles (not just in fashion but in all the media) so characteristic of mass culture's version of the postmodern.[5] Jameson's conclusion is that the "nostalgia film" differs significantly from the "older historical novel or film" in ways that reinforce the essential superficiality of postmodern subjectivity and its definition in and through the mechanisms of consumer capitalism:

> It seems to me exceedingly symptomatic to find the very style of nostalgia films invading and colonizing even those movies today which have contemporary settings: as though, for some reason, we were unable today to focus our own present, as though we have become incapable of achieving aesthetic representations of our own current experience. But if that is so, then it is a terrible indictment of consumer capitalism itself—or at the very least, an alarming and pathological symptom of a society that has become incapable of dealing with time and history.[6]

For Jameson, pastiche typifies both the special brand of simulated "history" offered by the nostalgia film and the more general disappearance of historicity in postmodern culture: "The disappearance of the individual subject, along with its formal consequence, the increasing unavailability of the personal style, engender the well-nigh universal practice today of what may be called pastiche."[7] Elsewhere, Jameson characterizes pastiche as "blank parody, parody that has lost its sense of humor," and thus has also lost the critical edge that is characteristic of its higher rhetorical form, irony.[8] I will begin my analysis with this insight, which will lead us to a more complex notion of the "consumer society" shaped fundamentally by contemporary television. But rather than moving relentlessly toward the old humanist (and Marxist) conclusions that television is intent upon turning its viewers into zombies (Pynchon's Thanatoids in *Vineland*), I will argue that television is merely participating in the larger rhetoric of an economy of representation, in which the principal aim is not the marketing of commodities but the production of narratives capable of being *retold* by their viewers. Such retelling, or "recitation," meets the essential criteria of Lyotard's "narrative cultures." There are two important consequences to this claim. In a positive sense, television is the medium of social consensus, and it is a medium capable of heterogeneous representations appropriate to a diverse society. In a negative sense, of course, contemporary television uses its mythic narrative for the purposes of control tied explicitly to the economic aims of capitalism. This in turn suggests that the "performative efficiency" of capitalism may have its own narrative repertoire, whose purposes may go well beyond the mere marketing of consumer commodities. More than a medium designed to advertise products, television aims first to sell *itself,* and by this I mean television's methods of representation and interpretation.

I place special emphasis on the term *retold* to distinguish this economy from an older capitalism in which *reproduction* is a primary aim. The "retelling" of mass media narratives relies on a certain narratological flexibility upon which both the principal media (film and television in my examples) and the viewer rely. "Consumer capitalism" as a *historical* development of traditional capitalism still presumes that the aim is the accumulation of capital and the theft of labor in the form of surplus value. In both cases, traditional Marxism insists on an *accumulation* and a certain repetition of the same. This is the basis for the Marxist critique of capitalism's substitution of *quantity* for *quality*—the quantity of time, money, or goods in the place of those qualitative measures of time, labor, and value that ought to be central to an ethically governed society. Thus, for Lyotard, the "destruction of narrative" involves the loss of those qualitative measures that permit an audience to understand the narrative function of recitation.

Pastiche is parody "that has lost its sense of humor" because it describes the combinatory and essentially intertextual rhetoric of postmodern capitalism. Pastiche is thus not some "secret law" or unrecognized feature of the cultural unconscious; it is merely one style among many designed to maximize the *circulation* of the commodity rather than promote its *consumption*. Once I have said that, then the term *commodity* no longer makes much sense in its traditional Marxist definition. Circulation *is* the postmodern version of *consumption,* and whatever is, in fact, consumed follows the laws determined by an economy built on maximal circulation of its products. This is, of course, an elaboration on Jean Baudrillard's observation that in postmodern economies, use value has been thoroughly absorbed by the circulation of exchange values.[9] A discrete commodity may mask the complex activities condensed in its nominal form; in fact, such masking is crucial to what Georg Lukács terms *reification* and the ways workers are alienated from what they have produced. In postmodern capitalism, however, there is no need to disguise the essential *narrativity* of the product; rather, such narrativity is fundamental to the commodity's "market value."

Television in particular works to construct an overall narrative framework in which diverse programming may appear to circulate in independent, often schizophrenic, ways.[10] New programs come and go with such rapidity that it is often difficult to tell whether one is watching reruns or this season's "new shows." The competition is so fierce among networks and the cable companies, as well as local stations, that it seems the only law that applies is the law of the marketplace. And the market seems to depend on constant change, generic variety, and passing fads. For instance, from 6:00 P.M. to 11:30 P.M. on Tuesday evening, May 4, 1993, *TV Guide* lists more than three hundred programs on twenty-one television channels, nineteen cable-television channels, and five premium ("movie") channels available in Los Angeles and Orange counties. It is little wonder, then, that many cultural critics view television as symptomatic of late capitalism, intent on offering specious "variety" to distract the viewer between commercials. For these critics, such diversity is little more than a repetition of the same tired clichés about bourgeois life, the promises of social mobility and wealth, the "sanctity" of the nuclear family, and the rewards for entrepreneurial zeal. If television has any narrative dimension, it is—for these critics—simply "the same old story." Once again, the "law" connecting different programs is one of repetition and the destruction of any historicity. We watch a succession of images, briefly connected within individual programs but each alien from the other.

Television relies on narrative connections that join different programs, even transcend network boundaries, in order to construct a "memory" in viewers. The circulation of television's representations depends on such memory, which in the simplest ways is built by means of thematic links, allusions to other programs (including parody and pastiche), quotation, and imitation. These techniques suggest a highly conventional mode of recollection, which may often be little more than the viewer's recognition of a certain television genre: sitcom, police drama, interview, talk show. But such conventionality is inherently repetitious, even in cases of parody, caricature, and pastiche. The narrative of television must also construct a certain temporal *mobility*, which relates the present program to a recognizable past. We may say that such television "history" is simulated, but it nevertheless works in ways analogous to most historical interpretations. It offers a means of organizing socially experienced events, and it thus possesses enormous power to influence the attitudes and values of its audience.

The most interesting ways that television constructs such memories transgress generic boundaries. Thus the ways that "fiction television" establishes narrative connections with the news, and the news influences the rhetoric of talk shows, documentaries, and docudramas deserve the most careful attention. These transgeneric narrations are, however, the most difficult to analyze, and I shall restrict myself here to a very limited set of examples drawn primarily from the intertextuality of fiction programs. In general terms, as I suggest in the title of this essay, such intertextuality might be described as the rhetoric of the televisual spin-off, were it not that the term *spin-off* refers technically to a series that borrows characters from another series.[11] To be sure, the term *intertextuality,* derived as it is from print cultures, only inadequately represents the different perceptual and cognitive processes involved in the formation of a televisual "memory" by way of related programs. The rhetorical "spin-off effect," broadened to include a wide range of programs and discursive practices, not all of which are technically specific to programs related only by shared characters, is a microcosm both of television's historical purposes and of postmodern production in general. In a sense, this spin-off effect epitomizes the aim of postmodern productivity: a "new" representation made possible by its prototype, and a representation whose novelty at once marks the exhaustion of the predecessor's marketability and the survival of a valuable residuum in the predecessor. The spin-off effect can also be used for testing my claims about television's narrativity, since it is often cited as prime evidence of television's repetitive and thus highly conventional rhetoric. For the sake of clarity, however, I shall distinguish between the general spin-off effect and technical spin-offs, as Todd Gitlin and others use the term, and refer only to programs with shared characters. In other instances, where there is a central allusion, quotation, or reference to other programs, I will use the term *intertextuality* for its technical precision (inadequate as the term must be for electronic media such as television).

In the early years of network television, programs were "renewed" by changing their titles or expanding their formats. Lucille Ball and Desi Arnaz's "I Love Lucy" evolved into the "Lucille Ball–Desi Arnaz Show." In a similar fashion, Jackie Gleason's unsuccessful "The Honeymooners" (1955–56) evolved from sketches that Gleason did on "The Cavalcade of Stars" (1949–52) and on his own "Jackie Gleason Show" (1952–61). Competitive programs like NBC's "I Dream of Jeannie" (1965–70), modeled after ABC's popular "Bewitched" (1964–72), did not significantly vary the basic model of "marketing" old packages in new wrappings, although they do suggest how the spin-off helps create a certain dialogue between networks. Today, that dialogue has grown far more complicated than the clichés about network competition and market shares suggest. Fox television's parody of the domestic sitcom, "Married with Children," effectively legitimated the new network in the midst of a spate of major network domestic sitcoms depicting bourgeois family life. In fact, the allusiveness of all these shows is intricate and incestuous, and "Married with Children"'s satire was quickly absorbed into the genre of the sitcom, much in the manner that the parodic qualities of "Soap," "Mary Hartman, Mary Hartman," and "Dallas" were conventionalized by the very allusions they made to other programs in their genres. The success of a program like "Married with Children" produces related programs: "Roseanne" and "The Ten of Us" are among the many responses by the major networks to Fox's challenge. It is worth noting here that these recent parodies of the bourgeois sitcom focus on working-class families. Like "The Honeymooners," "Roseanne," "Married with Children," and "The Ten of Us" rely on comedy that teeters ambivalently between a *critique* of the middle-class paradigm and a *confirmation* of working-class inferiority. In this way, social criticism is accommodated to the traditional aims of the domestic sitcom, which may help explain why these parodies are so easily and quickly defused.

The "historicity" of domestic sitcoms on television in the last half of the 1980s was intended to draw upon a presumed nostalgia for stable, middle-class life, associated traditionally with the coherence of the nuclear family. Nevertheless, this nostalgia has been supplemented by a certain realism that aims to address the social changes that have occurred in the United States. Double-income families, high unemployment, the homeless, high divorce rates, growing numbers of couples choosing not to have children, changing gender roles, and changing racial attitudes— all these sociological issues are reflected in contemporary domestic sitcoms. Few people seemed surprised by the public debate between then– Vice President Dan Quayle and the fictional character Murphy Brown (Candice Bergen) about "family values" during the 1992 presidential election campaign. The dialogue between the vice president and the fictional single mother and newscaster clearly set the stage for a disastrous theater of moralizing about the vanishing nuclear family at the Republican National Convention. When Murphy Brown responded finally and devastatingly to Quayle and the Republican party by displaying multicultural representatives of different kinds of families in the United States, "she" did so at the end of her fictional evening newscast. The confusion of fiction and reality bothered few because the social realism of fiction television has by now become such a convention.

Yet social realism by no means prevails in the family arrangements represented in these sitcoms. For every earnest sitcom organized in terms of a specific change in family life, there is one that focuses on a fantastic family, as the following examples from late 1980s television suggest: "My Two Dads" (*two* fathers, *no* mother), "Who's the Boss?" (working mother, housekeeper "hunk"), "Full House" (*three* fathers, no mothers), "Punky Brewster" (landlord and abandoned child), "Special Powers" (mother, daughter, and alien), "Alf" (nuclear family and adopted muppet), and "Small Wonder" (mother, father, son, and android).

Many of these programs grew out of the enormous success of "Eight Is Enough," "Growing Pains," and other domestic sitcoms based on the conventional middle-class family "soap" from the 1950s and 1960s: "Father Knows Best," "The Donna Reed Show," "Leave It to Beaver," and "The Patty Duke Show" were among the favorites. The network executives were not just relying on old stand-bys; they were hoping to adapt old forms to new social circumstances. This is why domestic sitcoms like "Bewitched," "I Dream of Jeannie," and "The Odd Couple" are important transitional forms; they connect the unself-conscious bourgeois domestic sitcoms of the 1950s and early 1960s with the later proliferation of "family romances" on 1980s television. These transitional sitcoms are also important because they introduced elements of fantasy that served specific purposes in legitimating television's *authority* over family life.

There are many reasons why domestic sitcoms from the late 1960s to the present have mixed fantasy and social realism. "Small Wonder," in which the "daughter" was actually an android that the father was "testing" at home, clearly domesticated technology and reinforced comforting solecisms about the human benefits of rapid technological development. "Alf" may have been no more than an extended advertisement for the cartoon figure and the several markets in which the character circulated. Both programs exploited liberal rhetoric about cultural diversity, racial tolerance, and "understanding the Other," even while they avoided focusing on *real* social others: African American, Hispanic, Chicano/a, Native American. An equally important consequence of this indulgence of socially liberal sentiments is the focus of such sympathies on "characters" self-consciously produced by the medium of television. In this regard, television may identify itself with the oppressed and excluded even as it continues to represent the values and ideals of the ruling class. Despite the laudable liberal aims of "Murphy Brown" in answering Vice President Quayle, the "display" of different families was strikingly at odds with the conventionally white, middle-class cast of the program.

I have discussed elsewhere how television programs from the mid-1960s to the mid-1970s self-consciously stressed associations of the "family" with the "media" in the interests of legitimating the television medium *and* its fictional forms.[12] Samantha ("Bewitched") and Jeannie were quite literally *empowered* by way of television's special effects. "The Odd Couple" was less ambitious, but its gay subtext encouraged a wide range of "special effects" in Oscar's and Felix's personal relations. In addition, Oscar Madison was a sportswriter and Felix Unger was a professional photographer, media professions that allowed the scriptwriters to cook up all sorts of scenarios organized around celebrity visits to the shows. Behind such celebrity visits, of course, was the legitimation of television itself, so that far more than advertising was involved in guest appearances by the singer Jaye P. Morgan or the sportscaster Howard Cosell.

In the 1980s, Presidents Reagan and Bush appeared with some regularity on fiction television as well as on the expected news and interview programs. By the early 1990s, the public debate between the vice president and "Murphy Brown"—that is, between the office represented by Quayle and the writers and producers "played" by Candice Bergen— merely confirmed what was already known by most viewers of commercial television: fiction television is as much a part of our epistemological topography as more informational programming. Complain as we do that the quiz show, talk show, and "town hall" television debate have taken the place of more educated and informed decision making, they have simply joined the wide range of programs that play a major part in the constitution of our social reality and our knowledge of it. These intrusions of the real-life news into fiction television have, of course, given greater credibility to sitcoms and melodramas, and they have also established narrative links between fiction television and the news, the talk show, and the political interview. It is remarkable how many of the adults in contemporary sitcoms work in some version of the mass media and how effectively this has helped to link television with family life.

The "magic" of television special effects and the celebrity guest have helped shape fiction television's claims to a unique combination of fantasy and realism. Viewed cynically, such devices are mere "hooks" for the viewer's attention, but they are connected to the more serious purposes fiction television has claimed for itself over the past two decades. Fiction television now offers a certain role-playing, or "acting out" of social possibilities. "The Cosby Show" has been justly criticized for representing the black family in terms borrowed from the white, upper-middle-class, professional family and thereby ignoring the *real* social conditions of most African Americans. But the actors themselves repeatedly emphasize the "role models" and social "ideals" they are offering African-American viewers as well as the importance of such representational models for white viewers. Such "trying out" of social models may be criticized for a host of reasons, but it suggests that television claims a certain utopian function that is integral to its bid for historical authority. In a revisionary fashion, "The Cosby Show" justifies all those tedious celebrations of the bourgeois family that were the television staples of the 1950s and 1960s. "Realism" is not the end, but rather a certain imaginative reinscription of social reality that will encourage the viewer to envision social "progress" behind the enormous social and economic upheaval of the years since the mid-1960s.[13]

This utopian dimension, however faulty we may judge it to be, transforms television's fictional narratives from mere nostalgia into serious historical interpretations. This point can be made more clearly by the explicit example of the intertextuality of Mary Tyler Moore's series of shows from the early 1960s to the 1980s. From her role as the beautiful and witty wife of Rob Petrie (Dick Van Dyke), head writer for "The Alan Brady Show," on "The Dick Van Dyke Show" to her part in the Mary Tyler Moore production company, which she started with her husband, Grant Tinker, Mary Tyler Moore has dominated fiction television for the past thirty years. A chronological list of Moore's major programs is in its own right a short history of fiction television in this period. "The Dick Van Dyke Show" (1961–66) was followed by a series of Mary Tyler Moore specials and variety shows between 1966 and 1970, including one coyly entitled "Dick Van Dyke and the Other Woman, Mary Tyler Moore" (April 13, 1969). "The Mary Tyler Moore Show" ran from fall 1970 to fall 1977, 168 episodes, and produced a long list of programs related either by shared characters (spin-offs), shared production company (MTM Productions), or shared celebrity: "Phyllis" (1975–77), "Lou Grant" (1977–82), "The Love Boat" (1977–83), and, of course, Valerie Harper's various spin-offs: "Rhoda" (1974–78), "The Nancy Walker Show" (1976–77), and the more recent "Valerie" and "Valerie's Family." Such a list hardly begins to describe the enormous productivity and power of MTM Productions, which has produced numerous other television programs and popular films. With its mewing-kitten logo, parodying the MGM lion's roar, MTM Productions represents itself as a Hollywood parvenu, but it is clearly one of the most profitable and powerful companies in the so-called industry.

Much of MTM's success has been based on its ability to work the intertextual rhetoric of fiction television. This rhetoric has a specific narrative history that has enabled subsequent programs to draw upon previous success and to produce a certain "memory" in the viewer. This memory is linked quite explicitly to the various fiction programs' claims to *interpret* social reality. To read this historical narrative in any responsible way would take me far longer than I have left in this essay, so I will venture only a few generalizations.

On "The Dick Van Dyke Show," Laura Petrie elaborates effectively the characters of Lucy ("I Love Lucy") and Gracie ("The George Burns and Gracie Allen Show"): wife of a show business insider, she is herself always on the margins of this world's excitement and celebrity. Unlike Lucy, Laura hardly notices what she might be missing, because her living room is an extension of Rob's office. The Petries' social life revolves around Buddy Sorrell (Morey Amsterdam), his wife, "Pickles," Sally Rogers (Rose Marie), and Mel Cooley, the producer of "The Alan Brady Show." In fact, Lucy has been divided into the beautiful, happily married Laura and Sally Rogers, the unattractive, single joke writer. Numerous episodes revolve around Sally's efforts to "get a date" and her anxiety about her age. The career woman leads an unenviable life of loneliness, self-doubt, and insecurity. She is always the maiden aunt, joking and crying at the same time, and much of what she adds to the humor of "The Alan Brady Show" comes from her own personal pain. With a bow in her hair and her bobby-soxer's hairdo, Sally is a case of arrested development. Professionally mature, she is represented as a sexually immature adolescent.

In "The Mary Tyler Moore Show," Mary plays Mary Richards, who finds herself in Sally Rogers's position, except that Mary is young and attractive. Mary moves to Minneapolis, "rebounding from a romantic disappointment and trying to build a career as a functionary [the associate producer] in the newsroom of a second-rate Minneapolis television station."[14] "The Dick Van Dyke Show"'s "working girl," Sally Rogers, is actually "split" into Mary Richards and Rhoda Morgenstern (Valerie Harper). Like Sally, both women work in the media, Mary as associate producer of the news at WJM-TV (Channel 12's "Six O'Clock News" in Minneapolis) and Rhoda as the window dresser at Hempell's Department Store. Like "The Dick Van Dyke Show," "The Mary Tyler Moore Show" repeatedly brings "work" home, and Mary's apartment is normally as crowded as the television offices. Unlike Sally's desolate apartment, Mary's apartment is the crossroads of public and private, of work and social life, much like the Petries' living room. Laura's married bliss is renarrated in "The Mary Tyler Moore Show" in the character of Phyllis Lindstrom (Cloris Leachman), who is also Mary and Rhoda's landlady. Laura and Rob's son, Ritchey, is transformed into Phyllis's daughter, Beth. Both children are the vehicles for expressing the adults' unconscious. In "The Dick Van Dyke Show," men are represented as abstractly desirable but actually repulsive to women. Only Rob's relation with Laura has any appeal, and his sexuality is almost entirely sublimated in his ceaseless jokes, smirks, and boyish body language. The apparently feminized world of "The Mary Tyler Moore Show" repeats this gendering. The stuffy Ted Baxter (Ted Knight) and the boyish but balding Murray (Gavin MacLeod) are Mary's coworkers at the station, and they are asexual figures, even as their own sexual desires are a source of comedy. Phyllis's husband, Lars, is another version of such alternatives to masculine authority. He is the absent presence that explains variously either his absence or Phyllis's compensatory need to meddle in everyone else's private life. More conventionally, perhaps, Rob is replaced by Lou Grant (Ed Asner), "the crusty but kindly news director," who serves as Mary's surrogate father, in effect giving body to the cultural unconscious of "The Dick Van Dyke Show."[15]

In "The Dick Van Dyke Show," work is sustained by the nuclear family and its domestic stability. In their offices, Rob, Sally, and Buddy lounge on comfortable sofas, read magazines, snack, exercise, argue, and otherwise behave as they would at home. In "The Mary Tyler Moore Show," the offices of WJM-TV are more business-like but are nonetheless the proper site for both community and significant *communication*. For Mary and Rhoda, life at home is an extension of the working community or a reminder of their domestic instability. The good, sound (albeit tough and often ironic) advice comes from Lou Grant; the frivolous, unrealistic, narcissistic advice comes from Phyllis Lindstrom. In one sense, of course, the two shows pretend merely to reflect the changing sociology of work, especially for women, from the 1960s to the 1970s, but the final purpose of such narration is not quite so realistic.

In "Lou Grant," the domestication of work takes on a distinctly postfeminist character, but one that is still ostensibly compatible with the feminist rhetoric of "The Mary Tyler Moore Show." When I say "the feminist rhetoric," I do not mean, of course, that "The Mary Tyler Moore Show" aligns itself with feminist politics. Rhoda's desperate efforts to find a man and Mary's endless worry about dates and romantic love clearly reflect the comedy-drama's attempt to refunction the bourgeois and patriarchal values of "The Dick Van Dyke Show" in terms "suitable" to the changing sociology of family, work, and gender. In "Lou Grant," the workplace is thoroughly domesticated, and actual "home life" is represented generally as privation. Lou's spare apartment merely emphasizes his single-minded commitment to his work, just as it plays on conventions from films in the 1940s and 1950s of the journalist's dedication to "public service."

Yet "Lou Grant" is a curious swerve in the pseudofeminist narrative that connects "The Dick Van Dyke Show" and "The Mary Tyler Moore Show." Instead of carrying yet further the story of women in the workplace, "Lou Grant" relies on the viewer's *memory* of this feminist motif to redeem an embattled masculinity. It is an instance of what Susan Jeffords terms "remasculinization," or the domestication of feminist politics by mass culture that others find characteristic of a postfeminist era.[16] Mary Richards is victimized by romantic love; she finds new commitment and confidence in her work. Lou is a victim of television's ruthlessness; fired from WJM-TV, he must make a new life for himself by returning to his professional roots as a newspaper journalist. His return to journalism plays on the public distrust of television news in the aftermath of the

Vietnam War. "Serious" journalism replaces the growing theatricality of television news for Lou, and such eccentrics as Dennis "Animal" Price (Daryl Anderson), the veteran photojournalist from the war, can be put to *work* in the interests of responsible news coverage. In this regard, our memories of Rob, Buddy, and Sally lounging in their office at "The Alan Brady Show" are complemented by recollections of Ted Baxter's vanity as the anchorman for the "Six O'Clock News" in Minneapolis and the general comedy of behind-the-scenes television news on "The Mary Tyler Moore Show."

Needless to say, "Lou Grant" remains a television representation of print journalism so that television may incorporate social criticism of. one of its primary genres, the news, within the fictional frame of this professional melodrama. Pursuing liberal causes with the support of his publisher, Mrs. Pynchon (Nancy Marchand), Lou adapts fitfully to a new workplace in which women are fantastically empowered. Lou's lonely private life, his bouts with alcohol, and his awkward "romances" allow sexual politics to encourage sympathy for the hard-pressed male. The gender role reversal from Lou Grant as news director in Minneapolis to Mrs. Pynchon as publisher of the *Los Angeles Tribune* plays on the feminist thesis that gender is a social construction shaped both by the subject's kind of work and by his or her social behavior. In short, "Lou Grant" pursues a reactionary argument with regard to sexual politics by refunctioning a liberal feminist thesis and focusing on the liberal "issues" that occupy most of Lou Grant's time in each weekly episode. What allows this illogical sort of argument to organize the narrative of Lou Grant is in part the "history" Lou brings with him from Minneapolis as the "crusty but kindly" surrogate father to Mary Richards. The influence of previous programs in this spin-off narrative is reinforced by frequent "guest appearances" by Mary Tyler Moore and Valerie Harper.

The stable home life of Charlie Hume (Mason Adams), the managing editor of the *Tribune,* does not serve as the same role model that the Petries' domesticity offers in "The Dick Van Dyke Show." Charlie protects his privacy, afraid of becoming as consumed by his profession as Lou, "Animal," and his surrogate children, the reporters Joe Rossi (Robert Walden) and Billie Newman (Linda Kelsey). But the nuclear family is not the source of communal values on "Lou Grant." Carrying the narrative logic of "The Mary Tyler Moore Show" a step further, "Lou Grant" argues that the working relations in the newsroom and on the streets are the only real bases for interpersonal relations. And work for the *Tri-*

bune, unlike the idle chatter of the scriptwriters for Alan Brady or the gossip at WJM-TV, Minneapolis, is distinguished by its political idealism. "Lou Grant" is, after all, a post–Vietnam War television drama, and it plays on the moral seriousness of any work connected with the mass media. But the political thematics contribute to the postfeminist aims of the program. Billie Newman is truly the "new man" insofar as she epitomizes the abilities of the professional newswoman to function successfully in this masculine world. In a similar manner, the maternal Mrs. Pynchon is thoroughly masculinized despite occasional, but generally *comic,* flirtation with Lou; such coquetry is almost always related to their "negotiations" over controversial stories. Billie relates to Joe as she would to a brother, and there is endless chatter about the "family" in the newsroom. Divorced at the beginning of the series, Billie does remarry, this time to Ted McLovey (Ed Potts), a baseball scout whose vocation suggests not only the integration of televisual news and sports but their semiotic relations as alternatives—at least in their ritualized forms—to home and family.

From Rob Petrie to Lou Grant, Laura Petrie to Billie Newman, and Sally Rogers to Mrs. Pynchon, these three shows enact a narrative that moves the nuclear family from suburban privacy to the workplace. The politics of the news (and implicitly the mass media) have replaced romance and even sexuality, substituting the *seriousness* of the news for the *frivolity* of interpersonal relations. Indeed, "Lou Grant" is primarily melodrama and only rarely punctuated by comedy. Whereas "Dick Van Dyke" and "Mary Tyler Moore" attempt to combine professional and private lives in the sitcom format, "Lou Grant" subordinates domesticity to work. "Lou Grant" seems to criticize its predecessors for their bourgeois commitments to family and individual satisfactions, and it offers hard work as the antidote to a narcissistic culture.

Yet the main characters' professions in all three shows involve the mass media—the "work" of television itself in the case of the first two series. The apparent concern with the changing sociology of the American workplace has served the less obvious purpose of legitimating television, the news, and even window dressing as serious businesses, whose work encompasses not only the economic purposes of ordinary labor but also the moral and human concerns normally belonging to the family and private life. Rob, Buddy, and Sally can hardly keep straight faces as they go about their "work" for Alan Brady; mass media is entertainment, slapstick, sight gags, and quotations from the Joke Book. Mary and

Rhoda struggle to keep their "careers" moving ahead, even though they are drawn repeatedly by the lures of marriage, children, and suburban gardening. Lou works through the night as the city sleeps, guardian of the public trust, defender of our right to *know*.

This analysis could be carried further to take into account the representation of labor, the family, and gender in "Phyllis," "Rhoda," "Valerie," and "Valerie's Family." For example, when Phyllis moves to San Francisco, she starts out as an assistant to Julie Erskine of Erskine's Commercial Photography Studio, but in the second season she takes a position as administrative assistant to Dan Velnti, an executive for the San Francisco Board of Supervision. Rhoda becomes a small businesswoman in New York, owner of Windows by Rhoda in "Rhoda." Comedy television, television news, print journalism, commercial photography, urban government, and even window dressing are all versions of *mass representation,* which is precisely the *work* of television. They are all essentially *immaterial* modes of production, unlike the work of Rhoda's husband, Joe Gerard (David Groh), who owns the New York Wrecking Company.[17] The "family" at work is the work of (representing) this new family, increasingly understood as the *community* constituted in and through the mass media. This may explain why the titles for such shows can interchange the celebrity—Dick Van Dyke or Mary Tyler Moore or Valerie Harper—with the name of the principal character—Lou Grant, Rhoda, Phyllis. Character and celebrity are synecdoches for the larger narratives in which they figure, and such narratives constitute the familiar community that is extended to the viewer. How we are to *know* these celebrities or "characters" depends on the *history* that has preceded them, and it is just this narrativization of history that is the principal work of fiction television.

Perhaps the apotheosis—or ultimate bathos—of this entire narrative (one that is, I need not remind you, *still running* as I write this) is Gavin MacLeod's metamorphosis from a balding Sally Rogers in "The Mary Tyler Moore Show" into the authoritative but compassionate captain of "The Love Boat," the most successful of the Mary Tyler Moore spin-offs (and also an MTM product). "Love Boat" utterly confuses work and domesticity, public and private, by turning the work of the Love Boat's crew into the social lives of its passengers. Their "home" is itself a floating bar and restaurant, offices and private bedrooms, a banal metaphor for the social and psychological transience of the American middle class in the postmodern era. On "Love Boat," characters work hard at their relationships, and the "product" is always displayed in the happy couples trooping two by two down the final gangway. Behind "Love Boat" are the conventions, characters, and narrative traces of MTM's prototypes, narratemes that have effectively allowed television to return to the "serious business" of sexual pursuit and the construction of that ultimate commodity, the nuclear family. Men and women may now *work* at love outside the framework of the suburban home. It is not just that Gavin MacLeod's character from "The Mary Tyler Moore Show" helps legitimate a series as shamelessly sexist and pornographic as "The Love Boat," although we understand precisely how his boyish, asexual charm in the former show could be recast as the disciplined, compassionate, but finally sexual captain of "Love Boat." It is rather that fiction television has itself been hard at work, not simply to contain the threats of feminist politics, the break-up of the nuclear family, and the changing workplace, but also to lend seriousness to the notions that life is spectacle, experience is *theater,* and the fictions of television are thus closer to postmodern "reality" than we would like to believe.

"The Love Boat" chronologically serves as a preface to the frenzied production of "family shows," of which domestic sitcoms are only one form, on television during the Reagan and Bush administrations. Its syndicated reruns continue to profile a sort of subtext for the domestication of television's fantastic medium and the related technological imperatives of postindustrial America in the same period. In a period in which middle-class life-styles and what I would term the "Californianization" of America gave new credibility to Veblen's *Theory of the Leisure Class,* the narrative work of MTM Productions played an important socializing role in the lives of Americans. It seems fair to add at this point that such work was also immensely profitable, not only when measured in dollars (although those came tumbling in) but also when judged according to the power of fiction television.

Today, fiction television quite openly claims to serve ethical, political, and historical purposes once reserved for educators, ministers, psychiatrists, and elected officials. Bill Cosby has argued that "The Cosby Show" takes the place of absentee parents in the generation of two-income families and latchkey children. The domestic sitcom is for Cosby quite literally an *extension* of the family, and thus it bears a special moral responsibility to represent conduct and judgments that can be easily adapted as models for real parents and children. Such an ethical dimension is bound up with television's growing bid for authority as the *inter-*

preter and *organizer* of history and thus the primary medium of social consensus. This historical authority is intimately tied to television's narrativization across the boundaries of its primary forms as well as to the narrativity that controls the internal coherence of those forms.

"Cagney and Lacy" and "Hill Street Blues" pioneered what I would term "instant fictionalization of the news," which is now a standard device of fictional television. When a Los Angeles policeman shot and killed an African-American child "armed" with a toy gun who had been left at home alone by his single, working mother, "Hill Street Blues" followed up the news story with an episode that fictionally engaged the moral dilemmas only weeks after the shooting had been reported, and well before the Department of Internal Affairs had completed its investigation. When Bernhard Goetz shot two African-American youths on a New York subway, touching off a heated debate regarding gun control, rights of "self-defense," racism, and urban paranoia, several police shows aired their own "interpretations." By the late 1980s, fictional programs of this sort often dramatized news stories within weeks, if not *days,* of the actual events. Such fictionalizations of actual events have influenced new documentary forms—such as Errol Morris's "Thin Blue Line"—that rely substantially on dramatic "reconstructions" of events and yet still claim to be closer to documentary than docudrama, insofar as they pretend to rely only on *plausible* evidence for reconstructions of events that otherwise could never be represented.

The incorporation of the news into fiction television has now produced a spin-off effect in the opposite direction: "news" organized in the manner of fiction television. Programs such as "Cops," "Unsolved Mysteries," and "Rescue 911" are edited from actual videotape ("Cops"), reconstructions of possible occurrences ("Unsolved Mysteries"), or reenactments of documented events ("Rescue 911"). Even more explicitly than such "television magazine" programs as "60 Minutes" or "Prime Time Live," they claim to "solve" actual problems by means of the special investigative powers of the medium of television. For the news reporters on "60 Minutes" and "Prime Time Live," the camera, the authority of the network, and the celebrity of the reporter enhance the usual moral purposes of investigative reporting in any medium. In "Cops," "Unsolved Mysteries," "Rescue 911," "Emergency Call," and a host of other such programs to emerge in the late 1980s, the ratiocinative powers of the television camera itself are emphasized. Of course, by "television camera itself," the intelligence and morality of the cameraman and editor are implied. What is primarily narrated in these new programs is the authority of technology to solve crises of violent crime or domestic emergency that each of us is likely to confront in everyday life. The television camera's reenactment of the "emergency" addressed successfully by the 911 telephone system claims its own pedagogical purpose. Not only does each "Rescue 911" teach the value of knowing how to use the emergency telephone system, but also it allows us to witness the techniques for successfully coping with common emergencies.

The spin-off effect is no longer merely a marketing device employed within the rhetoric of fictional television, complex as even this sort of "television history" can be. Today, television "spins off" of the news, and the obvious commitment of television news to the selection of newsworthy stories with *dramatic* possibilities applies to the network news organizations' fierce competition both for viewers and for stories adaptable to fictional programming, documentaries, docudramas, and a host of other television genres. The more complex the moral and social issues involved, the more *dramatic* such a story becomes, in proportion to television's bid to become our medium of interpretation and thus the principal authority in the shaping of social consensus.

It is obvious enough that such historical narrativity functions by way of a certain media *unconscious,* and that network executives, directors, and producers may still claim that their conscious purposes are controlled by ratings and the bottom line. Profit in the most obvious sense may still govern the consciousness of contemporary television, but rhetorical control and historical authority constitute its unconscious. The viewer's relation to this narrativity is complex and certainly far more "active" than media critics have ever been willing to grant. Watching a melodrama such as "Lou Grant" that "works through" the moral and social questions surrounding job discrimination on the gounds of age, race, or gender requires a certain reflection and moral judgment, but the viewer's judgment is conditioned by the conventions of the program itself and the television "history" of such conventions. Such "game playing" is even more active in programs like "Hill Street Blues" or "L.A. Law" that ask us to *decide* cases that are thinly fictionalized versions of news stories.

On this basis, I would speculate that the sitcom, so long the conventional foundation for fiction television, will soon disappear as an "entertaining" form. The situational ethics explored in "Full House" or "Who's the Boss?" already suggest that the comic functions are being replaced by the serious ethical concerns of game playing and have been influenced profoundly by the high seriousness of television melodramas and their complement, the evening news.[18] Television's narrative devices claim realism not in the traditional sense of providing an accurate representation of social reality, but much rather in the sense generally claimed by the novelist: to provide the interpretive frame in which social experience becomes understandable. Behind this aesthetic is the customary will to power of the author intent on substituting his form for the complexities of actual experience. We know now, I think, that the most insidious form of such narrativity works through the intertextual, generically dialogic, and antiformal modes of literary modernism, in which "literature" appealed by feigned confession of its own powerlessness—"these fragments I shore against my ruin"—to the constructive imagination of its reader. The antiformal experiments of high modernism appealed to the reader for their completion and social relevance, even as those works constrained this apparent "freedom" within the narrative boundaries of literature as modernism defined it. In a similar manner, contemporary television plays on its own apparent diversity, fragmentation, superficiality, and sheer entertainment value for the sake of "active" viewers who will discover its narrative laws, reproduce its "authority," and make its judgments their *own.*

This describes far better than Gramsci or Lukács what is meant by *hegemonic discourse,* and it works through narrative devices that are perfectly readable, albeit enormously complex, to media critics (including "literary critics") attentive to the ways narrative constructs history and establishes the horizons for social communication. As long as we treat these narrative devices as superficial, fragmented, merely *conventional,* we simply encourage this postmodern imperialism. Jameson says that academics have "traditionally had a vested interest in preserving a realm of high or elite culture against the surrounding environment of philistinism, of schlock and kitsch, of TV series and *Reader's Digest* culture, and in transmitting difficult and complex skills of reading, listening and seeing to its initiates." He goes on to argue that one version of postmodernism has attempted to refunction mass culture in the interests of what Brecht and Enzensberger optimistically viewed as the possibilities for a "popular culture" resistant to ideological domination by the media and capable of some measure of control over its *own* representation. "Many of the newer postmodernisms have been fascinated precisely by that whole landscape of advertising and motels, of the Las Vegas strip, of the late show and Grade-B Hollywood film, of so-called paraliterature with its airport paperback categories of the gothic and the romance, the popular biography, the murder mystery and the science fiction or fantasy novel."[19]

Yet the "refunctioning" of such "philistine" forms according to the traditional aims of high culture and serious representation is likely to be harder work than we first imagined. Jameson's critical strategy of ignoring commercial television and focusing instead on experimental video and whatever elements of the latter inform MTV has proven a critical mistake. Commercial television's simulation of history is not merely the production of what Jameson terms "pop history," in which our poor stereotypes and caricatures of the past are reflected in consoling and compensatory ways in the televisual mirror.[20] The history simulated on commercial television involves new modes of recollection, which are tied integrally to the different reception models involved in television viewing. The interests of mass media include the refunctioning of their forms, often in order to appropriate the political challenges of the Left, even when such appropriation is cynically designed to remain "current" or "fashionable." The inherently metafictional qualities of television's medium are always at work in its bids for political power, so that a mere critique of political contents will never touch the power of the fantastic that so enthralls us. As a *narrative,* television is the most complicated and influential mode of constructing and judging experience that we have had, however trivial we may find its individual narratological "units." It is as a complex narrative that television must now be interpreted, along with the means by which it constructs its own implied readers, whose "competencies" more than any other discursive standard constitute the terms through which our social consensus is structured *and* retold in our conversations, our behaviors, our dreams, and even our representations of ourselves.

Notes

1   Thomas Pynchon, *Vineland* (Boston: Little Brown, 1990), 337.
2   Fredric Jameson, Foreword to *The Postmodern Condition,* by Jean-François Lyotard, trans. Geoff Bennington and Brian Massumi (Minneapolis: University of Minnesota Press, 1984), xviii–xix.
3   Jameson, *Postmodernism or, The Cultural Logic of Late Capitalism* (Durham: Duke University Press, 1991), 70–71.
4   Jameson, Foreword to *Postmodern Condition,* 22.
5   Another view of the subversive potential of "nostalgia" and "retro" fashion is offered by Kaja Silverman in "Fragments of a Fashionable Discourse," in *Studies in Entertain-*

ment, ed. Tania Modleski (Bloomington: Indiana University Press, 1986). It is interesting that Silverman judges retro fashion to be one way of contesting "the binary
logic through which fashion distinguishes 'this year's look' from 'last year's look,' a
logic which turns upon the opposition between 'the new' and 'the old' and works to
transform one season's treasures into the next season's trash" (150). Silverman argues that a different, countercultural temporality is involved in retro:

> Because its elements connote not only a generalized "oldness," but a specific mo-
> ment both in the (social) history of clothing, and in that of a cluster of closely
> allied discourses (painting, photography, cinema, the theater, the novel), it re-
> inserts its wearer into a complex network of cultural and historical references. At
> the same time, it avoids the pitfalls of a naive referentiality; by putting quotation
> marks around the garments it revitalizes, it makes clear that the past is available
> to us only in a textual form, and through the mediation of the present. (150–51)

Silverman's argument is compelling, but it also seems to apply with particular force
to nostalgia on television. In this regard, television has already domesticated retro,
if not specifically in garments then in its temporal and discursive intertextuality.

6   Jameson, "Postmodernism and Consumer Society," in *The Anti-Aesthetic: Essays on
Postmodern Culture,* ed. Hal Foster (Port Townsend, Wash.: Bay Press, 1983), 117.
This view is complicated and elaborated but essentially unchanged in Jameson's
more recent *Postmodernism* (296): "Thus these films can be read as dual symptoms:
they show a collective unconscious in the process of trying to identify its own
present at the same time that they illuminate the failure of this attempt, which seems
to reduce itself to the recombination of various stereotypes of the past. Perhaps, indeed, what follows upon a strongly generational self-consciousness, such as what the
'people of the sixties' felt, is often a peculiar aimlessness."

7   Jameson, *Postmodernism,* 16.

8   Jameson, *The Anti-Aesthetic,* 114.

9   See Jean Baudrillard, "Beyond Use Value" and "Concerning the Fulfillment of Desire
in Exchange Value," in *For a Critique of the Political Economy of the Sign,* trans.
Charles Levin (St. Louis, Mo.: Telos Press, 1981).

10 Commenting on the difficulty that left-wing intellectuals have had trying to theorize commercial television, Jameson recalls "an ambitious conference on the subject
sponsored by *The Kitchen* in October 1980, at which a long line of dignitaries trooped
to the podium only to complain . . . they had no particular thoughts about television, . . . many then adding as in afterthought, that only one halfway viable concept
'produced' about television occurred to them, and that was Raymond Williams' idea
of 'whole flow' " (*Postmodernism,* 70). Of course, media critics and theorists like Rick
Altman have elaborated Williams's theory of televisual flow in works like Altman's
"Television/Sound," in *Studies in Entertainment,* ed. Modleski, 40–54. But Williams's
struggle to "read" cultural differences between British and United States television
programming in *Television: Technology and Cultural Form* (London: Fontana/Collins,
1974) should motivate us to develop more sophisticated theories and thus more successful means of interpreting what occurs in the narrative constructed by programming itself.

11 Todd Gitlin, *Inside Prime Time* (New York: Pantheon Books, 1983), 64–70.

12 See my "Metavideo: Fictionality and Mass Culture in a Postmodern Economy," in

Intertextuality and Contemporary American Fiction, ed. Patrick O'Donnell and Robert Con Davis (Baltimore: Johns Hopkins University Press, 1989), 214–35.

13   Bill Cosby's advocacy of strong family values is a complicated history that involves several media and must now be said to include the multicultural format and his patriarchal role on the revamped "You Bet Your Life." In the last half of the 1980s, however, "The Cosby Show" was complemented by Cosby's best-seller, *Fatherhood* (Garden City, N.Y.: Doubleday, 1986), which despite its primarily comic mode is clearly intended as pedagogical, as the "Introduction and Afterword by Alvin F. Poussaint, M.D.," makes explicit.

14   Les Brown, *Les Brown's Encyclopedia of Television* (New York: Zoetrope, 1982), 267. Other facts about these series are taken from Vincent Terrace, *Encyclopedia of Television Series, Pilots, and Specials,* 2 vols. (New York: Zoetrope, 1986).

15   Brown, *Les Brown's Encyclopedia,* 267.

16   See Susan Jeffords, *The Remasculinization of America: Gender and the Vietnam War* (Bloomington: Indiana University Press, 1989), 165–85.

17   Even Joe's work may be considered ironic commentary on the disappearance of the industrial age and its value system based on material production. As he "dismantles," the program constructs the ultimate "window" for the display of postmodern "goods" in the glass of the television screen.

18   Margaret Morse, "The Television News Personality and Credibility: Reflections on the News in Transition," in *Studies in Entertainment,* ed. Modleski, 76, concludes that television news is "a commodity" that becomes "lived reality" by way of its "ritual enactment." Hers is an interesting argument, but it suggests once again that the discursive paradigm for commercial television is one of repetition ("ritual") and thus lacks narrative depth and temporal mobility. To be sure, this is an early effort to theorize the very difficult question of what constitutes the televisual "form" of the news, but it is symptomatic of the media critic's tendency to trivialize the complex modes of narrative that distinguish commercial television from texts in print and even modernist film.

19   Jameson, "Postmodernism and Consumer Society," in *Anti-Aesthetic,* 112.

20   Jameson, *Postmodernism,* 25.

Daniel R. Schwarz

"Thirteen Ways of Looking at a Blackbird":

Wallace Stevens's Cubist Narrative

Phoenixlike, the relationship between literature and its contexts has been reborn as the field of cultural studies—a field that stresses power relationships among genders, races, and classes. New historicism and its child, cultural studies, have been skeptical of the older historicism's positivistic stories of A influencing B and of reductive drawings of the boundaries that divide foreground and background. While new historicism has sought to see literature as one of many cultural artifacts, these artifacts are usually seen in terms of socioeconomic production. But the stress on micropolitical and macropolitical relations should not prevent this welcome return to mimesis and to historical contexts from attending to other kinds of cultural frames. Specifically, the return from the formalism of deconstruction to mimesis should be a catalyst for examining and juxtaposing figures and movements without regard to simple patterns of influence. I am interested in examining cultural figures in configurations that shed new light on cultural history. My goal is to isolate the essential ingredients of modernistic culture, ingredients that spill over the borderlands between genres and art forms. While we have learned in recent years to be wary of locating essential or transcendent themes, it is still necessary to understand the genealogy of modernism and the figures who contributed to the modification of the cultural genetic code—particularly since these modifications live with us now in contemporary art.

As the high-modernist period—the period between 1890 and 1939— becomes distant, we need to locate the modernist turn of mind and see what distinguishes its ethos and its legacy. For today's younger gen-

eration, modernism bears the same approximate chronological distance
from their lives that the Victorian period does for those of us who were
born in the 1940s. Modernism provided not merely the texts but the
argument for New Criticism; namely, that a literary work was a self-
contained ontology and that there was no *formal* relationship between
the creator and his or her creation. Contrary to what was taught only
a few decades ago, modernist authors' lives do play a vital role in their
work. Moreover, we now understand that modernism is defined by cultural and historical contexts that provide a frame for understanding its
development. If ever there was a period in which authors' self-fashioning
in response to a confused and complicated cultural milieu was a central
subject, it was this one. Not only were religious beliefs and political assumptions called into question by the work of, among others, Darwin
and Marx, but the very notion of what constituted reality was under-
mined by the discoveries of modern physics.

Stressing canonical texts and paintings within the high-modernist
tradition, this essay takes part in the exciting dialogue within the profession about the possibilities of cultural criticism. Although as coeditor
of this volume I enthusiastically embrace the other explicit and implicit
concepts of culture represented in it, my essay speaks in part from a traditional definition of culture as the distinguishing patterns of the quality
of life of a period—the patterns regarded as excellent in arts and letters.
I am committed to a humanistic version of cultural studies, one that
enters a dialogue with Marxist and poststructural cultural studies but is
not restricted to them.

This essay addresses how Wallace Stevens used, modified, and transformed what he considered to be essential cultural material: the American tradition of Emerson; the romantic tradition of Wordsworth, Keats,
and Shelley; and the symbolic tradition of Pound; and, in particular, the
experiments in modern painting that he knew and wrote about. Indeed,
he designed "Thirteen Ways of Looking at a Blackbird" (1917) to be a
debate about the direction of American poetry.

By presenting a heteroglossic dialogue among cultural influences, I
draw upon Bakhtin as one of my theoretical models. While my work has
been continually modified by the theoretical and narratological revolution of the past few decades, I always begin my inquiries as a humanist
and as one influenced by the Aristotelian tradition. That tradition defines
genre by insisting on the question "What kind of text are we reading?"

It focuses on the structural organization and the progressive movement from beginning to middle to end; and it responds to the structure of effects—the text's *doesness*—that is the result of the author's conscious and unconscious decisions.

A title like "Thirteen Ways of Looking at a Blackbird" invites us away from the world of doing and into the world of beholding. Stevens wished to emphasize the contemplation of reality, not reality itself. The blackbird is something of an *x* factor whose identity changes in relation to the speaker's mood and context. As the title and insistence on verbs of looking, knowing, and seeing emphasize, the poem is about what we know and how we know it. Each stanza brings the blackbird into some relation with the mind. The speaker is like a surveyor using the blackbirds as an instrument to measure the geography of the mind. From the outset, the play on "eye" and "I"—introduced in the last line of stanza I and the first line of stanza II—emphasizes the stress on one person *looking*. We might think of "Thirteen Ways of Looking at a Blackbird" as both a poem and a *theory* of poetry. As Robert Morris has remarked, "From the origins of such terms as 'theory' (from *theoria*—to look at) and 'idea' (from *idein*—to see) to Plato's metaphor of the cave, the visual is both privileged and concealed in language."[1] Within this poem is a dialogic debate among diverse possibilities of American poetry. Implicitly enacted in the poem are the following positions with regard to American poetry: (1) American poetry should follow symbolic modes, such as Pound proposed; (2) it should follow the even more nonmimetic example of abstract modern painting; (3) it should follow the native tradition of Emerson and Whitman; and (4) it should find the note of high romanticism in the tradition of Wordsworth, Keats, and Shelley. I shall argue that this dialogue among diverse poetic principles is essential to understanding Stevens's entire canon.

Isn't Stevens saying that the blackbird—like a metaphor—is whatever and wherever one wants it to be? And although the blackbird flies from the circle of visual perception, as in stanza IX, it returns or—mysteriously—is still there in stanzas X, XI, XII, and XIII as an object of contemplation and as a catalyst for meditation and creativity. Indeed, the speaker's rhyme in stanzas IX and X emphasizes that when the blackbird is "out of [his] sight," it is still hypothetically possible to evoke it in his mental "light":

IX

When the blackbird flew out of sight,
It marked the edge
Of one of many circles.

X

At the sight of blackbirds
Flying in a green light,
Even the bawds of euphony
Would cry out sharply.[2]

Thus the poem stresses that sight has little to do with seeing; the "insight" of memory and fantasy—both indispensable for the creative process—is just as real. As in "The Snow Man" (1921), both what is there and what is not there are real:

For the listener, who listens in the snow,
And, nothing himself, beholds
Nothing that is not there and the nothing that is.

The text defines the essential Emersonian distinction between me and not-me, between the freedom of the observer to perceive and the world on which his mind acts. In "The American Scholar" Emerson writes: "The one thing in the work, of value, is the active soul. . . . The soul active sees absolute truth and utters truth or creates. In this action it is genius."[3] Yet at the end of Stevens's poem, as we shall see, the distinction is blurred and the blackbird is depicted as a function of the speaker. Similarly, the poem itself begins in an I/not-I relationship with the reader and collapses by its very tautological structure into a function of the I-reader. While Stevens wrote that "this group of poems is not meant to be a collection of epigrams or of ideas, but of sensations," the effect of such a group is to insist on recuperation in terms of something we can understand.[4] That is, as the poet comes to terms with a difficult, abstruse, and resistant subject, so readers come to terms with—bring into the ken of their understanding—a complex, abstract, seemingly arcane, and resistant poem. But because the poem is as much about the exploration—the quest—for innovative form as it is about its nominal subject, readers experience the creative process: the dialogue between the formal ingredients (the abstract discourse) and the story that always, like an underground stream, threatens to emerge above the surface as the *agon*.

While its spare diction and syntax look forward to Stevens's later lyrics, "Thirteen Ways of Looking at a Blackbird" has a much harder, flatter surface, one that not only puzzles and distances readers but makes them uneasy. Stevens is obliterating conventional expectations of narrative and three-dimensionality. One is struck by what is absent from the poem: politics, relationships, the presence of the speaker's psyche—although that, as we shall see, is revealed obliquely by the speaker's choice of scenes and his development of metaphors. Rereading, one realizes how often the speaker is outrageously importing nonempirical and unconventional assumptions. At such a distance as implied by "twenty snowy mountains," how could the speaker see the moving eye of the blackbird?

I

Among twenty snowy mountains,
The only moving thing
Was the eye of the blackbird.

What does it mean in stanza II to be of three minds?

II

I was of three minds,
Like a tree
In which there are three blackbirds.

Is it an intensification of the ambivalence of being of two minds, while introducing a poem that stresses the multiplicity of perspectives? If—to pursue the logic of Stevens's metaphoricity—one is like a tree, is one then capable of growth or is one wooden or rigid in one's responses?

Stevens conceived of poetry as a performance for an audience, but one that required readers' participation; in "Thirteen Ways of Looking at a Blackbird," he is emphasizing the visual element and inviting his readers to see a poem as if it were a visual performance, a kind of modern dance or a series of paintings. Yet the very need for utterance—of articulating in the first and third person the responses to the blackbird—shows the impossibility of his attempt to write a kind of visual silkscreen where abstract detachment from reality takes the place of mimesis. For Stevens, as for Joyce—particularly in *Ulysses* and *Finnegans Wake*—language takes precedence over ways of conveying feeling and emotions; the mimetic code triumphs over the pure and abstract within the work; and themes and values emerge about how people live and die, create and desire. Just as Joyce in the "Sirens" episode of *Ulysses* goes as far as he can go in exploring the possible fusion of music and language, Stevens in "Thirteen Ways of Looking at a Blackbird" explores the possibility of visual poetry.

Undoubtedly Stevens was influenced by imagism. It is well to recall Pound's definition of an imagist poem in his 1914 essay "Vorticism": "In a poem of this sort one is trying to record the precise instant when a thing outward and objective transforms itself, or darts into a thing inward and subjective."[5] We might recall Pound's famous haiku-like example of an imagist poem, "In a Station of the Metro": "The apparitions of these faces in the crowd: / Petals on a wet, black bough." Pound used free verse forms to render an impression in a single metaphor or to juxtapose an object with several objects, each standing as a metonymy for the other. A. W. Litz has written of how "Thirteen Ways of Looking at a Blackbird" varies the haiku form; the poem is also indebted to Japanese prints in which a single setting is rendered from different viewpoints and at different seasons of the year or of the mind.[6] The stanzas are deeply indebted to the cryptic form of haiku, an unrhymed form limited to seventeen syllables, divided rigorously into three lines of five, seven, and five syllables; its usual topic is a brief evocation of something in nature. In its highly stylized presentation and its use of folk and religious references, "Thirteen Ways of Looking at a Blackbird" also suggests a sequence of scenes from a Noh play.

The thirteen stanzas are like pictures at an exhibition—we might even recall Mussorgsky's musical composition of that name—or, to propose another metaphor familiar to Stevens, a cubist painting where disparate elements are combined into one flat surface. In a sense the poem has a radial center—the blackbird or the perception of the blackbird—around which concentric circles of impressions revolve. Indeed, are the thirteen stanzas not like so many still lifes, a form that minimizes the presence of the human subject, narrative, and storytelling? As if each stanza was a still life in a room, the reader stands at the center and chooses which to observe. At the same time each stanza is a cinematic scene progressing to greater, if tentative, revelation. Perceiving the poem as a visual entity, we notice that the imposing empty space on the page calls attention to, and provides demarcation for, the dearth of words, almost the way frames define and mark the space outside and inside paintings.

Certainly the influence of impressionism and cubism is strong in "Thirteen Ways of Looking at a Blackbird." As Michael Brenson notes, "Cubism shattered the autonomy of the individual subject and integrated it with its environment. It made instability, indeterminacy and multiple points of view staples of modern art. It was more comfortable with metamorphosis and change than with permanence."[7] Stevens became fascinated with cubism at the 1913 Armory Show: "Were [cubists] not attempting to get at not the invisible but the visible? They assumed that back of the peculiar reality that we see, there lay a more prismatic one of many facets. Apparently deviating from reality, they were trying to fix on it. . . . [T]he momentum toward abstraction exerts a greater force on the poet than on the painter. I imagine that the tendency of all thinking is toward the abstract."[8]

In *Adagio*, Stevens quotes Braque's emphasis on the doing as crucial to art: "Usage is everything. (*Les idées sont destinées à être deformées à l'usage. Reconnâitre ce fait est une preuve de désinteressment* [Georges Braque, Verve, no. 2]."[9] According to William Rubin, cubists made "the very process of image formation virtually the subject of their pictures."[10] From cubism Stevens derived his sensitivity to light and shade, his experiments with layered textures, his presentation of images in several pictorial planes, his wit and playfulness, and his abstractness oddly intermingled with the embrace of daily life. Such poems as "The Emperor of Ice Cream" and "The Man on the Dump" recall Picasso's and Braque's passion for vernacular material, particularly their sensory appreciation of the objects and interaction of the gregarious and classless world of the café. Wasn't Stevens's idea of Florida, especially Key West, based on experiences and fantasies of this kind? Wasn't Key West his version of bohemian life in Paris? Poems like "The Snow Man" and "Tea at the Palaz of Hoon" follow the cubist tendency to dissolve the distinction between figure and ground and eliminate a single point of perspective, and they also eliminate what Emily Bardace Kies has called "a comprehensible recession in space."[11] Stevens, like Braque, focuses on the connection between things, the composition; but like Picasso, he is riveted by the peculiarities of individual things, the specificity.

If we substitute "writing" for "painting," what William Rubin says of Braque is true of the early Stevens: "Braque's reverence for the language and the craft of painting distances him from his subject." Like the cubists, Stevens took odd combinations of man-made and natural forms and fused them into homogeneity, but it was a homogeneity that was tentative and disjunctive. Stevens fulfilled Rubin's definition of the collage: "The essense of collage, then, is the insertion into a given context of an alien entity—not only of a different medium but of a different style or, as the Surrealists would later insist, even of a motif drawn from a different context of experience or level of consciousness." One could say that "The Man with the Blue Guitar" and "Notes toward a Supreme Fiction" are elaborate collages. Too, Stevens's nonmimetic use of color—as, say, in "Anecdote of the Prince of Peacocks"—recalls the cubists' use of color as "an autonomous sign disengaged from the morphological depiction of an object." Like Braque, Stevens liberated color from mimesis and freed color from "the need for space-denoting modulation as well as from the contouring of objects."[12] Stevens followed Braque and Picasso in taking art outside the mimetic system of representation with which we are familiar and making a new system based on new juxtapositions, odd assemblies of objects, and discontinuous relations that barely held together—a system that each perceiver had to resolve into his own hypothesis of unity, a hypothesis always challenged by the anarchy of disunity. Yet the flight from verisimilitude was accompanied by a desire to fuse familiar perceptions into odd and striking combinations. Stevens, like the cubists, depended on the visible world of immediate experience for his donnée, but he created a teasing balance between abstraction and representation.

Stevens found in collage not only a lyrical impulse but also a model for narrative possibilities. Moreover, he adopted the cubists' example of playing on, within one work, a continuum stretching from the most recognizable (a blackbird in "Thirteen Ways of Looking at a Blackbird") to the most abstruse abstractions:

> I was of three minds,
> Like a tree
> In which there are three blackbirds.

For Picasso, as Rubin puts it, "collage, construction and *papier collé* . . . were about alternate ways of *imagining* reality. . . . The collage principle, we recall, is by definition conflictual and subversive, and sorts well with Picasso's anarchic tendencies, his personification of the *agent provocateur.*"[13] Writing of Picasso's May 1912 collage, "Still Life with Chair Caning," Kies notes, "Such an unpredictable, playful, and provocative combination of objects, illusions, and paint exemplifies Picasso's acrobatic imagination and subversive spirit."[14] Like Picasso, Stevens enjoyed the role of aesthetic joker. Stevens, for all of his respectability and desire for order and control, had another self in his poetry that gave voice to his libidinous, anarchic side, a side that flouted bourgeois values and expectations.

By its flat plane, sense of story, and reductive, almost hawklike overview, "Thirteen Ways of Looking at a Blackbird" places readers at a distance and situates them far from the expected intimacy of lyrical poetry. We take for granted conventions of sense and meaning, Stevens implies, but his rhetoric—as a structure of tropes that generates a structure of effects—invites us to create an alternative group of assumptions and to see where that takes us. As wittily and playfully as Paul Klee and other surrealists, he turns our expectations upside down and proposes observations on the relationship between the linguistic and the visual. The "eye" in the first poem is the objective world that exists beyond the perception of self. So, too, is the mark on the page, the disruption of blankness, the notation that makes meaning.

The empty space on the pages on which the poem appears is a visual metonym for the limitless spaces of the mountains. Among other things, the print (or signs left by words) is both tracks that a bird might leave in the snow and the printing on the page. The typography of the poem—the spare stanzas, each with its own demarcation of a Roman numeral—emphasizes the presence of occasional black marks on a white page. Just as the twenty mountains in stanza I provide a vast space for the perception of the birds and their potential activity, so the pages offer the promise of meaningful signs. Does not the generous space surrounding the rather scant typography on the page visually mime the blackbird against the sky, particularly against the twenty mountains?

The striking presence of black within diverse scenes—black set against the white of snowy mountains (I) or within a snowscape (XIII)—climaxes in its juxtaposition with the astonishing appearance of green light into the black-and-white mindscape in stanza X:

> At the sight of blackbirds
> Flying in a green light,
> Even the bawds of euphony
> Would cry out sharply.

Does not Stevens have in mind the ersatz order proposed by those upholding the moral law in his 1922 poem "A High-toned Old Christian Woman"? But as he makes clear in a letter to Henry Church, he also had in mind rigorous academics who were reluctant to admit the diversity of the universe. "What was intended by [stanza] X," wrote Stevens, "was that the bawds of euphony would suddenly cease to be academic and express themselves sharply: naturally, with pleasure, etc."[15]

The sequence of thirteen related poems recalls pointillist paintings that fix one moment in space and isolate it from a temporal process. Isn't each miniature poem like a collection of pointillist dots that cohere on the surface? The poems may owe something to pointillism's freezing moments in time and place by applying dots or tiny strokes of color elements to a surface so that, when seen from a distance, the dots or strokes blend luminously together. Indeed, like the tracks of the print covering the white page in "Thirteen Ways of Looking at a Blackbird," the white ground is systematically covered with tiny points of pure color— or black—that blend together when viewed from a distance, producing a luminous effect. The optical mix of Seurat has a grayish aspect, which Baudelaire attributed to the molecular quality of nature; not only imagism but the desire to look at nature in miniature—stimulated by pointillism and Baudelaire—may have influenced Stevens.

As much as a surrealistic collage by Ernst, Stevens undermines our traditional expectations of what we see. For Stevens, aspiring in 1917 to a pure poetry, abstraction was an aristocratic mode of thinking that would take one away from the pedestrian, utilitarian, and philistine world of *doing* into an aesthetic realm of *being*. He aligned himself with those modern painters—dadaists, surrealists, suprematists—who searched for forms and icons that would give man a different view of his reality. Does not the very preoccupation with black suggest such abstract compositions as Malevich's *Suprematist Composition: Red Square and Black Square?* Surely Stevens had in mind—even if he does not mention it— the red-winged blackbird.

Haddam in stanza VII is a rich image implying the paradox that traditional and experimental modes of mimesis are often mutually dependent on one another for meaning.

> VII
> O thin men of Haddam,
> Why do you imagine golden birds?
> Do you not see how the blackbird
> Walks around the feet
> Of the women about you?

Haddam, Little Haddam, and East Haddam are small, well-to-do New England villages on the Connecticut River's east bank, where old established family lines have been perpetuated from generation to generation and where roads have names like Petticoat Lane. Thus Haddam stood in Stevens's mind for suburban and tradition-bound resistance to challenges to moral and artistic convention and for spiritual undernourishment. The homophonic pun in stanza VII on Haddam/Adam wittily suggests that the enthusiasm for enervated and mannered art follows Adam's loss of innocence and the corruption of the enclosed garden of nineteenth-century America. But does Haddam not also suggest Hadim in the Byzantine Empire, where—as Yeats stressed—exotic figures such as golden birds were created by artificers and nonmimetic iconographic art reached perfection? Does not the poem continually propose seduction away from our everyday world only to show us that such a seduction is evanescent if not impossible?

As W. J. T. Mitchell has suggested, the further the abstract painter goes from language and narrative, the more we as audience need to recuperate our experience in language.[16] According to the Horatian maxim, *ut pictura poesis* (as in painting, so in poetry). Much as when observing abstract painting, the reader of "Thirteen Ways of Looking at a Blackbird" must reorient himself or herself to nonmimetic experience and must resituate himself in a mode of perception that requires his own verbal intelligence. Just as we must formulate our response to abstract painting in words, so we must verbalize a response to remote and esoteric poetry. Ironically, the very desire to overcome puzzling rhetoric and inchoate representation requires a response in words that situates the puzzling artistic experience within our own experience. Paradoxically, abstract painters themselves rarely want their visual texts to be understood as abstract. Mitchell quotes Rosalind Krauss's remark that the "greatest fear" of abstract artists is that they "may be making *mere* abstraction, abstraction uninformed by a subject, contentless abstraction."[17] A spring 1989 exhibit of Joan Mitchell's work at Cornell's Johnson Art Museum and the ensuing discussion it generated underlined for me once more that the more abstract the artist, the more it is necessary to recuperate art in terms of the mimetic code.

Let us consider the significance of the blackbird. Black stands for night, for death, for black magic and the black mass, and for limiting and enclosing light and understanding. It is the color of the devil. God created life from black chaos, and life will presumably end in blackness. We come from the blackness of the womb, where conception takes place in darkness, and we return to the blackness of the grave. Stevens's speaker never forgets that black neither transmits nor reflects light. It is the color of repetition without variety.

In the first stanza, the eye of the blackbird seems a center point of a mindscape, a center point representing energy and life, but also the specter of death. Does the blackbird not also suggest the ominous bat—indeed, the bloodsucking vampire bat—with a suggestion of the vampire myth? The three blackbirds become possible metonyms for the three crosses in the traditional crucifixion scene when Christ was killed. This possibility is reinforced by the continuing presence of death and shadows in the poem, and even—to describe the bird's flight—by the use of the verb "crossed" and its association with sharp, knifelike or nail-like "barbaric" icicles in stanza VI:

> VI
> Icicles filled the long window
> With barbaric glass.
> The shadow of the blackbird
> Crossed it, to and fro.
> The mood
> Traced in the shadow
> An indecipherable cause.

Do we not feel a threat of ritualistic death—inexplicable death such as the crucifixion—in stanza VI: "The mood / Traced in the shadow / An indecipherable cause"? Does not the redness of the red-winged blackbird—admittedly unstated but perhaps more ominous and *present* because it is ostentatiously suppressed as a kind of missing signifier—carry a hint of blood?

Stevens also evokes the sinister nursery rhyme "Four and Twenty Blackbirds":

> Sing a song of sixpence,
>   A pocket full of rye;
> Four and twenty blackbirds,
>   Baked in a pie.
>
> When the pie was opened,
>   The birds began to sing;

Was not that a dainty dish,
  To set before the king?

The king was in his counting-house,
  Counting out his money;
The queen was in the parlour,
  Eating bread and honey.

The maid was in the garden,
  Hanging out the clothes,
There came a little blackbird,
  And snapped off her nose.

"There came a little blackbird / And snapped off her nose" implies the threat of sexual violation, of debilitating illness such as leprosy where the nose might actually fall off, and of death. While the king is in his countinghouse—the patriarchal dominant male believing he is in control of his fortune and his world—and the queen is in her parlour—her domain, according to convention—the live birds flying out of a pie overturn traditional expectations of order and reality. To a child reading the nursery rhyme, the birds emerging from a pie or attacking the maid present a frightening image. On first reading, my own children were horrified by the illustrations in their *Mother Goose*. Since blackbird was a slang term for both blacks and indentured servants, the nursery rhyme implies a reversal of class hierarchy in the form of a social uprising of the dispossessed.

Let us turn once again to the reason that Stevens writes from thirteen different perspectives, as if he were not of "three minds" but of thirteen. It emphasizes Stevens's need to take multiple perspectives in a post-Christian world where one no longer sees one world descending from and depending on God. Thirteen is a number associated with black magic and bad luck, as in Friday the thirteenth—the day, according to legend, when Christ was crucified. And thirteen is the number of people, including Jesus, at the Last Supper. In early Christianity the number acquired a magical or at least iconic quality because its constituent numbers, one and three, suggest the Trinitarian perspective. Thirteen is also associated with the coming of adulthood and maturity, as in the Jewish bar mitzvah.

Given that there are thirteen months in the Jewish biblical calendar, thirteen emphasizes the cycle of life and renewal implicit in the poem's return to a realistic placing—in stanza XIII—of the blackbird in an expected setting: a winterscape where "The blackbird sat / In the cedar-limbs." The poem does begin and end in winter; if the autumn of stanza III precedes the spring of stanza XII, isn't that Stevens's way of emphasizing the arbitrariness of temporal sequence in literature and of showing that perceptions and memories can willfully scramble chronology?

III
The blackbird whirled in the autumn winds.
It was a small part of the pantomime.

. . . .

XII
The river is moving.
The blackbird must be flying.

Do the seasons have to be in order? Could more than one year be implied by the sequence of poems? It is as if, after summoning the blackbird from the natural world to the metaphorical, after recreating it in his own ontology and allowing it to accrete with symbolic meaning, in a final tour de force Stevens returns it to the natural realm. Thus the poem itself is not only about the cyclical and renewing process of seasons and natural creation, it is about the process of poetic creativity—of metaphoricity—and about the poet's ability to use the copula to create ex nihilo what he chooses. Thus, Stevens proposes, if I may reductively paraphrase his hypothesis: "Let the blackbird be whatever identity I wish it to be. Let optative become indicative." In a very real sense the persona uses the blackbird as a visual icon to explore his limits, to survey his own mind. The process by which something from nature takes on its own life within the mind—the mind's potential to create its own ontology in whatever illuminating distortions it wishes—is the subject of the poem.

Yet the blackbird's flight, walk, sound, shadow, and whistle are present as phenomenological evidence of an actual bird. Within stillness and silence—a world of "pantomime" and "innuendo" and "shadow"—and within the poem's vast mindscape is the ubiquitous blackbird. Within the ontology defined by the speaker, the blackbird insists on movement and process and sensation. Defined in terms of present participles—"moving" (stanza I), "whistling" (stanza V), and "flying" (stanzas X, XII)—the bird is the poem's active principle, a principle that deflects attention from past and future and, almost like a flat plane in painting, releases the reader from three-dimensionality and the world in which he or she feels comfortable, in part by freeing her from causes and consequences. Indeed, within the poem's imagined world, the bird is the only principle of life and movement until one reaches the "moving" river—seemingly related to the return of the bird in spring—and the "snowing" of the concluding stanza.

> XIII
> It was evening all afternoon.
> It was snowing
> And it was going to snow.
> The blackbird sat
> In the cedar-limbs.

Even in Stevens's effort to create a highly stylized poetry, the presence and pressure of a living bird define the rhythms of birth and of death, of desire and of creativity. That he can address an unpromising subject in stark terms signifies a coming to maturity of the artist's creative imagination; thus the poem is about the process of creating. And we read "Thirteen Ways of Looking at a Blackbird" with such great Romantic lyrics about birds as "Ode to a Nightingale" and "To a Skylark" in mind. Is Stevens not playfully alluding to such poems? Do we not see the blackbird in the intertextual context of Shelley's "To a Skylark" where the speaker marvels at the wondrous bird: "The blue deep thou wingest, / And singing still dost soar, soaring ever singest"; and in Hopkins's "The Windhover," with the suggestion that the beauty of the bird's flight is a metaphor for Christ's intervention on behalf of man? In Keats's "Ode to the Nightingale," the speaker speaks of the nightingale that

> In some melodious plot
> Of beechen green, and shadows numberless
> Singest of summer in full-throated ease.

Although Stevens's blackbird evokes no such idyllic image as Keats's or Shelley's, and no such epiphanic religious moment as Hopkins's, isn't the blackbird's whistle and whirling flight evidence of life in the flat, lifeless plane? Isn't the association with green a harbinger of spring?

By reducing the bird to its minimalist essence, doesn't the poem both elegize and parody a romantic tradition of hyperbole about the song of a bird? Doesn't Stevens make common ground with Hardy's gloomy vision of the darkling thrush in the poem of that name whose joyful song so contradicts the speaker's gloom and despair that he transforms the bird's "full-hearted evensong" as if it were a precursor of suicide?

> An aged thrush frail, gaunt, and small,
> In blast-beruffled plume,
> Has chosen thus to fling his soul
> Upon the growing gloom.

Yet Stevens's abstract and detached style also reflects an anaesthetic quality that recalls the speaker of "Prufrock"—another 1917 poem—imagining the sky as a patient etherized upon the table. Does not "Thirteen Ways of Looking at a Blackbird" call forth a wasteland despair that again recalls Eliot and reminds us that Stevens is both an American heir of Emerson and Melville and a high modernist with kinship ties to Eliot, Joyce, Lawrence, and Yeats? Isn't there, too, the elegaic note of high modernism in this poem that *refuses* to see the bird as symbolic of nature's wonders and of nature's capacity for uplifting the spirit and causing it to sing lyrically?

The blackbird's mark is not only everywhere, even as the moving shadow on the windows of icicles, but its whistle is the catalyst for present inflections and later innuendoes—in other words, for causes and consequences. Yet it is defined in terms of traces, of recalled or imagined perceptions rather than actual ones: the memory of "just after" the blackbird's whistling, the innuendo of its sound or appearance, the recollection of the bird after it is out of sight. It is almost as if the blackbird images poetry; for, like poetry, it is a catalyst for perceptions that transcend and intensify the natural world, even as it remains grounded as part of the natural world. Just as empty space defines content, in stanza V the poem emphasizes how silence and sound define one another:

> V
> I do not know which to prefer,
> The beauty of inflections
> Or the beauty of innuendoes,
> The blackbird whistling
> Or just after.

As a modulation of sound that becomes an innuendo only after it is domesticated into the ken of understanding, inflection bears the approximate relationship to innuendo that signifier bears to signified or image to thing imaged. Isn't the poem about the presence in imagination and memory of inflection, innuendo, and indecipherable cause? In a sense, the text is a dreamscape with puzzling and ambiguous "inflections" and "innuendoes."

The blackbird also represents desire and sexuality. The strong phallic suggestion—the idea in stanza IV of the blackbird as a necessary completion of the sentence about a man and a woman—carries over into the entire sequence:

> IV
> A man and a woman
> Are one.
> A man and a woman and a blackbird
> Are one.

To a 1917 middle-class culture accustomed to thinking that white is more beautiful than black—as Thomas Jefferson had averred—and yet deeply fearful of the mystery of black people, whom they saw from a distance but rarely knew, wouldn't the black phallus itself be a threatening and disturbing image? Doesn't the sexual reading derive from the political innuendo of blackbirds jumping out of the pie and uprooting the king's orderly household? In stanza VII does not Stevens excoriate the men of Haddam/Hadim for favoring their artifices—their golden birds—while the blackbird pays attention to the women around them?

But the blackbird is also a metonymy for the desire to write poetry; it is pen and penis, it is the instrument of creation. Surely, in stanza VII, the bird's walking around the feet of women is deeply sexual, giving way in stanza VIII to the wooing of "noble accents"—do we not hear a homophonic play on sexual *ascent* and tumescence?—and "lucid, inescapable rhythms" that are both creative and sexual:

> VIII
> I know noble accents
> And lucid, inescapable rhythms;
> But I know, too,
> That the blackbird is involved
> In what I know.

The penis is often figured in common talk as a bird; just as a bird in flight is an image of a sexually aroused penis, so a limp bird—and perhaps a disappearing one—is an image for a flaccid penis. Isn't its flight from sight the detumescence following desire and a premonition of death (note the echoes of the seventeenth-century metaphysical poet's equation of sexuality and death), as well as the necessary lull following the intensely creative and passionate act of creating poetry? In "Circles," hadn't Emerson written that the eye is the first circle of understanding while the horizon beyond is the second? The sharp cries of "bawds of euphony"— looking forward to "A High-toned Old Christian Woman"—testify to the effectuality of pen and penis, to the agony and the pleasure deriving from fulfillment of desire, and to the longing for more sensuality.

As the essence of the not-I world and the instrument of sexual and creative desire, the blackbird expands to become a life principle, and that life principle must include the inevitability of death. Thus the blackbird represents not only desire and sexuality but also mutability and mortality. In terms of a historical context for the death motif, the blackbird also suggests the fighter-bombers that were used for the first time in World War I, and which from the ground were conceived as metallic birds. It was in 1917 that the German Red Baron, Manfred von Richthofen, was shot from the sky by a British Sopwith Camel. The blackbird's shadow—appearing twice in stanza VI and once in the speaker's premonition of his funeral cortège in stanza XI—hovers over the poem as if it were the possibility of death. Among other things the cortège signifies the temporary death of the penis in detumescence. Yet as the sequence proceeds, the speaker begins to reveal himself, until in stanza XI he foresees the chilling picture of his own death. Does not the shadow of his "equipage" suggest his funeral cortège?

> XI
> He rode over Connecticut
> In a glass coach.
> Once, a fear pierced him,
> In that he mistook
> The shadow of his equipage
> For blackbirds.

We think not only of the transformation of Cinderella and her "glass coach" at midnight but of Emily Dickinson's "Because I Could not Stop for Death":

> Because I could not stop for Death—
> He kindly stopped for me—

> The Carriage held but just Ourselves—
> and Immortality.

But for Stevens, immortality exists only in the survival of his poetry.

The poem concludes with a dialectical debate between life and death, between affirmative and negative ways of seeing, between forward time and scrambled, confused time. Looking becomes a kind of knowing, although knowing itself—"know" recurs four times: three times in stanza VIII and once in stanza V—contains the inversion of not knowing implied by the homophonic relation between "know" and "no." (The play on "know" and "no" looks forward to the ambiguity of the last line of "The Snow Man," where the possibility of knowing is contained in the concept of nothingness: "[T]he listener, who listens in the snow, / And, nothing himself, beholds / Nothing that is not there and the nothing that is.") Both of the last two stanzas use the present participle to affirm that the very action of perceiving overcomes death and stasis. In stanza XII the speaker's ability to perceive the process of the cosmos is related to perceiving movement on a clear day: "The river is moving. / The blackbird must be flying." But in stanza XIII, the poem ends only with snow— recalling and giving new meaning to the "snowy mountains" of stanza I. For the actuality and promise of snow imply the possibility of ice and suggest the barbaric, threatening icicles of stanza VI, including the threat of phallic intrusion that recalls the nursery rhyme suggested by the title.

Although snow also implies the possibility of water and renewal, suggesting the green light and spring and seasonal change, there are other strong hints of death and despair. The cedar-limbs suggest cedar coffins, which recall the glass coach of stanza XI, and the transparent icicles, which reflect the continuing movement back and forth of the ominous blackbird foreshadowing death and evil. As we have seen, the blackbird, among other things, is a ubiquitous and ominous reminder of death and imminent doom, and its shadow is far different from the shadows from which Keats's nightingale sings. Since the speaker had compared himself to a tree, the return of the blackbird to the cedar is a reflexive turn and return to the self. Wherever one turns, one finds oneself—and one's fate imaged by the blackbird is a version of the self. Just as the very poem enacts the speaker's own compulsive inclination to address the same subject, the blackbird is itself a trope for necessity or Fate—the force beyond ourselves that we cannot quite control. Thinking, no doubt, of the innuendo of coercion and necessity in "The blackbird must be flying" (stanza XII), Stevens wrote that stanza XII addresses "the compulsion frequently back of the things that we do."[18]

The poem enacts the essential dualism of life, the dualism imaged by Nietzsche in the Apollonian/Dionysian conflict, where, as Robert Morris puts it, "the deference (and mania) for temperance, moderation, justice, clarity, individual identity, clear distinctions of forms, and intellectual precision is pitted against the formlessness of the wild, the uncontainable, the mystical shattering of individual identity for ritual unity, and the hubris of jubilation and manic play."[19] The Dionysian mode is represented by major aspects of the poem: the unpredictable and uncontrollable blackbird, whose flight "whirled in the autumn winds" and whose whistle cannot be controlled; the reversal of expectations: "I am of three minds" and "I was like a tree"; the "barbaric glass" created by icicles; and, of course, the presence of sexuality and the specter of death. These aspects challenge the Apollonian aspects: flatness and abstraction, the controlling "eye"—*e y e* and "I" as the vertical pronoun—the artificial golden birds imagined by the "thin men of Haddam" (Hadim), the man-created "noble accents and lucid, inescapable rhythms" (which are mocked—or overridden—by the blackbird's "whistle" and "whirl"), and the "circle" of the speaker's field of perception.

In "Thirteen Ways of Looking at a Blackbird," we should see Stevens as an American poet with a mythopoeic imagination who is trying to reinvent reality outside temporal movement. Stevens wishes to free us from conventional notions of time, of the relationship between past and present. "It was snowing and it was going to snow." The poem moves forward and backward through past, present, and future as if Stevens were trying to obliterate time; the poem exists without past and future on a flat plane. The poem is at once timeless and rootless, even as it is absolute and eternal, and in those senses, transcendent; it glorifies the perception of the "eye" and "I" at the expense of all else. Isn't the eye the camera's eye that seems to demand the self-effacement of the subject? And yet, at the same time, the nonmimetic code—including the absence of the familiar red-winged blackbird and the continuing paradoxical appearance and disappearance of the bird—belies the power of the eye and focuses on inner ways of seeing. Doesn't the monochromatic quality of the poem and the stance of detached, neutral objectivity—a stance that cannot exclude sexuality and death, both of which continually intrude and even dominate almost in spite of the speaker's efforts to control—owe something to this? The subject of the poem includes self-effacement and its impossibility; for time and self intrude their presence despite Stevens's effort to write minimalist art. According to Helen Vendler, "'Thirteen Ways of Looking at a Blackbird' depends wholly on contraction, on the simple declarative sentence reduced almost to the infantile."[20] The impulse to minimalism present in imagism and in haiku is also an American phenomenon: the succinct remark, the fixing phrase, is the antithesis to—and another version of—American hyperbole. Isn't the perception that hyperbole and understatement are on a continuum the essence of art by such poets as John Ashbery and Robert Creeley as well as visual artists like Jasper Johns, Robert Rauschenberg, and Andy Warhol? Like them, Stevens makes art out of banal subjects—as he does here and will do again in "The Emperor of Ice Cream" (1922) and "The Man on the Dump" (1938).

Notes

1   Robert Morris, "Words and Images in Modernism and Postmodernism," *Critical Inquiry* 15 (Winter 1989): 345.
2   Wallace Stevens's poems are quoted from *Collected Poems* (New York: Vintage Books, 1954).
3   Ralph Waldo Emerson, "The American Scholar," in *The Portable Emerson,* by Carl Bode in collaboration with Malcolm Cowley (New York: Penguin Books, 1946), 56.
4   Wallace Stevens, *Letters,* ed. Holly Stevens (New York: Knopf, 1966), letter no. 279.
5   Ezra Pound, "Vorticism," *Fortnightly Review,* new series, 96 (September 1914), reprinted in *The Modern Tradition,* ed. Richard Ellmann and Charles Feidelson, Jr. (New York: Oxford University Press, 1965), 150.
6   A. Walton Litz, *Introspective Voyager: The Poetic Development of Wallace Stevens* (New York: Oxford University Press, 1972), 66.
7   Michael Brenson, "Picasso and Braque: Brothers in Cubism," review of Museum of Modern Art exhibit *Picasso and Braque: Pioneering Cubism, New York Times,* September 22, 1989.
8   Stevens, *Letters,* no. 655.
9   Stevens, *Opus Posthumous,* rev. ed., ed. Milton J. Bates (New York: Knopf, 1989), 186.
10 William Rubin, Introduction to *Picasso and Braque: Pioneering Cubism* (New York: Museum of Modern Art, 1989), 16.
11 Emily Bardace Kies, *Picasso and Braque: Pioneering Cubism,* exhibit pamphlet (New York: Museum of Modern Art, 1989).
12 Rubin, Introduction to *Picasso and Braque,* 22, 38, 40.
13 Rubin, Introduction to *Picasso and Braque,* 37–38.
14 Kies, *Picasso and Braque.*
15 Stevens, *Letters,* no. 387.

16   See W. J. T. Mitchell, "*Ut Pictura Theoria:* Abstract Painting and the Repression of Language," *Critical Inquiry* 15 (Winter 1989): 348–71.

17   Rosalind Krauss, *The Originality of the Avant-Garde and Other Modernist Myths* (Cambridge: Harvard University Press, 1985), 237; quoted in Mitchell, "*Ut Pictura Theoria,*" 357.

18   Stevens, *Letters,* no. 387.

19   Morris, "Words and Images," 345.

20   Helen Vendler, *On Extended Wings: Wallace Stevens's Longer Poems* (Cambridge: Harvard University Press, 1969), 78.

Ingeborg Majer O'Sickey

The Narratives of Desire in Wim Wenders's

Der Himmel über Berlin

Der Himmel über Berlin (*Wings of Desire,* 1987) was directed by the West German filmmaker Wim Wenders and cowritten by Wenders and the Austrian poet, novelist, and playwright Peter Handke. Although *Himmel* neither foregrounds Berlin's position as a divided city nor problematizes the fact that the citizens of this city were forced to live separately for over a quarter of a century, *Himmel* occupies a unique place in German cinematic history in that it is the last film to be made of Berlin before the city was unified in November 1989.

The film uses Berlin's cityscape for the hero's initiation into manhood. Subtending my argument is the claim that this initiation is pre-scripted in classical Oedipal fashion as the story of a white, male hero who embarks on a quest that will ultimately result in a masculinist subjectivity. Moreover, in the process of production, a particular *Geschichte* (story *and* history) is appropriated in a way that adds to already existing cultural narratives that reproduce (rather than illuminate, subvert, or critique) mistakes of *Geschichte,* creating an effect that is particularly evident in the film's representations of the Turkish and Jewish people in Berlin. This process of appropriation ultimately resembles the gestures of colonization and border politics that are now evolving in the recently united Germany. The hero's appropriation of the city's territory thus resembles his takeover of Woman, who is figured as a psychopolitical terrain similar to the city, and both appropriations ultimately serve as narrative components for the hero's quest for a masculinist subjectivity.

Since Wenders is considered a member of the film cottage industry called the New German Cinema (NGC), it is important first to consider

Himmel in terms of its position within West German films of the 1970s and 1980s. From its inception in 1962, the NGC has had as one of its goals to critically illuminate Germany's inability and/or unwillingness to look at its compliance with the Nazi regime. To this end, Wenders's colleagues in the NGC (Margarethe von Trotta, Rainer Werner Fassbinder, Helga Sanders-Brahms, and Alexander Kluge, to name only a few) have thematized as well as problematized *Vergangenheitsverdrängung* (denial of Germany's psychopolitical past) as a way toward their personal *Vergangenheitsbewältigung* (working through the scars of Germany's Nazi past).[1] These filmmakers stress that the racist policies and sexist politics that characterized the National Socialist regime have not simply been erased. Many see the German people's unwillingness to look at their involvement with the Nationalist Socialist regime as a stumbling block that has prevented them from creating a nonracist and nonsexist society. In their work, NGC filmmakers shake up the belief in an ideological tabula rasa (the so-called *Stunde Null,* "zero hour") after 1945, insisting that, on the contrary, many citizens in the Federal Republic of Germany continue to harbor a desire for a racially pure and patriarchal society. To this end, many NGC filmmakers weave into the tales of their films their disagreement with the arbitrary nature of the so-called denazification program (which was shaped and brought to a hasty end by West Germany's recruitment into the cold war), their objection to West Germany's remilitarization, and their frustration with West Germany's wholesale acceptance of the ideology of the capitalist West. Going beyond the attempt to shake West Germany out of its national amnesia of the twelve years of National Socialist rule, these filmmakers often draw analogies between attitudes in present-day Germany and former fascist ideology and policies. Notable examples of such efforts are R. W. Fassbinder's *FRG Trilogy,* a project he began in the mid-1970s; Ebbo Demant's 1979 made-for-TV film *Lagerstrasse Auschwitz;* and the omnibus film *Deutschland im Herbst* (1978).[2] In addition to these ideology critiques, feminist NGC filmmakers such as Helga Sanders-Brahms (*Deutschland, Bleiche Mutter,* 1980), Margarethe von Trotta (*Schwestern,* 1979, and *Bleierne Zeit,* 1981), Jutta Brückner (*Hungerjahre in einem reichen Land,* 1987), Marianne Rosenbaum (*Peppermint Frieden,* 1983), and Michael Verhoeven (*Nasty Girl,* 1991) use their films as vehicles to reveal the continuities of oppressive social policies and practices faced by Jewish men and women, German women, and other marginalized people from the Third Reich to today's Germany. These films expose what might be called the dysfunctionality of Germans in private and political spheres.

Wenders approaches *Vergangenheitsbewältigung* in a radically different way from these filmmakers. Although he does not jettison history in *Himmel* in order to offer Germans "a new vision" (his words), he uses it in a nonconfrontational way in that he aesthetisizes *Spurensuche* (uncovering historical traces). In *Himmel* he expresses a position he articulated in 1976: "I think it is of primary importance to hold on to the will to create a new beginning; not to lose one's energy."[3] This *Einstellung* (both in the sense of cinematic "take" and political vision) sets Wenders apart from other filmmakers of the NGC. Whereas his colleagues' underlying belief is that the German people cannot create an equitable society unless they confront their past and present actions, Wenders believes that the work of *Vergangenheitsbewältigung* saps the German people's energy and forecloses a chance for utopian energies. Whereas the filmmakers behind the *Hitlerwelle* (Hitler wave), as it became known in the West German press, thematized in many of their productions a disillusionment with the course the new Federal Republic of Germany had taken since 1945, Wenders's film attempts to vault over the implications of difficult passages in Germany's history. This move fits his goal, which is to awaken "utopian energies" in his audience. Thus, rather than holding up for critique cultural narratives that sanction notions of racial purity, nationalism, and gender relations based on patriarchal interests, Wenders's narrative in *Himmel* attempts to captivate his viewers with a spectacularly executed visual feast. His film, which he has called "an epos to peace," is designed not to raise consciousness but to teach "the audience to learn amazement."[4]

The Angel of History: *Vergangenheitsbewältigung*

"At the origin of Narrative, desire," Roland Barthes tells us in *S/Z*. Keeping this thought in mind, let us briefly consider the opening sequence of *Himmel*. For eight long seconds the screen is completely filled with the expanse of the sky over West Berlin; in a gradual fade-in an enormous eye appears, within which, using a multiple image montage, the rooftops of the tenement buildings that line the Wilhelmian residential ring slowly develop, similar to the gradual way a photograph develops in the darkroom. This shot is followed by a dissolve shot that shows the protagonist, the angel Damiel, standing on the bombed-out part of the tower of the Gedächtniskirche (the Kaiser-Wilhelm Memorial Church) in the posture of surveyor overlooking the cityscape, while a chorus of murmuring voices can be heard rising up from below.

This remarkable scopic confession is followed by nearly twenty minutes (comprising about 110 scenes) of narration of West Berlin as a body of text as the angel Damiel (and later his friend Cassiel) takes us on a tour of West Berlin.[5] The film thus opens self-consciously with the description of its own operation in terms of the scopic drive: the eye of the camera thematizes the film's visual pleasure, its *Schaulust.* Teresa de Lauretis's remarks about the significance of the scopic drive in terms of psychocultural narratives emphasize the importance of the scopic drive in cinema as it reinscribes the "sex-gender system": "The scopic drive that maps desire into representation, and is so essential to the work of the film and the productive relations of imaging in general, could be itself a function of social memory, recalling a time when the unity of the subject with the world was achieved and represented as vision. Together, narrativity and scopophilia perform the 'miracles' of cinema."[6]

It is through this framework of narrativity and scopophilia that my remarks about *Himmel* are refracted. The opening sequence and the film's first twenty minutes or so present us with such an explicit statement of the hero's visual pleasure that it alerts us that the narrative to follow is based on the hero's desire for a masculinist subjectivity. It therefore does not come as a surprise that the film not only reveals its operation in terms of the scopic drive but links this operation quite explicitly to narrative as its raison d'être as an art form. We see this linkage in the way *Geschichte* (in the sense of story *and* history) and the act of storytelling (in the sense of making meaning by unifying experience) are openly celebrated in the film as a life-giving and lifesaving activity, and as the organizing principle for community and individual life *tout court.*

The authority to narrate is conferred upon the male characters in the film. It is reiterated in and through Homer, the film's bard, who appears throughout the film explicitly explaining this function of narrative. In a less explicit way, it is reiterated by Peter Falk, who, referencing the character of Colombo, personifies the idea of narrativity *as* detecting pleasure. The angel Cassiel, on the other hand, functions as the *prohibition* of narrative; the successful completion of the hero's narrative function is Cassiel's loss: the romantic quest for the woman (Marion) is set up against the background of the destruction of the homoerotic relationship between Damiel and Cassiel. As the appearance of the woman in the film is used to restore "order," the men's relationship is broken up and sorted into a narrative that explicitly casts Damiel as a hero, whose function it is to find the woman and to fantasize her into a being who will complete him. In this function, Cassiel is, to use Vladimir Propp's term, the donor as well as the *Symtomträger* (bearer of symptoms that emanate from societal taboos) for the hero's achievement of a masculinist subjectivity. Cassiel is appropriately described by the text we overhear from a reader in West Berlin's public library (the Staatsbibliothek) as "the angel of temperance" and of "solitude and tears who 'shews forth the unity of the eternal kingdom.'"[7]

The male protagonist of the film, the angel Damiel, who is often the I/eye of the camera, can be said to personify the entire operation of the film-in-process. It is his desire for a unified subjectivity that fuels the engine that propels the narrative forward. In light of his narratological function, it is likely that Damiel is not only an angel in the conventional sense of "messenger" and "bearer of good tidings" but also the "Angel of History" of Walter Benjamin's ecphrasis of Paul Klee's drawing *Angelus Novus*.[8] This connection indicates not only that the angel's backward glance is encoded in the film as a "drama of vision" but that the code of the Angel of History engenders a particular kind of narrative drama (or narrativity) as a work of *Vergangenheitsbewältigung*.

The cityscape of West Berlin also plays an important narrating role in the film's work of *Vergangenheitsbewältigung*. The angels' home, the Staatsbibliothek, is the repository of hundreds of thousands of narratives of all sorts; the film set of yet another film, an air-raid bunker that functions as the site where the story of Holocaust victims is referenced, tells a kind of story of the Third Reich and World War II; parts of the Berlin Wall with graffiti are visually engaged to reference the border between East and West; the circus is presented as the stage upon which a narrative of human play and creativity is enacted; and finally, the sky *and* heavens (*Himmel* means both) above the Berlins represent the place that evokes the stories of both the life-destroying air raids during World War II on the entire city and, later, the lifesaving airlifts for thousands of West Berliners.

Since the places that take part in the film's narrative are assimilated into the West, the absence of East Berlin is figured as a kind of *Vergangenheitsverdrängung*. In many ways we can see the film's depictions of the Berlin Wall as a sign of the tensions inherent in narrative closure:

the narrative of remembering the past in the angel's function as Angel of History is in conflict with the narrative of the hero's inscription of his initiation into manhood. The wall as the visible sign of this conflict is, as I will discuss in more detail below, figured as a border that represents and problematizes the representation of (sexual) difference itself.

The Drama of Remembering as *Vergangenheitsbewältigung*

The images of the city as representations of memory traces recall Walter Benjamin's distinction between "universal history" ("its method is additive") and "materialistic historiography" ("based on a constructive principle").[9] "Universal history" encodes historical events of prewar Berlin in the view that Damiel and Cassiel have when they periodically rest on the wings of the Siegesengel Victoria. To the east the angels direct our view to the Brandenburger Tor (Brandenburg Gate), which glosses two centuries of German history: Napoleon marched through it victorious over the Prussians in 1803; Kaiser Wilhelm I marched through it victorious over the French in 1871; Nazi torches illuminated its columns on the *quadriga;* tanks of the Red Army rolled past it in 1945; demonstrating workers were put down there in a bloody attack by the East German regime in 1953; Erich Honecker's troops divided the city in two in the *Schutzwall gegen die Faschisten* (the protective wall against the fascists) on August 13, 1961.

Whereas the film encodes the Benjaminian notion of "universal history" by following the additive method, Wenders's engagement of Benjamin's concept of materialist historiography is an extremely restricted one. This point becomes clear when we consider the film's failure to validate the social reality of West Berlin's "foreign" population, most of whom live in West Berlin's district of Kreuzberg.[10] Although Kreuzberg has an important role in the film as the site where Damiel's metamorphosis from angel into human takes place and where he sells his armor in a German antique shop in the Goebenstrasse, the Turkish cultural and commercial life of Kreuzberg is absent from the film. Furthermore, signs of the racial tensions (graphically depicted in graffiti with racist slurs in subways, on tenement walls, and so on) among the white European Germans, the Turks, and the German Turks are made invisible in the film.[11] Images of Turks are used as stand-ins for "the other" rather than as social agents in their own environment or as subjects in history. Thus, the presence of Turkish women in West Berlin is referenced only in their servile relationship to white employers (we see them, for example, in the Staatsbibliothek at night, vacuuming); or reduced (as in one shot where a Turkish woman is shown completely alone in a high-tech laundromat) to an image that serves to contrast "exotic" Woman with the Western world of high technology. A seemingly innocuous scene, Damiel's brief encounter with a German Turkish boy after Damiel comes out of the antique shop, puts the absence of references to Turkish cultural life into sharp relief. To the boy's request for directions to the Akazienstrasse, Damiel responds with such rapid-fire instructions that the boy cannot understand his German.[12] Thus, even in the German Turkish boy's neighborhood, it is Damiel who owns the city. By taking away the possibility of understanding from the boy, Damiel steals the boy's ability to venture out of "his" neighborhood. In the act of *naming*, Damiel takes the authority to narrate (the city) as his.

Looking at the film's colonizing gesture vis-à-vis West Berlin's Turkish and German Turkish population enables us to read Wenders's film as a cultural narrative of a city that reproduces the ideological operation that is always already present in such narratives. The film's hegemonic gesture points to broader implications of its mythic assimilation of the wall as the sign that functions to obliterate differences (cultural, ethnic, sexual, political, and psychopolitical ones). Indeed, as I have mentioned, it is remarkable that *Himmel,* the last film about Berlin before the city was politically unified, does not narrate the city as culturally, politically, and psychologically divided. It is also remarkable that the film erases East Berlin as a fact of urban life; except for the border guards patrolling no-man's-land at the wall, East Berliners are absent from *Himmel über Berlin.* This is important because the wall that separated the West from the East in Kreuzberg is the site where the protagonist achieves full narrating power as a Western masculinist subject.[13] Thus, when we refract the film through recent Western narratives about re/unification, a number of connections come to mind. The city is mapped, I have suggested, into the geography of the film as a mythical place. As such its function is to retell the story of a unified city. This can be done only by suppressing (psycho)cultural differences (differences frequently expressed in West Germans' racist attitudes toward their Eastern neighbors), and thus the social function of the story as a narrative denies other narratives that contradict it.[14] Clearly, as we have seen in the way Turks are referenced in the film and by the absence of East Berliners, *Himmel* tells a story of coherence that excludes conflicting narratives.

The narratives of unification have also authorized a denial of conflicting narratives. Beginning at least with the March 18, 1990, elections in East Germany, the talks between East and West clearly show that conflicting stories—those of once-powerful emancipatory movements that were swallowed up by a tide in which the power of the deutsche mark determined the victory of the Christian Democratic Union in East Germany—were suppressed. Left-wing intellectuals who were once at the forefront of the revolution and who formed the New Forum, the League of Women, and the Coalition of Lesbians, among other groups, called for slowing the tempo of the discussions so that the creation of a separate social democracy could be considered. As these groups were drowned out by unification rhetoric and squeezed to the margins, their fear that the former German Democratic Republic would become a colony of the West became a reality: the East German citizens of working age have already lost their basic right to employment; children have lost the right to guaranteed state-funded child care; under the current system, in which child care responsibilities are left to women, this in turn undercuts previous attainments of gender equality in the workplace. Furthermore, East German women are very close to losing the right to make their own decisions concerning reproduction.[15] Tatiana Bohm, the human rights activist and a minister in the East German transitional government that existed from January to April 1990, spoke to the hegemonic gesture that characterizes such narratives in the press: "In the U.S. papers, it is as if unification with West Germany was the only goal of our movement. . . . And reunification on West German terms. As if the GDR people had no other desire than immediate merger with the Western world. No one remembers the demands that were formulated in the fall: that emerged from the peace, human rights, women's and ecology movements."[16]

Although not speaking specifically about *Himmel*'s treatment of West Berlin's Turkish population or the absence of East Berliners, bell hooks indicts precisely this kind of colonizing gesture in *Himmel* in her compelling article "Representing Whiteness: Seeing *Wings of Desire*":

> If, as [Wenders] suggests, the angels are "a metaphor for history, a particular memory," we would all have seen these angels differently had they not been predominantly male and all white. In many ways the film attempts to create a space of otherness, where white masculinity can be reconceptualized and white patriarchal imperialist

history critiqued. Such a project raises questions about whether the alternative narrative he constructs actually subverts or challenges the old. Wenders' work represents a trend in white avant-garde aesthetic circles toward revisioning old narratives, presumably to create new and different stories—narratives of opposition. *Wings of Desire* does not fulfill this promise. It does not tell a new story.[17]

The argument that hooks offers, that representation in *Himmel* is marked by a politics of identification and positionality, speaks to the manner in which the social reality of the East Berliners and the Turkish people in West Berlin is treated in the film. It is her charge of Wenders's work as representative of a "trend in white avant-garde aesthetic circles" that is significant for the following discussion of Wenders's experimentation with form in the depiction of the history of the Jewish experience in Nazi Germany. This experience is narrated as a fiction in a film within the film, starring Peter Falk in the character of Colombo (the frame story of the film within the film is that the American detective Colombo is hired in 1945 by a man who wants Colombo to find his brother's son in Germany). First, Wenders's choice of Peter Falk must be problematized on the level of a cinematic code. Casting a well-known actor in one of the film's roles, and casting him as his television personality, assimilates, or perhaps grafts, this persona to the new plot. The "fictional" Colombo (who has appeared on TV screens for years in Germany as well) is made integral to the plot, and he, or the TV show, becomes the "prior reality" that the film addresses and from which it derives its meaning.

Second, still keeping this cinematic code in mind, we must contrast Wenders's use of documentary footage of non-Jewish Berliners' sufferings during the air raids of World War II with the way a part of German Jewish history during the Third Reich in Berlin is referred to by way of a detective story. The documentary footage, which depicts 1945 air raids on Berlin, and archival photos of the corpses of non-Jewish Berliners who perished in the bombing attacks on Berlin are blended in as Cassiel's memory flashes while he is on his way to the location of the film within the film. Positioning this archival material in contiguity to the "fictional" representation of the deportation of the German Jews makes Wenders's aesthetic choices even more problematic. Furthermore, the juxtaposing of "truth" and speculative "fiction" (i.e., documentary versus fictional representation) within the film as text-in-process must be seen in the context of post–World War II German (especially East

German) cultural narratives that deny and/or erase the Shoah. It is precisely this kind of *Vergangenheitsverdrängung* that the Angel of History
(in Benjamin's sense) is said to fight against.[18]

Adding to these difficulties are the innocuous lines given to Homer
(played by Curt Bois) as he walks around the now desolate Potsdamer
Platz. Reminiscing nostalgically about the bustling commercial center
that it once was, Homer recalls the Nazi takeover with these words:
"The department store Wertheim used to be here too. And then, there
were suddenly flags, over there. . . . The entire plaza was full of them.
And then the people, they weren't friendly any more and the police
weren't either." Here, too, Wenders's choice of actor is significant. Bois,
a German-Jewish actor, is well known to the older generation of Germans for his work with Bertolt Brecht and Max Reinhart and for his
escape from Nazi Germany in 1933. Wenders's choice of an actor whose
work and, to some degree, whose life story are part of the German cultural consciousness is difficult to reconcile with the lines Curt Bois (as
Homer) is given to recall the Third Reich.[19]

When Homer's nostalgic trip into the past is put side by side with the
choice of ideologically weighted discourse in the heroine's long speech
toward the end of the film, it is difficult not to indict the film as a reproduction of a celebration of fascist ideology. In her final, extraordinarily
aestheticized speech to Damiel, Marion uses terminology that resonates
so strongly with the language used during the Third Reich that few
people would use it today without putting it inside quotation marks:

> Wir sind jetzt mehr als nur zwei. Wir verkörpern etwas. Wir sitzen
> auf dem Platz des Volkes, und der ganze Platz ist voll von Leuten,
> die sich dasselbe wünschen wie wir. Wir bestimmen das Spiel für
> alle! Ich bin bereit. . . . es wird eine Geschichte von Riesen sein, un-
> sichtbaren, übertragbaren, eine Geschichte neuer Stammeltern.

> [Words that are weighted with Nazi ideological baggage are itali-
> cized in my translation]: We are no longer merely two people. We
> sit on the *plaza of the people,* and the entire plaza is crowded with
> people who want the same thing we do. We determine the future for
> all! *I am prepared.* . . . It will be the story of *giants,* invisible, trans-
> ferable, a history of new *tribal* parents.[20]

Finally, the historical inaccuracy of the events referenced in the film
within the film adds another layer of problems to this narrative. The

sequences that portray Colombo on the set of the film within the film present Jews in a bunker, awaiting their deportation by the Nazis. The year is 1945. This inaccuracy in the film's otherwise meticulous attention to historical detail is remarkable. If, in 1945, any Jews remained of the 140,000 who constituted the Jewish community in Berlin before 1933, they were in hiding. No deportations of Jews from Berlin in 1945 are recorded. The deportations to Auschwitz began on July 11, 1942, and of the more than 55,000 Berlin Jews who were deported to the concentration camps, as few as 6,000 Berlin Jews lived to see liberation in 1945.[21]

It is possible that Wenders is interested in critiquing the general misinformation about the Nazi period in general and the Shoah in particular; it is also possible that he is trying to critique the exploitation of it in dramatizations on American TV, for instance, or that he wants to confront the (im)possibilities inherent in representations of historical events. Whether or not any or all of these speculations obtain, Wenders's use of a part of Jewish history in Berlin as a pretext to experimenting with form must be criticized. The film enters not only into the recent narratives of revisionist historians both in Germany and the United States, but also into the cultural narratives marked by an ignorance in the younger generation in both parts of Germany of the events of twelve years of National Socialism and by a denial of these events on the part of many members of the older generation.

Marion/Marionette: East Berlin as Woman

Wenders does not use experimental forms to expose the classical cinema's filmic apparatus in the representation of women in *Himmel*. Rather, his film *reproduces* what de Lauretis says of classical narrative film generally: "Cinema works for Oedipus. The heroine therefore has to move on, like Freud's little girl, and take her place where Oedipus will find her awaiting *him*."[22] When Damiel finds the heroine, twenty minutes into the film, the heterosexual romance script is activated in the terms of classical narrative cinema. These terms include the equation of the binary pair female=passive/male=active. As we have seen, Damiel traverses the western territory of the city and takes possession of it in barely concealed voyeurism. In a similar way he traverses and takes possession of the woman. She, like the city, is a body displayed to be looked at. The text of the city, which is activated through the scopic drive, is engaged not only as a particular city-narrative of history and social relations but as female body in an allegorical sense as well as in a metonymic substitution. In this latter narrative strategy the hero's desire to conquer the city's body glides almost seamlessly into the desire to conquer the heroine's body. This movement is most suggestively similar to a sexual conquest when Damiel, after his first twenty minutes of roaming the city, "leaves" the body of the city through a tunnel before he enters the womblike circus tent, where he finds his object of desire, Marion. The allegorical element, conversely, can be seen in the fact that their first meeting is prescripted in the film by way of a resemblance that Damiel and Marion briefly share: rehearsing on the trapeze for the evening performance, she appears as a "winged creature," wearing feathers. Her trainer refers to her function as *colombe* (dove, symbol for peace), but she also, within the chain of signification of the film, personifies Nike—the Siegesengel Victoria—the same figure to which Damiel frequently returns to rest and which he, too, may be said to personify.

In many ways East Berlin, signed as a "dark continent," can be theorized as the *absent* woman in the film. Like Marion, it has no story, except insofar as it is assimilated to the story of the West. Marion is an exile (from somewhere in France), and as a narrative component that completes *his* story, she has no authority to narrate. Similarly, East Berlin, which is narrated solely in terms of the mythologized wall that separates it from the West, has the function as narrative component that betokens the desire for unity. In the same way that East Berlin's difference is assimilated into the name "Berlin" in the title of the film, the woman's difference is erased as she is fantasized into a mythical other. Both erasures are made in the service of the hero's ascent to a masculinist subjectivity. In light of the mythic assimilation of the wall, and keeping in mind that narrative or storytelling is, as de Lauretis puts it, "the mapping of sexual difference into each text,"[23] it is not surprising that the site where sexual difference is constructed is the border separating the East from the West. In its narrative function as the sign of difference the wall works to obliterate all obstacles, be they the foreign residents in Kreuzberg, the racial tensions in West Berlin, the psychopolitical scars of a divided city, or East Berlin's residents. Thus, inasmuch as the female character is figured in her acquiescence to being made feminine (Woman with a capital W), the space where sexual difference is mapped is allegorically gendered female.

The erasure of the woman and her rescription into Woman can best be illustrated with the sequence that immediately follows Damiel's (and the spectators') first view of Marion. During the rehearsal Marion finds out that she has lost her job as a trapeze artist because the circus has run out of money. She walks to her trailer on the circus grounds and enters it. Damiel follows her there. While she reclines on her bed, wondering about her future, Damiel takes visual possession of her. I say "possession" because since Marion cannot see Damiel see her, she is figuratively blinded. As a number of film theorists have shown, the female character's inability to return the gaze in classical narrative cinema encodes an absence of the female character's own desire. In other words, since she cannot return his gaze, she cannot participate in the narration of her desire. Thus, on one level still personifying Nike ("a goddess without story," without individuality, often de-faced),[24] the subjective camera (the I/eye of the camera and the hero) "gives" her (a) vision—that is to say, a face. But her face is created also by an economy of gazes that goes back and forth between the angel and the film's spectators. Most of the shots are alternating close and medium-long shots of Marion from a position to the side of her, with some crucial point-of-view shots that encourage spectators to identify with the angel.

But the male protagonist's appropriation of Marion is not limited to the voyeuristic. In what I call "auditeurism" the male protagonist listens in on the heroine's thoughts and delivers them to us through the agency of his power. Again the spectator is implicated, this time in the role of coauditeur. The spectators' voyeuristic and auditory role, which is in this way reflected back to them, can be extremely difficult to accept since it demands of them a position that essentially "informs" against the female character in the film.[25]

In the manner that Marion's thoughts are delivered in the economy of auditeurism, they can be said to ventriloquize male desire. First, for a blank page: "plus rien penser, to think of nothing. Just to exist. Berlin. I am a stranger here and still it's all familiar. To wait at a photomat and to come out with a different face . . . a story could start this way. . . . How should I think?" And second, at the end of the sequence, in a ventriloquization of his desire for a dream woman: "I must always be ready and every man in the world will look at me. Longing. Longing for a wave of desire that rises up in me. . . . Desire to love."[26] In this double construction through the agency of voyeurism and auditeurism, Marion, like the goddess Nike, henceforth helps move the protagonist's story forward, wearing the face he has designed for her to wear, thinking thoughts that reflect his desire.

Marion's final evening performance similarly reveals how scopophilia is engaged in the narrative construction of desire as the hero's. In this long sequence, Marion is working the trapeze while the male figures in the ring and on the bandstand bond through looks at the performing female body. Several cross-cut shots establish a link between Damiel and the trainer and between the male members of the band as they look at the woman on the trapeze. In the two shots where the looks of the members of the band and Damiel are fused, Marion's performance is sexually most suggestive: she takes off her robe to the band's drumroll and lets it fall to the ground. She then drops into a split and ends in an explicitly sexual pose. Whereas Marion is displayed as a (sexually) *receptive* body in the trailer, on the trapeze she is displayed as a (sexually) *performing* body. In both positions she connotes what Laura Mulvey calls woman's "to-be-looked-at-ness." Clearly, the fact that Marion performs as a trapeze artist allows the relay of male looks to be fused in a particular way. As Mulvey explains, the function of the displayed woman in cinema generally and the "device of the show girl" allow "the two looks [the characters' and the spectators'] to be unified technically without any apparent break in the diegesis." In this way "the woman displayed has functioned on two levels: as erotic object for the characters within the screen story, and as erotic object for the spectator within the auditorium, with a shifting tension between the looks on either side of the screen."[27]

In Marion's last scene in *Der Himmel über Berlin*, we see the culmination of the film's process of mapping sexual difference. The scene follows an inexorable logic: the consummation of the heterosexist script is presented in a shot of the angel-turned-man with Marion-turned-marionette performing on a rope that he swings around. This image points to a reversal of the characters' positions: whereas Damiel begins as an angel without a visible, material body, Marion begins as a sexualized body; whereas his conversion from angel to man grounds him, her conversion into the principle that is to complete him mythologizes her into the ideal Woman.

In Wenders's trajectory both the city and the woman are de/scribed into the classical narrative so as to fit the desire of the male hero. While both the male and female protagonists are, of course, Wenders's (and in a more limited sense, also Peter Handke's) instruments and vehicles for the filmic reality of *Himmel*, the authority to narrate is conferred on the male hero. Thus, whereas Damiel's role is to narrate himself into the puppet master in charge of narrating an idealized Marion/ette, the female figure has no such structuring role. There is a grim analogy in the image of Damiel as the puppet master and Marion as marionette: it reads like the narratives surrounding the unification talks and postunification politics, with Helmut Kohl as the puppet master and East Germany dangling on a rope as he swings it round and round.

Notes

I presented versions of this essay at Syracuse University (January 1990) and the International Conference of Narrative in New Orleans (April 1990). My thanks to Mike Arnold and Janice Carlisle for their editorial help. For critical readings and suggestions I thank Beverly Allen, Linda Alcoff, Doug Anderson, Konstanze Bäumer, Dympna Callaghan, Peter Goldman, Jane Marcus, Sally Miles, and Robyn Wiegman, as well as the members of the critical studies group at Syracuse University.

1   The terms *Vergangenheitsverdrängung* (denial of the past) and *Vergangenheitsbewältigung* (coming to terms with the past) have become popular to describe the ways Germans have dealt and still deal with the legacy of the Third Reich. *Vergangenheitsverdrängung* and *Vergangenheitsbewältigung* are commonly used to describe an either/or situation: either an individual or a group of people deny all of the National Socialist past, or they come to terms with all of it. It isn't that simple, of course. The dichotomy established by these terms entails that one is always to a certain degree present in the other.

2   A joint effort by several prominent NGC filmmakers, *Deutschland im Herbst* addresses the government's violent reaction to terrorism in West Germany in 1977 (the Schleyer kidnapping and the Mogadischu drama) through the lens of Germany's Nazi past.

3   "Was ich für entscheident halte, ist der Gendanke, sich den Willen zu bewahren, neu anzufangen. Die Energie nicht zu verlieren" (my translation); Robert Fischer and Joe Hembus, *Der Neue Deutsche Film, 1960–1980* (Munich: Goldmann Verlag, 1981), 16.

4   Ira Paneth, "Wim and His Wings," *Film Quarterly* 42 (1988): 2–8.

5   I say "West Berlin" when talking about the movement of the characters in the film, since as far as I can determine, the angels spend only twenty-three seconds in East Berlin. I am indebted to Konstanze Bäumer, whose help in identifying places in the film was invaluable.

6   Teresa de Lauretis, *Alice Doesn't: Feminism, Semiotics, Cinema* (Bloomington: Indiana University Press, 1984), 67.

7   Wim Wenders and Peter Handke, *Der Himmel über Berlin. Ein Filmbuch* (Frankfurt am Main: Suhrkamp Verlag, 1989), 28.

8   In one scene of the angels' tour through the Staatsbibliothek, we overhear someone read a text that refers to this: "In 1921, Walter Benjamin bought Paul Klee's drawing *Angelus Novus.* It hung in his various studies until his escape from Paris in June

1940. In his last writings, *Theses on the Philosophy of History* (1940), he interpreted the drawing as an allegory of the backward glance at history" (Wenders and Handke, *Der Himmel,* 23). I am grateful to Beverly Allen for this reference.

9   Walter Benjamin, *Illuminations,* ed. Hannah Arendt, trans. Harry Zohn (New York: Schocken Books, 1969), 262.

10   Of all the federal states of the Federal Republic of Germany, West Berlin has the highest proportion of "foreign" residents: 12.5 percent (figures from 1985), compared with 7.6 percent in the other federal states. The largest group of West Berlin's foreign residents (in 1985, 44.9 percent) is composed of people from Turkey. Many Turks live in Kreuzberg, the smallest and most densely populated district in West Berlin; they make up 20 percent of the entire district and on some blocks as much as 50 to 60 percent; see T. H. Elkins and B. Hofmeister, *Berlin: The Spatial Structure of a Divided City* (London: Methuen, 1988), 221, 225.

11   Second-generation Turks living in Germany, who make up a large percentage (accurate numbers are not available at this point) of the people referred to as Turks, are by definition German Turks.

12   This scene is particularly problematic in that the German Turkish boy's reaction is rendered comically; the struggle of German Turkish children with the German language is well known as one of the major problems for West Berlin's "foreign" population.

13   Damiel's immediate assimilation to the West is powerfully encoded in a number of ways: his clothing, his admiration for things American and for Peter Falk, his ambitions, and so on are clearly marked as late Western capitalist, specifically United States American.

14   This formulation is guided by Rachel Blau DuPlessis's discussion of the social function of mythic narrative, *Writing Beyond the Ending: Narrative Strategies of Twentieth-Century Women Writers* (Bloomington: Indiana University Press, 1985), 107–8.

15   The right to decisions concerning reproductive freedom, formerly granted only to East German women, was recently, if only (in June 1992) provisionally, accorded to West German women as well.

16   Laura Flanders, "A Western-Style Hangover for East German Feminists," *Zeta* 3 (1990): 105.

17   "Representing Whiteness: Seeing *Wings of Desire,*" *Zeta* 2 (1989): 37. I am indebted to hooks's fine essay in many ways, and especially for inspiring me to think beyond issues circumscribed by my own positionality.

18   In his extrafilmic statements Wenders's position is clearly different from this filmic one; it is marked by an acute sense of responsibility toward German Jews: "If there is any response to my parents' generation or to the one before it, it is the way they treated history after 1945. They tend to make everyone forget, which made it impossible to deal with" (cited in hooks, "Representing Whiteness," 37).

19   Wenders and Handke, *Der Himmel,* 58–59. Similarly problematic, in light of Wenders's references to Walter Benjamin in the film and considering Benjamin's flight from the Nazis and his subsequent tragic death in 1940, is that Wenders fails to present the *Geschichte* of the Berlin Jews in the sense of Benjamin's materialistic historiography.

20 Wenders and Handke, *Der Himmel,* 162–63. The image of the plaza recalls the 1934 National Socialist party Congress in Nuremburg—indeed, Marion's lines evoke an image of Leni Riefenstahl's representation of the masses of people greeting Hitler in the film *Triumpf des Willens,* where, not so incidentally, Hitler's plane emerges out of the sky in an opening shot similar to the opening shot in *Himmel.* Marie Luise Gättens offered a different response to Marion's speech when I raised this point during the discussion that followed my talk "Marion/ette: Desire in Wim Wenders's *Wings of Desire*" at the Narrative Conference in New Orleans in April 1990. She reads the entire scene as parodic. I disagree with this reading because, when seen in the entire process of the film, it would be the only instance where parody is used in the love story.

21 Carolin Hilker-Siebenhaar, ed., *Wegweiser durch das jüdische Berlin. Geschichte und Gegenwart* (Berlin: Nicolaische Verlagsbuchhandlung Beuermann GmbH, 1987), 11, 368.

22 de Lauretis, *Alice Doesn't,* 153.

23 de Lauretis, *Alice Doesn't,* 121.

24 Marina Warner, *Monuments & Maidens: The Allegory of the Female Form* (New York: Atheneum, 1985), 130.

25 This demand does not have to be fulfilled, of course. As feminist film theorists have shown (Elizabeth Cowie, Janice Doane, Laura Mulvey, Constance Penley, and others), there are many positions other than identification with the male gaze that spectators can take up. Given the powerful drive toward identifying with the hero's desire, it will be, at any rate, a lonely position if she or he chooses not to inform against the heroine.

26 Wenders and Handke, *Der Himmel,* 49–50.

27 Laura Mulvey, "Visual Pleasure and Narrative Cinema," in *Feminism and Film Theory,* ed. Constance Penley (New York: Routledge, Chapman and Hall, 1988), 62.

Paul Morrison

"End-Pleasure": Narrative in the Plague Years

It's not simply that there are no more perfect moments; rather, there never has been one, at least not for gay men. Hence the audacity of the now notorious Robert Mapplethorpe retrospective: "The Perfect Moment" refuses to know itself as a gay rake's project, as the story of gay sexual crime and punishment. But also the futility, for every "perfect moment," every individual photograph, has been recuperated as, read in relation to, the allegedly inexorable logic of AIDS. True, Mapplethorpe was famous long before "The Perfect Moment"; in our post-Warholian culture of celebrity—artistic and sexual—he was a minor star. But in death, after death, everything about Mapplethorpe, everything about the controversy occasioned by him, is structured by a fact that is presented simply, openly, as one among many, but which surreptitiously structures and determines all: Robert Mapplethorpe died of complications arising from AIDS. His name has appeared in print in forms as various as "Mapplewood," "Mappleton," and "Mapplesex"; it is frequently misspelt as "Maplethorpe." (Or normalized as such: there seems to be a determined effort to efface the perversity that would spell "maple" "mapple" or pronounce "mapple" "maple.") But no matter what form the name assumes—Jesse Helms has apparently never pronounced it the same way twice, a rhetorical ploy he could only have learned from Archie Bunker, who is in this, as in all things, his better—the acronym is invariably noted and noted accurately. All artists or authors, the very category of the author or artist, died some time ago. Or at least the academy issued a generalized death notice. But when it is death-by-AIDS, the death of the artist is again news.

Not that this should surprise: it took the death of an artist or actor from AIDS for AIDS to become news. Consider *Life* magazine, September 1985: "AIDS was given a face everyone could recognize when it was announced that Rock Hudson, 59, was suffering from the disease [*sic*]." Some twelve thousand of the already sick (by the official count) had to find representation in that face; for the six thousand already dead (and still counting), it was too late. And today that face denotes only AIDS: "The faceless disease [*sic*] now has a face. But it is not the ruggedly handsome face of *Giant* or *Magnificent Obsession* or even *Pillow Talk* that will be Rock Hudson's greatest legacy. Instead, that legacy will be the gaunt, haggard face of those poignant [for whom?] last days."[1] This might seem homophobic enough, but it does scant justice to a "legacy" that elides even the "instead," the caesura between the "ruggedly handsome" and the "haggard" face. The contemporary response to the spectacle of Rock Hudson's once normative masculinity—the love scenes are now regularly met with laughter and smirks—argues a haggard face that retroactively structures the handsome one, a culture that alleges to see the death skull beneath the youthful skin. AIDS is not, then, simply the cause of Hudson's death, but the belatedly revealed truth of his life: the role he can no longer play, if only because he once played it with such dexterity, is that of a heterosexual. Hence the laughter, the purely defensive response of a homophobic culture to the knowledge that here (as elsewhere) its normative spectacle of heterosexual masculinity was (and frequently is) a gay man.

The "legacy" of Rock Hudson or Robert Mapplethorpe presupposes a cultural context in which AIDS continues to be received, its changing demographics notwithstanding, as *the* narrative of gayness, subjective and objective genitive.[2] The reduction of "The Perfect Moment" to a story of gay sexual crime and punishment; the reception of a Rock Hudson and Doris Day love scene as an occasion for knowing smirks: both represent the revenge *of* narrative *on* gayness, the assimilation of the "male homosexual" to the fully satisfying teleology that, in our standard technologies of self-fashioning and self-knowledge, he is said to resist. It is now conventional to speak of AIDS as "an epidemic of signification"; Thomas Yingling characterizes it as "profoundly unimaginable, as beyond the bounds of sense . . . an epidemic almost literally unthinkable in its mathematical defeat of cognitive desire."[3] And, in one sense, so it is. But this is to assume that our culture finds genocide unthinkable, little less impracticable, and that it construes the lives of gay men and women as nonexpendable, neither of which seems to me unproblematically so. AIDS is related to a phenomenon "almost literally unthinkable in its mathematical defeat of cognitive desire," I want to suggest, but in the mode of resolution or reconstitution: the epidemic has *resolved* rather than *occasioned* a crisis in signification—the crisis that has always been gay sexuality itself.

The Freudian narrative of psychosexual development, which remains even today the most pretigious technology of self-fashioning and self-knowledge, construes homosexuality as a simple failure of teleology, as sexual impulses that have yet to find resolution and stabilization in heterosexual genitality, in proper object choices and organ specificity. *Three Essays on the Theory of Sexuality,* for example, acknowledges sundry perversions—homosexuality, fetishism, scopophilia, exhibitionism, sadism, masochism—as "abortive beginnings and preliminary stages of a firm organization of the component instincts" of a law-abiding sexuality. Perversion is distinguished from heterosexual genitality primarily in terms of its relation, or nonrelation, to "discharge," which Freud terms "end-pleasure": "This last pleasure [the pleasure of genital orgasm] is the highest in intensity, and its mechanism differs from that of the earlier pleasure. It is brought about entirely by discharge: it is wholly a pleasure of satisfaction and with it the tension of the libido is for the time being extinguished."[4] Like the well-made narrative, normative sexual activity issues in climax, from which comes, as it were, quiescence; like the well-made narrative, moreover, normative sexual activity is end-haunted, all for its end. The perversions of adults, as Leo Bersani notes, are thus intelligible only as "the sickness of *uncompleted narratives*."[5]

Yet the celebration of the "highest satisfaction" is not without its ambivalence: like the wicked queen in the fairy tale who fears that someone, somewhere, may be more beautiful than she, the highest satisfaction is haunted by the possibility that it is not. A pleasure that is coincident with the extinction of libidinal energy, if only "for the time being," necessarily suggests that "the end of sex, the goal of sex" is also "its end, its disappearance": normative "end-pleasure" pursues the end of pleasure.[6] The perversions of adults thus become intelligible as multiple narratives, endless narratives, nonnarratives—everything that our culture designates or denigrates as "promiscuity," which is simply a sexuality that does not pursue, lemminglike, its own end or disappearance. Here is Freud once again:

The attainment of the normal sexual aim can clearly be endangered by the mechanism in which fore-pleasure is involved. This danger arises if at any point in the prepatory sexual processes the fore-pleasure turns out to be too great and the tension too small. The motive for proceeding further with the sexual process thus disappears, the whole path is cut short, and the prepatory act in question takes the place of the normal sexual aim. . . . Such is in fact the mechanism of many perversions, which consists in lingering over the prepatory acts of the sexual process.[7]

The normative teleology is endangered not only "by the mechanism in which fore-pleasure is involved" but by any teleology that is simply for pleasure, any sexual economy in which pleasure does not work toward its own effacement. Bersani notes that the now ubiquitous public discourse on gay sexual practices—the heated fantasies of gay men having sex twenty to thirty times a night—presupposes a thoroughly preternatural standard of sexual heroics.[8] Unless, then, one assumes the discourse to be hortatory, which seems unlikely, it must be construed as fantasy. Simon Watney argues its affinities with nineteenth-century speculation (no less heated) on the prostitute's capacity for multiple orgasms,[9] which seems reasonable enough: both are forms of pleasure strictly superfluous to the (re)productive deployment of the body; both presuppose a capacity for end-pleasure or discharge that does not mean an end to pleasure. But then the prostitute's capacity for pleasure is conventionally analogized to disease, and the homosexual's to death. This perverse coupling of Eros and Thanatos betrays a generalized cultural sadomasochism—even the most extravagant of Mapplethorpe's S/M photographs seem positively life affirming in comparison, but it relieves the wicked queen's anxieties. Gays, like girls, might think they just want to have fun, but we now know better. The sickness of uncompleted narratives is simply recast as a fully motivated, fully coherent narrative of sickness: the perverse, the promiscuous, just want to die.

The compulsion to make of AIDS the narrative of gayness, or gayness the narrative of AIDS, brooks no opposition, least of all from gay self-representations themselves. The reduction of "The Perfect Moment" to the story of gay sexual crime and punishment, for example, violates Mapplethorpe's own organizational principle for the exhibit: the show is based not on the narrative order of the one after another but on the juxtaposition of discrete "portfolios," relations of spatial juxtaposition. The retrospective would thus seem subject to—indeed, it would actively seem to solicit—the critique Susan Sontag directs against photography in general:

> Photography implies that we know about the world if we accept it as the camera records it. But this is the opposite of understanding, which starts from *not* accepting the world as it looks. All possibility of understanding is rooted in the ability to say no. Strictly speaking, one never understands anything from a photograph. . . . The camera's rendering of reality must always hide more than it discloses. As Brecht points out, a photograph of the Krupp works reveals virtually nothing about that organization. In contrast to the amorous relation, which is based on how something looks, understanding is based on how something functions. And functioning takes place in time, and must be explained in time. Only that which narrates can make us understand.[10]

The fetishization of narrative as the precondition of all understanding— as opposed to an ideologically specific form of the same—is itself open to critique. It would require but little ingenuity, for instance, to expose the ideological interests served by the privileging of understanding over "the amorous relation," the preference for a metaphysics of depth over an erotics of surfaces. Nor would it be difficult to argue that photography presupposes a narrative context, if not content.[11] But Sontag's point is well taken: "The Perfect Moment" is without significant narrative content. Conspicuously so, in fact, although to little avail. For nothing about gay life or gay sexuality is now admitted as "unrelated, free standing particles"—the latter is Sontag's characterization of still photography—for nothing escapes the teleology of AIDS as the narrative of gayness.[12] All the perfect moments are retroactively made to line up—as in a police lineup, although here everyone and everything is guilty—in the narrative logic that reduces Robert Mappleton or Maplesex or Maplethorpe to the-artist-who-died-of-AIDS.

"The fear of AIDS," Sontag argues, "imposes on an act whose ideal is pure presentness (and a creation of the future) a relation to the past that is to be ignored at one's peril."[13] Yet Sontag's own formulation seems itself incapable of imagining the ideal it imagines AIDS to threaten: by definition, the experience of "pure presentness" can have no investment in "a creation of the future," even so modest a future as breakfast the next morning. (Edna St. Vincent Millay to a trick: "Let me make it plain / I find this frenzy insufficient reason / for conversation when we meet again.") Pure presentness can be maintained as sexual ideal, moreover, only if all sexual activity aspires to the condition of perversion, which the normative technology construes as lingering in, dilating upon, the sexual present. ("This danger arises when at any point in the prepatory sexual processes the fore-pleasure turns out to be too great and the tension too small.") But our culture is unwilling to entertain such a possibility, even if its most prestigious theoretician of sexuality unwittingly invites it. And in the plague years, the invitation can be declined without fear of missing the best party in town. "So remember when a person has sex, they're having it with everybody that partner had it with for the past ten years." The grammar of this 1987 pronouncement from the secretary of health and human services is no less atrocious than its politics—fantasizing about all the others might up the erotic ante, but it hardly constitutes safer sex. The point, however, survives its formulation: perversion is not the experience of pure presentness but a narrative in which every perfect moment is potentially contaminated by its past, and hence threatening to its future. Pure presentness becomes, instead, pure repetition, the unending return of the same.

All of which to say: it's back: the marriage plot and its attendant ideology: the erotics of scarcity, monogamy, the prudent administration and distribution of desire. For the Sontag of *AIDS and Its Metaphors,* this is the pressure exerted by—or is it the redemptive promise of?—the plague years:

> The catastrophe of AIDS suggests the immediate *necessity* of limitation, of constraint for the body and for consciousness. But the response to AIDS is more than reactive, more than a fearful and therefore appropriate response to a very real danger. It also expresses a positive desire, the desire for stricter limits in the conduct of personal life. There is a broad tendency in our culture, an end-of-the-era feeling, that AIDS is reinforcing; an exhaustion, for many, of purely secular ideals—ideals that seemed to encourage libertinism or at least not provide any coherent inhibition against it—in which the response to AIDS finds its place. The behavior AIDS is stimulating is part of a larger grateful return to what is perceived as "conventions," like the return to figure and landscape, tonality and melody, plot and character, and other much vaunted repudiations

of difficult modernism in the arts. The reduction in the imperative of promiscuity in middle class life, a growth of the ideal of monogamy, of a prudent sexual life.[14]

But which is it? A reactionary pressure that has gained momentum because of the epidemic or the transcendent good that will emerge from it? Is Sontag one of the "many" for whom the "positive" desire to "constrain" the non-HIV-positive body—as if to anticipate the larger social project of an imposed quarantine on those who did not heed "the reduction in the imperative of promiscuity"—is in fact a positive development? Is Sontag to be counted among those for whom the return of "plot and character," the hoariest of all narrative conventions, is an occasion for gratitude? Or is she merely functioning as an amanuensis to a culture that now believes it has forged a "coherent inhibition" against "libertinism," a narrative of perversion and promiscuity that need no longer begrudge the deviant their fun?

Frankly, it's difficult to say. The journalistic *style indirect libre* of the prose would suggest the latter, the argument of *On Photography,* the fetishization of narrative as the precondition of all understanding, notwithstanding. It is difficult to imagine, moreover, so distinguished an apologist for the avant-garde recommending a repudiation of "modernist" innovations altogether. Not surprisingly, then, both *Illness as Metaphor* and *AIDS and Its Metaphors* rethink the earlier commitment to narrative as the precondition of all understanding: "I decided to write about the mystifications surrounding cancer. I didn't think it would be useful—and I wanted to be useful—to tell yet one more story in the first person about how someone learned that she or he had cancer, wept, struggled, was comforted, took courage . . . though mine was also that story. A narrative, it seemed to me, would be less useful than an idea. For narrative pleasure I would appeal to other writers."[15] These reflections on *Illness as Metaphor* stand as preface to *Aids and Its Metaphors,* which suggests that they are no less proleptic than retrospective. Certainly the project of the latter, the attempt to "retire" metaphor from the discourse of AIDS, would logically involve a rejection of narrative. As Paul de Man observes, "From the recognition of language as trope, one is led to the telling of a tale, to the narrative sequence. . . . The temporal deployment of an initial complication, of a structural knot, indicates the close, though not necessarily complementary, relation between trope and narrative, between knot and plot." Or Peter Brooks: narrative "operates as metaphor in its affirmation of resemblance"; it brings into relation different actions, combines them through perceived similarities, and appropriates them to a "common plot," which requires "the rejection of all merely contingent (or unassimilatable) incident or action."[16] The identity of these surd elements is never specified, but in a culture that effectively knows only one "common plot"—every Jack shall have his Jill—they are easily guessed.

But *AIDS and Its Metaphors* does not just say no to narrative, its gesture of refusal notwithstanding. Indeed, "narrative pleasure" reasserts itself in a fully coherent, fully motivated narrative of gay sexual pleasure as death or death wish:

> An infectious disease whose principal means of transmission is sexual necessarily puts at greater risk those who are sexually more active—and it is easy to view as a punishment for that activity. True of syphilis, this is even truer of AIDS, since not just promiscuity but a specific sexual "practice" regarded as unnatural is named as more endangering. . . . Addicts who get the illness by sharing needles are seen as committing (or completing) a kind of inadvertent suicide. Promiscuous homosexual men practicing their vehement sexual customs under the illusory conviction, fostered by medical ideology with its cure-all antibiotics, of the relative innocuousness of all sexually transmitted diseases, could be viewed as dedicated hedonists—though it's now clear that their behavior was no less suicidal.[17]

Although Sontag seems fully at home with the empty moralism of terms such as "promiscuity," she is apparently less comfortable with what she proceeds to call, euphemistically and thus nonspecifically, "a specific sexual 'practice.'" (She means perverse "end-pleasure," pleasure taken the wrong end round, fucking or getting fucked in the ass, which she regards as unnatural and "more endangering." But what is actually "more endangering"—and it apparently bears repeating—is unprotected anal intercourse, or the way that "the specific sexual 'practice'" is practiced. "An infectious disease whose principle means of transmission is sexual" does not "necessarily" put at risk those "who are sexually more active," although statements like Sontag's, which associate "promiscuity" qua "promiscuity" with AIDS, do.) True, Sontag seems only to be rehearsing various homophobic constructions of the epidemic—"it is easy to view," "regarded as," and so on—against which she might be expected to define her own position. By the time we read of "their vehement sexual customs," however, it is not homophobia but gay sex itself that is predicated on culturally determined illusions, received opinion: AIDS is not a catastrophe that the powers that be have allowed to happen, but the result of gay men's "illusory conviction . . . of the relative innocuousness of all sexually transmitted diseases." By the time we reach the end of the paragraph, moreover, all is retroactively made "clear": "their behavior was . . . suicidal," full stop. Like all good stories of a certain kind, the narrative of AIDS is both fully motivated (the active agent is not a virus, which would hardly do, but a gay community intent on collective suicide) and in possession of a final twist (this suicidal intent is not just received opinion, as it might first appear, but the belatedly revealed truth of things). No matter that gay men initially knew nothing of the existence of AIDS or the means of transmitting HIV infection while practicing their "vehement sexual customs": narrative retroactively brings to light causalities that always were operable, even if they passed temporarily unrecognized or unacknowledged as such. (How else to read an otherwise illegible oxymoron: inadvertent suicide?) [18] Freud maintains that people fall in love in order not to fall ill. People, not perverts: *they* have sex in order to die. Or so our culture insists and Sontag reiterates. There are, then, only two forms, two narratives, of "end-pleasure": an end-pleasure that pursues an end of pleasure and an end-pleasure that issues in death.

Narrative retroactively brings to light causalities that always were operable, even if they passed temporarily unnoticed or unacknowledged as such: if Mapplethorpe's photographs of "their [and his own] vehement sexual customs" cannot be assimilated to normative technologies of self-fashioning and self-knowledge, those "customs" can always be read in relation to the cultural fantasy that projects its own murderous homophobia as the "suicidal" impulses of gay men practicing "their vehement sexual customs." *AIDS and Its Metaphors* is the perfect (if unwitting) amanuensis of this cultural fantasy, which renders its larger project little more than gestural: "My aim was to alleviate unnecessary suffering— exactly as Nietzsche formulated it. . . . *Thinking about illness!*—To calm the imagination of the invalid, so that he should not, as hitherto, have to suffer more from thinking about his illness than from the illness itself— that, I think, would be something! It would be a great deal!" [19] Perhaps this would be a great deal, but it is difficult to know how the belatedly revealed knowledge that a sex life or drug habit always was "suicidal" serves to release the sick from the suffering of self-incriminating thinking about their illness.

Clearly Mapplethorpe did not suffer from this homophobic fantasy: the refusal of narrative that is "The Perfect Moment" is very much a refusal to reduce AIDS to the belatedly revealed truth of his life. Not that the retrospective constructs a closet for the sick. "The Perfect Moment" includes, for example, the highly theatrical and frequently reproduced *Self-Portrait* of 1988: the death skull is not, as it were, hidden beneath the skin, but theatrically foregrounded, as if to insist that no hidden psychology or pathology ("it's now clear that their behavior was . . . suicidal") structures AIDS. The self-portrait, moreover, is but one "moment" among many, and the various moments are not rendered retroactively (or posthumously) less "perfect" for its inclusion: "vehement sexual customs," an innately diseased sexuality, did not kill Robert Mapplethorpe. But if "The Perfect Moment" refuses to make the death skull the belatedly revealed truth of Mapplethorpe's life, critics have evinced no such reluctance. Consider Dominick Dunne, *Vanity Fair,* February 1989: Mapplethorpe's work is "a documentation of the homoerotic life in the 1970s at its most excessive, resulting, possibly, in the very plague that was killing its recorder." Or Susan Weiley, *Artnews,* December 1988: Mapplethorpe's erotic images "provoke a shudder similar to the one we feel looking at the smiling faces in photographs of the Warsaw ghetto."[20] "It's now clear": homosexuality = death.

It's not clear, however, that the collective imagination requires calming. The previous administration in Washington, to cite but the most obvious example, did not seem unduly agitated by the epidemic. George Bush did plant a tree in memory of an "innocent [read: nongay, nondrug-using] victim of AIDS," which is more than his predecessor can claim, but this is hardly evidence of an overly excited response. And the project of calming the imagination—for Sontag, this means retiring the metaphors, particularly the military metaphors, that allegedly structure the discourse of AIDS—needs to recall that the slogan of AIDS activism, "Fight Back, Fight AIDS," is not reducible to so much tropological play. (A lesson that has not been lost on cancer activists, a disease against which Sontag herself fought the good fight.) It is, of course, easier to contemplate with equanimity—which in no way precludes compassion or pity—a phenomenon that is construed as the logical result of an innately suicidal sexuality. Liberal readings of the epidemic, for example, tend to follow Sontag in rejecting the metaphor of "plague," but only to recover the moral calm of, say, a Pat Robertson. For it makes no practical difference whether AIDS is construed as punishment from above

("God's way of weeding His garden") or within ("their behavior . . . was suicidal"): Sontag's New Age psychology is as much an apology for homophobia (it too is a gay "disease") as that old-time religion. Not that *AIDS and Its Metaphors* is without practical efficacy. Sontag is altogether too successful in calming the imagination, and the wrong imagination at that. Responsibility for the epidemic resides not with a generalized and genocidal homophobia ("on the whole," Sontag blithely notes, the medical establishment has been "a bulwark of sanity and rationality"); rather, it is the "essence" of homosexuality itself.[21]

Now all this might seem unduly harsh: Sontag is not the enemy, and Lord knows—if only because He is to be counted among them—there are enemies enough to go around. Sontag is not unique, moreover, in rehearsing, despite the best of intentions, the cultural fantasy that construes AIDS as the narrative of gay sexual crime and punishment. Indeed, given the available alternatives, "inadvertent suicide" can easily be made to seem the most benign of narratives, the least homophobic of plots: "Back in the bathhouse, when the moaning stopped, the young man rolled over on his back for a cigarette. Gaetan Dugas reached up for the lights, turning up the rheostat slowly so that his partner's eyes would have time to adjust. He then made a point of eyeing the purple lesions on his chest. 'Gay cancer,' he said, almost as if he were talking to himself. 'Maybe you'll get it too.'"[22] "Their vehement sexual customs" is here reduced to "his," and "inadvertent suicide" is refigured as willful murder: this is the notorious Patient Zero of Randy Shilts's *And the Band Played On*, a novel whose success—it is soon to become what it has always labored to be: a TV miniseries—is inseparable from its homophobia. Gaetan Dugas answers, of course, to the most conventional of narrative exigencies: the novel traditionally figures structural injustice as individual villainy, and Gaetan Dugas is very much the villain of a nineteenth-century multiplot novel. Part 2 of *And the Band Played On* takes as its epigraph a passage from Emerson's "Self-Reliance": "All history resolves itself quite easily into the biography of a few stout and earnest persons."[23] Altogether too easily, as it happens. Granted, the "history of AIDS," like "the history of sexuality," may be its discursive construction, but this is hardly a compelling argument for resolving a history of criminal silence and institutional homophobia into the biography of a few stout and earnest persons, Randy Shilts and friends, and one particularly "dedicated hedonist." *And the Band Played On* is finally the story of the bad faggot too many people slept with and the good faggot too few people listened to: Gaetan Dugas and Randy Shilts. "THE MAN WHO GAVE US AIDS"—I am quoting from the *New York Post,* which obligingly gave Shilts the headline his book so obviously solicits—is also the story of "THE MAN WHO GAVE US THE MAN WHO GAVE US AIDS." Patient Zero makes Randy Shilts's name.

There are, then, good faggots: they have—the term is from the Auden poem "September 1, 1939," although the Larry Kramer play has given it new currency—"normal hearts":

> What mad Nijinsky wrote
> About Diaghilev
> Is true of the normal heart;
> For the error bred in the bone
> Of each woman and each man
> Craves what it cannot have,
> Not universal love
> But to be loved alone. . . .
> There is no such thing as the State
> And no one exists alone;
> Hunger allows no choice
> To the citizen or the police;
> We must love one another or die.[24]

I cannot pretend to speak for or from "the normal heart," but this seems to me exactly wrong: "What mad Nijinsky wrote / About Diaghilev" is not the norm, although the assertion that it is can only serve the cause of the regime of the norm. For even if one were to concede Auden his biologism—and it is a generous concession: hunger is hardly meaningful in isolation from its social distribution and regulation—the physiology of hunger cannot be conflated with the poetics of love. (People do get hungry without first reading about it in books; they do not fall in love without prior literary experience.) The hunger that "allows no choice / To the citizen or the police" is anything but a physiological dispensation: the conflation merely invites the psychoanalytical cop into the heart of the gay citizen, the better to render those other cops—I mean those whose uniforms bear the official sanction of the state—superfluous to the regulation of the bedroom or T-room. "We must love one another or die": the virtual reiteration of the Freudian injunction might better read, "we must become heterosexuals manqué or die."

And nothing is now easier to become: in a world in which twelve steps will take you virtually anywhere you want to go, in which the self-help manual is all that remains of culturally significant literary experience, ersatz heterosexuality is open to us all. Gay literature itself provides any number of how-to narratives: Paul Monette's *Afterlife,* for instance, is virtually a crash course in the pursuit of the normal heart. True, this story of a trio of self-proclaimed AIDS "widows" has the good sense to question the validity of its organizing category: one such "widow," Sonny Cevathas, returns from a memorial service for his lover only to find "the locks changed at the Bel-Air house,"[25] which is hardly the normal experience of the heterosexual heart-in-mourning. But if a certain local irony is directed against the categories of heterosexual privilege, it is belied by a deeper complicity in narrative forms of the same. For in *Afterlife,* only the sexualities have been changed, and only to protect the ideological innocence of the normative plot. "Do you love him?" Mr. Inman, Senior, asks his son Mark, an AIDS "widow" who has returned home to tell his father that he is both gay and HIV-positive. "I guess," Mark concedes, "but not like *you* mean," a response that is met with paternal puzzlement: "At this the father finally turned and looked at his son. Not judgmental, not even ironic, just curious to know how many meanings love could have."[26] Just one meaning, as it turns out, which means, in practice, ersatz heterosexuality: Mark learns to love Steven as his father learned to love Roz, his second wife. Like the hunger that allows no choice to the citizen or the police, love allows no choice to the gay son or the straight father, for love means the privatized, bourgeois couple; love is the heterosexual policing of desire. Freud characterizes perverse sexual activities as "ethically objectionable, for they degrade the relationships of love between two human beings [he never entertains the possibility of "among"] from a serious matter to a convenient game attended by no risk and no spiritual participation."[27] This is clearly not the liberal apologist for sexual diversity and tolerance, but so much the better: perversion must struggle against Freud (and the Mr. Inmans of the world) to reclaim its "ethically objectionable" character. And never more so than today. For even in the plague years, perverse sexual activity can be attended by minimal risk; even now, perversion can avoid participation in the poetics of bourgeois spiritualization.

Afterlife notwithstanding. It is finally unimportant, for example, that gay "widows" do not enjoy the same legal privileges as their straight counterparts, for they too can find a place, be put in their place, in that most impoverished of all arrangements: the marriage plot. The Freudian injunction is modified—we must learn to love each other because we are dying—but it is otherwise business as usual:

> "That's all there is, son. Someone to love. You ask anybody here." And he [Mr. Inman] gestured grandly over the Pitch 'n' Putt, but also included the mid-rise condos banked on every side, full of seniors in lonely efficiencies. "They've either been married for forty years, and they are holding on to what little time they got left, or they're widowed and only half alive. The lucky ones are like Roz and me, we get another chance. We know it's not for long. Two years, three years—just like you say. But that's all there is, so you take even a little."[28]

Afterlife recognizes no difference between the politics of the father's triglyceride and the son's T-cell counts: death is acknowledged only as the most universal of dispensations. And so it is: we are all, as Pater (following Hugo) famously remarks, *condamnés*. A universal dispensation does not, however, a neutral biological fact make: if nothing else, AIDS is a reminder that the death sentence, like hunger, is meaningless in isolation from its cultural distribution and regulation. Even the most lyrical evocation of the dominion of death, moreover, need not issue in a counsel of despair (or heterosexuality). The conclusion of Pater's *Renaissance,* for example, refuses the conventional wisdom that maintains that enough is as good as a feast: "our one chance lies in expanding . . . [the] interval, in getting as many pulsations as possible into the moment," [29] a formulation that virtually rehearses (or anticipates) our most canonical formulation of perversion. But then *The Renaissance,* particularly its concluding moments, proved something of a scandal. Sex and death, as Yeats maintained, may well be the only subjects worthy of a serious mind. The inevitability of the latter, however, need not serve as an argument for the (re)productive deployment of the former. Pater, for one, refuses to advance that dreariest of all possible social imperatives under the guise of a metaphysical heroism: the perpetuation of the bourgeois family is not a sublime lie against time. On the contrary: the inevitability of death is an argument for "getting as many pulsations as possible into the moment," as many perfect moments as possible.

The Renaissance does not labor to reconcile us to, to congratulate us for, what it terms our "listlessness": this seems to me the true source of its scandal. Boredom, as Bataille reminds us, has long since replaced religion as the opiate of the masses (or at least the professional classes),

and it may be that the primary spiritual agenda of the novel is to reconcile us to it. Certainly Mark Inman, after having been schooled in the
discipline of heterosexual love, learns that he has desired too much, too
many, which he thus comes to acknowledge as too little—he leaves his
father only to meet with and reject the advances of "a young god": "How
many times had he walked this dock in a horny swoon of desire, too
late to drive to the bars in Miami? He'd always been up for another encounter like this, the chance to plunder beauty. That was the point: you
could never have enough. But now he could feel himself recoiling, because if he'd lost the pleasure of this, then what was left?"[30] This is the
entire point of *Afterlife:* pre-AIDS gay sexuality could never satisfy, for
in pursuing too many bodies, it was content with too little spiritual en-
tanglement. And so *Afterlife* teaches Mark to recoil from this pleasure,
to accept the end of pleasure, the very little that is left him, as the great
good that emerges from the devastation of the plague years. The gay
body becomes for Mark what it has always been for the novel: the prisoner of the soul. Good pecs, for instance, betray a pathological taste for
promiscuity; Sonny Cevathas is a hunk, which means that he can only
end badly. Steve Shaw is the man for Mark, if only because Steve has developed a potbelly, which the novel construes as the outward sign of an
inward grace: a capacity for monogamy. This allegorization of the body
is less flexible than, say, the handkerchief code—the red flag in your
right pocket can easily be switched to the left—for it is concerned not
with mobility of the body's perversions but with the dispensation of the
soul. Appropriately, then, Mark turns from the young god's good pecs to
Steve's big belly, and the two learn to ape, albeit in an empty formalism,
the life of Mr. and Mrs. Inman.

   If AIDS thus provides the opportunity for reclaiming the gay subject
for the marriage plot—that is, if it resolves rather than occasions a crisis
in signification—AIDS can only be construed retroactively as perverse
resistance to that plot. "Having so much sex makes finding love impossible": this is spoken by Ned, the Larry Kramer figure in *The Normal
Heart,*[31] but the sentiment underwrites all normalizing plots. There is a
sexuality that pursues its own end or disappearance, the erotic pes-
simism that calls itself love, and there is perversion; there is the normative pursuit of an end to pleasure and the perverse end-pleasure that
issues in death. Here again is Ned in *The Normal Heart:* "I said the gay
leaders who created the sexual liberation philosophy in the first place

have been the death of us all. Mickey, why didn't you guys fight for the right to get married instead of the right to legitimize promiscuity?"[32] It's now clear: their behavior—our behavior—always was suicidal. We must, then, learn to love each other or die or learn to love each other because we are dying. It makes little difference which: the point is that no one need begrudge us our fun.

Notes

1 As quoted in Richard Meyer, "Rock Hudson's Body," in *Inside/Out: Lesbian Theories, Gay Theories,* ed. Diana Fuss (New York: Routledge, 1991), 274.
2 As D. A. Miller notes in a devastating—which is to say, thoroughly judicious— review of Sontag's *AIDS and Its Metaphors:* "Neither the epidemic's changed demographics nor the changes in our awareness of them have much altered its poetics. . . . AIDS remains centrally a gay disease, the disease of gayness itself"; see Miller, "Sontag's Urbanity," *October* 49 (Summer 1989): 95.
3 Paula Treichler, "AIDS, Homophobia, and Biomedical Discourse: An Epidemic of Signification," in *AIDS: Cultural Analysis/Cultural Activism,* ed. Douglas Crimp, *October* 43 (Winter 1987): 32; Thomas Yingling, "AIDS in America: Postmodern Governance, Identity, and Experience," in *Inside/Out,* 291–92.
4 Sigmund Freud, *Three Essays on the Theory of Sexuality,* 4th ed., trans. James Strachey (New York: Basic Books, 1962), 63, 76.
5 Leo Bersani, *The Freudian Body: Psychoanalysis and Art* (New York: Columbia University Press, 1986), 32.
6 Bersani, *The Freudian Body,* 33.
7 Freud, *Three Essays,* 77.
8 Leo Bersani, "Is the Rectum a Grave?" in *Cultural Analysis/Cultural Activism,* ed. Crimp, 211.
9 Simon Watney, *Policing Desire: Pornography, AIDS, and the Media* (Minneapolis: University of Minnesota Press, 1987), 33–34.
10 Susan Sontag, *On Photography* (New York: Farrar, Straus and Giroux, 1977), 20–21.
11 See Paul Morrison, "Coffee Table Sex: Robert Mapplethorpe and the Sadomasochism of Everyday Life," *Genders* 11 (Fall 1991): 18–19.
12 Sontag, *On Photography,* 20.
13 Susan Sontag, *AIDS and Its Metaphors,* in *Illness as Metaphor and AIDS and Its Metaphors* (New York: Doubleday, 1989), 99, 20–21.
14 Sontag, *AIDS and Its Metaphors,* 166.
15 Sontag, *AIDS and Its Metaphors,* 101.
16 Paul de Man, "The Epistemology of Metaphor," in *On Metaphor,* ed. Shelden Sacks (Chicago: University of Chicago Press, 1979), 21–22; Peter Brooks, *Reading for the Plot: Design and Intention in Narrative* (New York: Knopf, 1984), 91.
17 Sontag, *AIDS and Its Metaphors,* 114.
18 This entire paragraph is indebted to Miller's "Sontag's Urbanity," 95.

19 Sontag, *AIDS and Its Metaphors*, 101–2.

20 As quoted in Richard Meyer, "Imagining Sadomasochism: Robert Mapplethorpe and the Masquerade of Photography," *Qui Parle* 4 (Fall 1990): 74.

21 Sontag, *AIDS and Its Metaphors*, 169.

22 Randy Shilts, *And the Band Played On: Politics, People, and the AIDS Epidemic* (New York: St. Martin's Press, 1987), 198. On the relation between Shilts's "viciously homophobic portrait of 'Patient Zero'" and the structure of traditional narrative, see Douglas Crimp, "How to Have Promiscuity in an Epidemic," *October* 43 (Winter 1987): 239–52.

23 Shilts, *The Band Played On*, 9.

24 Larry Kramer, *The Normal Heart* (New York: New American Library, 1985), epigraph. I make no pretense of doing justice to the complexities of Auden's poem; I am concerned only with the meanings it has been made to bear in light of its use as epigraph to Kramer's play.

25 Paul Monette, *Afterlife* (New York: Avon Books, 1990), 5.

26 Monette, *Afterlife*, 177.

27 Sigmund Freud, "'Civilized' Sexual Morality," *The Complete Works of Sigmund Freud*, trans. James Strachey (London: Hogarth Press, 1953–74), 10:200.

28 Monette, *Afterlife*, 178.

29 Walter Pater, *The Renaissance* (Chicago: Pandora Books, 1978), 238.

30 Monette, *Afterlife*, 180.

31 Kramer, *Normal Heart*, 61.

32 Kramer, *Normal Heart*, 85. An expanded version of "'End-Pleasure': Narrative in the Plague Years" appears in the first volume of *GLQ: A Journal of Lesbian and Gay Studies*.

Part Three

Cultural

Reconstructions

and

Revisions

Caroline McCracken-Flesher

Cultural Projections: The "Strange Case" of Dr. Jekyll,

Mr. Hyde, and Cinematic Response

Robert Louis Stevenson's *Strange Case of Dr. Jekyll and Mr. Hyde* got off to an inauspicious start.[1] In a letter to F. W. H. Myers, Stevenson blamed "the wheels of Byles the Butcher [which] drive exceedingly swiftly" for its inception.[2] Further, not only did he blame "financial fluctuations" and importunate tradesmen for the story's creation, he also credited some of its crucial scenes to "the Brownies"—to a dream.[3] And those scenes, along with the initial text, were consigned to the flames at Stevenson's wife's instigation because, according to her, they failed to do justice to the tale's implicit moral.[4]

Yet from the ashes rose a deeply moral tale. Through a series of narrative envelopes, Mr. Utterson the lawyer delves into the truth of his friend Henry Jekyll's mysterious life and the repulsive Edward Hyde's equally mysterious death. From a series of disparate circumstances, and from the dead Dr. Lanyon's last, horrified writings as well as the vanished Jekyll's "Full Statement of the Case," Utterson discovers that Dr. Jekyll, in a self-serving experiment, has separated out and unleashed his evil nature, and that the evil nature—whatever it involves—has suppressed and supplanted the mixed, but socially functional, being that was Henry Jekyll. Utterson reveals, and by effacing himself brings home to the reader, the terrible duality of man and the awful insubstantiality of the flesh.

But Stevenson's story has proved a phoenix in more ways than one. Not only is the tale Stevenson called his "shilling shocker" still read, through stories, plays, and movies, it is constantly re-presented.[5] Within a year of its publication, Stevenson's novel appeared on the stage, and even as I write, the Theatreworks/USA company is getting ready to present on the University of Wyoming campus *Jekyll and Hyde,* "a contemporary musical about a teenager and the alter ego he creates in his chemistry labortory" (*sic*).[6] The early cinema dramatized Stevenson's novel with equal promptness and even greater frequency. The first two versions came out in 1908, and America produced at least ten others before 1920. Indeed, each decade filmmakers have offered numerous presentations of the tale; in 1989–90, television contributed two versions to the glut.[7]

Such a plentitude of data begs analysis. It invites the critic to ask whether Stevenson's text is truly *re-presented* in each version, or whether it is merely *represented;* do variations on Stevenson's text go beyond those required by generic transformation from printed page to stage or to cinema screen? And if they do—if the story, play, or movie only represents Stevenson's tale—what force determines its changes? Further, the data push us to question why Stevenson's text is so persistently re-presented—or represented. If we can discover what it is that generations of authors and stage and screen directors have put into *Dr. Jekyll and Mr. Hyde,* and what characterizes their additions, we must still ask why this text so frequently merits their attention. Do they derive something from the text as well as giving something to it?

Clearly, the many versions of *Dr. Jekyll and Mr. Hyde* encourage us to examine more deeply the influence of the re-presenter on the text, and the influence of the text on the re-presenter. In fact, *Dr. Jekyll and Mr. Hyde*'s multiple re-presentations invite us to apply Reader Response theory. Ultimately, indeed, they may enable us to pursue and extend it. Reader Response critics have long argued that the act of reading effectively rewrites any given text, and contemporary literary theorists concur as increasingly they discover that all communication takes place through and in spite of the play of the signifier. In other words, critics and theorists agree that by virtue of the reader's participation, the text as it is read is never the text as it was written; the meaning of the text lies somewhere between text and audience rather than solely with the author. This observation, however, has proved difficult to support. The problem lies in the data available: the text and the reader's assessment of his or her response. When the critic focuses on the text, s/he can determine only how it predetermines response; when s/he focuses on the reader's perception, the analysis is compromised by the reader's retrospective and subjective report and the critic's own directing questions.[8] Both critics and theorists, then, need data that manifest in and

of themselves the interpenetration of reader and text, for only through
such data can we hope to trace the operations of response, can we discover how far the reader reads and how far and why s/he rather rewrites
the elements of an "originary" text in the moment of reading.[9] The many
versions of *Dr. Jekyll and Mr. Hyde,* particularly the movie versions that
situate themselves as re-presentations of Stevenson's originary text, that
claim not to revise their source text but simply to stand in its place, to
some degree constitute such data. With their faithfulness to the originary text's primary structures but their tendency to relocate its values
and renegotiate its significations, these cinematic representations suggest just how far the reader stands subject to the text—and how far the
text stands subject to the reader.

But what reader operates in a cinematic representation of a text? To
what extent is a film director a reader—never mind *the* reader—given
the corporate and public nature of the cinematic project? Jerome Christensen clarifies, with respect to this last, that "it is not the producer,
director, writer or star who is the *auteur* but the corporate body that com-
prises those functions."[10] Yet, however multiple the cinematic purveyor
of Stevenson's text, in its re-presentation/representation of *Dr. Jekyll and
Mr. Hyde* it inevitably enacts a reading of the tale. And since the cinema
corporation's reading is channeled through the director, I will invoke the
director as the representative corporate reader.

To proceed, bearing these caveats in mind: *Dr. Jekyll and Mr. Hyde's*
multiple remakes indeed confirm that texts stand subject to their readers,
that they are rewritten through the act of reading, as Reader Response
critics have suggested. Repeatedly, the movie versions of Stevenson's
originary text deviate from the novel beyond their generic requirements,
thus demonstrating that the reader (cinema corporation/director) to
some degree dominates the text. Yet the many versions of *Dr. Jekyll and
Mr. Hyde* more interestingly suggest that texts stand subject not to the
reader per se, but to the contemporary cultural complex as it is channeled through the reader. When we map a Jekyll and Hyde movie's divergences from the originary text across its director's contemporary cultural
complex, we discover that the director's interpretive response is encoded
according to culturally determined expectations and anxieties. To the degree that director and author participate in the same semiotic systems,
the text that constitutes the director's response matches the author's; to
the degree that they do not, the director's text differs. The re-presented
text, then, stands inevitably *represented* according to the play of the sig-

nifier within the matrices of culture. It manifests the interpenetration not just of originary text and of reader (director), but of text as cultural construct and of reader as culturally determined intertext. Finally, if we consider side-by-side multiple representations of Stevenson's text, and if we follow not their divergences from but their similarities to the originary text and to one another, we discover that if culture constructs narrative through the act of reading, the originary text's narrative matrix simultaneously restructures the intersecting culture. In sum, then, through movie representations of Stevenson's novel we discover that in reading, we describe culturally determined but narratively delimited circles.

A quick comparison of three movie versions of Stevenson's tale provides preliminary data that reveal whether and how *Dr. Jekyll and Mr. Hyde* stands subject to its readers' (directors') rewriting. For this comparison I have chosen John Robertson's 1920 silent film starring John Barrymore, Victor Fleming's 1941 version with Spencer Tracy, and the titillatingly titled *Dr. Jekyll & Sister Hyde,* directed by Roy Ward Baker in 1971 for the British company, Hammer Film Productions.[11] All three movies initially were selected by circumstance—no others were immediately accessible on video when I began my research. So it is the more significant that all three figure themselves as re-presentations of Stevenson's text, and yet that all three represent it in quite individual ways. Clearly, some factor imported by the director works to refigure the text.

But what is that factor? How far do the movies re-present Stevenson's text? Each holds to Stevenson's oppositional structure; through the intervention of a serum, each sets good and evil at odds in the persons of Jekyll and Hyde. In each, Jekyll's experiment yields tragic results. Yet each movie figures good and evil through characters absent in Stevenson's novel. Moreover, each represents evil in ways quite foreign to Stevenson's text. For Stevenson, Hyde's evil remains unspecified, although Jekyll attempts to define it in his "Full Statement of the Case":

> The pleasures which I made haste to seek in my disguise were, as I have said, undignified; I would scarce use a harder term. But in the hands of Edward Hyde, they soon began to turn towards the monstrous. When I would come back from these excursions, I was often plunged into a kind of wonder at my vicarious depravity. This familiar that I called out of my own soul, and sent forth alone to do his good pleasure, was a being inherently malign and villainous;

his every act and thought centered on self; drinking pleasure with bestial avidity from any degree of torture to another; relentless like a man of stone. (116)

Jekyll cites Hyde's depravity, his monstrosity and malignity, but he does not define those qualities. Similarly Utterson, Jekyll's lawyer friend and ultimate nemesis to Jekyll/Hyde, cannot define what in Hyde repels him.

> Mr. Hyde was pale and dwarfish, he gave an impression of deformity without any namable malformation, he had a displeasing smile, he had borne himself to the lawyer with a sort of murderous mixture of timidity and boldness, and he spoke with a husky, whispering and somewhat broken voice; all these were points against him, but not all of these together could explain the hitherto unknown disgust, loathing and fear with which Mr. Utterson regarded him. "There must be something else," said the perplexed gentleman. (25)

Even Hyde's deeds prevent us from deciding how and why his evil functions. When Hyde tramples over the child and murders Sir Danvers Carew, the crimes seem motiveless. London is at a loss to understand. The movies, by contrast, specify Hyde's evil. In them, it takes the form of clearly defined social deviance.

In the three analyses that follow, I consider how the Robertson, Fleming, and Baker movies figure evil, and I trace the extent to which each different figuration emanates from the changing concerns of twentieth-century culture in Britain and America. With this information we should be able to assess to what degree this narrative in particular—and narrative in general—stands subject to reconstruction by the reader's culture.

John Robertson: *Dr. Jekyll and Mr. Hyde* (1920)

In the 1920 version of *Dr. Jekyll and Mr. Hyde,* Jekyll appears an unusually fine fellow. He differs from his predecessor in Stevenson in his youth, dedication, and idealism. His friends actually call him "London's Saint Anthony." How does this paragon fall? Stevenson's doctor effectively tempts himself. In his "Full Statement," Stevenson's Jekyll details the self-serving assumptions that led him to experiment:

> I saw that, of the two natures that contended in the field of my consciousness, even if I could rightly be said to be either, it was only because I was radically both; and from an early date, even be-

fore the course of my scientific discoveries had begun to suggest the most naked possibility of such a miracle, I had learned to dwell with pleasure, as a beloved daydream, on the thought of the separation of these elements. If each, I told myself, could but be housed in separate identities, life would be relieved of all that was unbearable; the unjust might go his way, delivered from the aspirations and remorse of his more upright twin; and the just could walk steadfastly and securely on his upward path doing the good things in which he found his pleasure, and no longer exposed to disgrace and penitence by the hands of this extraneous evil. (106–7)

By contrast, Robertson's doctor falls to external temptation—and temptation from an unlikely source, at that. Jekyll's prospective father-in-law (an addition to Stevenson's text, as is the fiancée) on a whim tempts him to indulge in the experiences that, he claims, construct a valid old age. Sir George Carew challenges Jekyll, "In devoting yourself to others . . . aren't you neglecting the development of your own life? . . . A man has two [selves]—as he has two hands. Because I use my right hand, should I never use my left? Your really strong man fears nothing. It is the weak one who is afraid of—experience."[12] In 1920, it would seem, Youth falls to the temptations of Age.

To what temptation does Jekyll yield? When Stevenson's doctor falls, he indulges no single proclivity, but this later doctor's fall is primarily sexual. Moreover, while Jekyll's predilection for sex becomes a constant in later movies, director John Robertson figures it here with an odd specificity—across alcohol. Consider the signs: Jekyll's initial temptation occurs over after-dinner drinks with Carew; to enter the music hall, site of the doctor's subsequent sexual temptation, Jekyll and Carew must pass drunks in various states of inebriation; inside, Jekyll's sexual fall is precipitated over a drink with the music hall's Italian dancer. When Hyde later seeks sexual pleasures, he finds them behind a speakeasy door; behind that door Hyde finds not only sex but also a man who imagines he is crawling with red ants and who clearly suffers from delirium tremens. Yet Hyde's identification with the evils of drink goes even deeper. If entomological manifestations symptomize alcohol poisoning, then it is surely significant that Hyde himself seems spidery. He has long fingers; he moves jerkily and scuttles along the streets like an insect; he even appears to bite his women—and his male victims—on the neck. But most obviously, when he repossesses Jekyll at night, he takes the form of a giant, hairy spider that succubus-like, climbs upon the bed and sinks into Jekyll, making him Hyde.

While Stevenson's tale depends on Jekyll's imbibing a mysterious potion, the potion itself stands subordinate to the phenomenon of transfiguration. Further representations of Stevenson's tale similarly give it little prominence. How, then, do we read Robertson's foregrounding of the potion by linking it to alcohol? If we map this addition to Robertson's originary text across his contemporary cultural complex, we discover an intriguing coincidence: 1920 was the first year of Prohibition. Although Prohibition began during the war years, it was federally legislated in 1919 and fully enforced in 1920. And in 1920, many Americans stood torn between their desire to drink and their disgust at drinking's results. The year's-end papers manifest the confusion, printing stories advising how to get a drink at New Year right beside articles on the successes of dry agents, whose job it was to enforce the legislation. In the *New York Times* New Year's Day article, "Sober Crowds Jam Streets of City on New Year's Eve," we find a wavering tone typical of contemporary reports about alcohol. A few paragraphs demonstrate the point:

> In the wicked age just past a kind of mob intoxication, not entirely psychological, took possession of the tens of thousands who surged . . . around Times Square, placing all on about the same level of exhilaration. Last night the big crowd was roughly divided into two classes, the vast majority who were cold sober and a small minority who were hopelessly to the contrary.
>
> New Year's Eve, it appeared, was being appropriately celebrated in new whisky. Early in the afternoon, policemen were picking off the sidewalks men who complained thickly that they had had but a single drink. But their consolation was that they had paid as much for it as for an old-fashioned night of wild revelry. Dollar notes fell on the bars like nickels.[13]

So in Hyde's figuration across alcohol and through its negative entomological signs, we see in operation both a contemporary fascination with drink and an anxiety concerning its transformative power.

But where does Robertson's Sir George come in? Why is he the tempter? And why must Sir George fall to Hyde? Moreover, why does Robertson's Jekyll commit suicide? In Stevenson's text it is impossible to distinguish the hand that administers the poison. And why does Robertson's aged and spidery Hyde transform back into the young and pure

Henry Jekyll in death? Stevenson withholds that luxury from his character. I suggest that all these phenomena serve an age/youth dichotomy foregrounded from the beginning of Robertson's text and stemming from contemporary cultural concerns. For some the 1920s seemed the age of youth; as manifested in the Roaring Twenties and the Lost Generation, the young were considered both freer and more responsible than their elders, who had drawn a generation into war. Youth, then, quite logically stands privileged in Robertson's text—to the point that Jekyll is tempted to experience by Age, and so is not responsible for his fall into Hyde or for Hyde's sins. Indeed, he dies a romantically self-sacrificing death to protect his beloved from himself as Hyde, thus regaining his youth and purity; he even stands absolved from blame in the destruction of his aged tempter.

The figure of the hoary spider makes especially clear how society's fears modify both one another and Stevenson's text. The spider conflates contemporary fears about alcoholic excess, on the one hand, and the vampirism of age, on the other, as they are channeled through the director. Its presence in the movie reveals just how precisely the director's culturally determined reading is written across Stevenson's text.

Victor Fleming: *Dr. Jekyll and Mr. Hyde* (1941)

Victor Fleming's *Dr. Jekyll and Mr. Hyde* similarly loads Stevenson's text with culturally determined significations. But because Fleming directed at a later date (1941) and therefore channeled a different cultural complex, his movie not surprisingly figures good and evil in different ways. In one element, however, it duplicates the concerns of Robertson's text: Fleming's movie, like Robertson's, stresses the dichotomy between youth and age. But it also reverses the valuation Robertson accorded the two terms. Thus, unlike his predecessors in other movie versions of the tale, Fleming's young Dr. Jekyll, while brilliant, appears only alloyedly good. Specifically, although he is indeed tempted to noble ends—to expel extreme evil—he shows little concern for the means to those ends. While the movie begins with Jekyll apparently showing compassion for a man whose soul has been divided by trauma, with remarkable speed that compassion resolves into interest in an experimental subject. Indeed, when Jekyll drinks his potion himself, he does so only because that experimental subject has died. Further, the older males are the ones who seem most concerned for the individual and for society at large.

Fleming foregrounds his particular configuration of the selfish and the social in youth and age, respectively, as early as his second scene. Here, Jekyll and his superior, Dr. Heath, discuss whether Jekyll should experiment on the subject come suddenly to hand:

> *Heath:* I can't allow it, it's a matter of ethics, Jekyll.
> *Mrs. Higgins* [subject's wife]: Please Dr. Jekyll, may I go in and . . .
> *Jekyll:* No, no. Not now Mrs. Higgins. Bear up now, that's how you can help.
>   Good heavens, man, it's the greatest opportunity I've ever had. The more I see of the case the more I realize it.
> *Heath:* My dear Jekyll, you know how we all admire your work, and possibly this case does come within the scope of your research; that's why I'd like to bow to your opinion. But as head of the staff of this hospital I cannot . . . Listen, Jekyll. Tell me straight out. What do you think you could do for this man?
> *Jekyll:* I might have a chance of curing him.
> *Heath:* A chance!
> *Jekyll:* Yes, I've been experimenting with animals.
> *Heath:* Yes, but what might work with animals might not with a human being. Your—your chemicals may be deadly.
> *Jekyll:* No, not one animal has died.
> *Heath:* But it might. No. It's too dangerous. You go too outside the known medicine.
> *Jekyll:* But I am no witch doctor.
> *Heath:* But who's called you a witch doctor? You told me yourself that it still had to be proved. I can't allow you to—to experiment with—well, after all, the man's a human being.
> *Jekyll:* You mean he was a human being—and he might be again, if you'd keep your hidebound ethics out of this. Sometimes we have to gamble. Or haven't you the courage to face what might be the most daring . . .

Fleming's Jekyll stands revealed here as both compassionate and vauntingly ambitious. On the one hand, he treats Mrs. Higgins considerately; on the other, he sees her husband as "the greatest opportunity I've ever had." Indeed, as Higgins now exists, with his evil foregrounded, Jekyll sees him as less than human. Heath, by contrast, while admittedly somewhat pompous and even elitist, nonetheless sees Higgins precisely as a "human being." Where Jekyll sees an opportunity to advance his research, Dr. Heath sees the difference between an animal and a person. Consequently, he opposes Jekyll's experiments on ethical grounds, for the sake of the subject—a point the movie stresses at the beginning and again at the end of the scene.

Repeatedly, Fleming emphasizes this reverse polarization of good and evil across youth and age. Consider the scene that precipitates Jekyll's experiments. In the versions of Stevenson's tale offered by Robertson and Fleming, Jekyll begins his research, and therefore his fall, after a dinner with his seniors. But where Robertson's Jekyll is led into temptation by a few older men figured as dangerous debauchees, Fleming's reacts against massed doctors, a bishop, and a general, all socially concerned pillars of society. These men discuss not the pleasures of experience but the responsibilities of life, carefully and conscientiously pursuing the nature of the soul and the problems of experimental science. Their conversation, which considers Jekyll's experiments quite seriously, if it views them with caution for the issues they raise, reveals that they see themselves working each in his own province, but cooperatively and congenially for the common good. So if the dinner proves a fiasco, it is because young Dr. Jekyll refuses to see behind his companions' age and authority to their care and conscience. As he earlier dismissed his medical superior for his "hidebound ethics," now he assumes his seniors' self-interest and affords them neither his attention nor his respect.

Fleming's movie not only aligns age and authority, it also allies them to an equally positively valued Church and State. Consider the movie's narrative envelope. In the opening scene, we join the congregation of a pristine Christopher Wren church as the bishop rises to intone:

> With purity in our hearts, with right thinking in our minds, we arm ourselves with intolerance of all evil. So it is, on this glorious Sabbath morning and in this momentous year of eighteen hundred and eighty-seven, we naturally turn our thoughts towards that way of life as exemplified by Victoria, our beloved queen, for this week begins Her Majesty's Golden Jubilee. From her heart has come an ever-increasing flow of virtue and moral blessing. She came upon a world sadly mired in the ways of the flesh, but during her reign the forces of good have achieved notable and great victories over the forces of evil, and though we know not the time, nor the season, we know that in God's own time evil shall be wiped out by good.

In Victoria's accession to the throne the bishop reads a moment of national and religious certainty, a moment that gives hope, it seems, to the present. The movie's end, interestingly, asserts exactly the religious and social order the bishop projects. Jekyll has retreated behind his wall of chemicals to protect himself and Hyde, who, as Dr. Lanyon has pointed out, constitutes a kind of blasphemy against society and religion both. (On the night Hyde murders Ivy, a barmaid turned prostitute, he transforms back into Jekyll before Lanyon. Lanyon exclaims, "You've gone beyond. You've tampered with . . . you've committed the supreme blasphemy.") Refusing to admit how deeply his character stands compromised by Hyde, Jekyll repeats, again and again, "I've done nothing. I'm Dr. Jekyll. I'm Dr. Henry Jekyll." As a result, he has to be forced to reveal himself. Notably it is Lanyon, who has managed to unite interest in Jekyll's noble aims with loyalty to his elders and their ethics, and who now stands at the head of a number of policemen, who forces Jekyll to reveal his other side. Once that side is manifested in Hyde, Lanyon kills him with three ritualized shots. The movie then closes with Poole, the butler, repeating the Twenty-third Psalm over the body as a church bell tolls in the distance.

This configuration of age with the authority embodied in Church and State is particularly striking in that it inverts and supplements the significations not just of Robertson's movie but also of Rouben Mamoulian's 1932 version, to which Fleming's owes much of its structure, its female characters, and their dramatization.[14] In Robertson's movie, age lacks authority and is largely a force for evil; in Mamoulian's, age enjoys authority but in its conservativeness abuses that authority. When Fleming adds to the paradigm Church and State, he goes beyond Mamoulian, Robertson, and even Stevenson.

What could cause Fleming so massively to reencode not just Stevenson's text but its multiple representations? Some crisis seems to be forcing on Stevenson's tale a conjunction between age and authority and Church and State. What kind of crisis might have such a pervasive effect? Contemporary circumstances again provide an explanation. By 1941, World War II was well under way, and by the end of the year, America had entered the fight against the Axis powers. But while Fleming was filming, America was still wrestling with the question of how legitimately to participate in the war. A *Washington Post* article from December 27, 1941, manifests the depth of the nation's ethical conflict even after Pearl Harbor:

> At a season of the year when peace and good will is chanted from
> every country, castle and hamlet, we Americans in consort with all
> other liberty-loving peoples on earth are feverishly engaged in shap-
> ing implements of destruction. . . . we are doing precisely the things
> the tyrants are doing, those whose methods we abhor. . . . The fact
> that these tyrants are forcing their subjects to do that which we are
> doing freely, may suggest but does not adequately explain the dif-
> ference.[15]

Clearly, America was weighing just ends against potentially compro-
mising means, and its dilemma is dramatized across Jekyll and Hyde.
Consider one crucial scene: before taking the potion, Jekyll asks his gatekeeper whether, if he had a balloon that could travel to the moon and
the pilot died, he would take the pilot's place; the gatekeeper replies that
he would—so long as he had a way to return. In other words, the gatekeeper questions whether his initial means will allow him to reestablish
order after his trip, after accomplishing his experimental end. Jekyll,
who does not listen to this lower-class and yet notably older and authoritative figure of the fates, becomes subject to his means and must be cast
out. Yet, in becoming subject to his means, in being re-created as purely
evil, Jekyll justifies his death at society's hand to the point where it can
be ritualized through Lanyon's three shots and sanctified by the Twenty-
third Psalm. He enables society to fulfill the divinely mandated task set
for it in the first scene, when the congregation disrupted by Mr. Higgins's
evil outburst rises and sings,

> Where'er you meet with evil
> Within you or without,
> Charge for the God of battle
> And put the foe to rout.[16]

Jekyll dramatizes the risks even in a just war, but he opens a way for
society to participate in that war.

   A quick comparison of Fleming's movie with Stevenson's novel, then,
confirms that Fleming too encodes Stevenson's text according to contemporary concerns. But placing Fleming's movie in a matrix with
Stevenson's novel and the Robertson and Mamoulian movies reveals a
somewhat more complex relationship between text and reader/director.
Although the successive acts of directing each supplement the text ac-

cording to prevailing cultural concerns, they do not necessarily modify the originary text to the same extent or even at the same points. The director's concerns may to a greater or lesser degree match those manifested through the originary text. Indeed, after a period of divergence, cultural concerns—or at least the representations appropriate to them— may cycle back together. So after a generation of purity, manifested in Robertson's and Mamoulian's movies, Jekyll regains his original mixed personality through 1940s anxieties over the legitimacy of personal power and of war to suppress it. Moreover, while a culture can cycle back over time to share some of an earlier period's concerns, it can also share those concerns only to invert them. Age and authority figure prominently in the cultural paradigms of the 1920s, 1930s, and 1940s but are positioned quite differently as the decades progress. Thus, insofar as we can argue from movie representations of *Dr. Jekyll and Mr. Hyde,* a given reading manifests not just the reader's divergences from but also his or her coincidences with the text. But does the matrix configured in this process of response depend only on the distribution of the reader's concerns across the text? Does Stevenson's text simply constitute a structure to be filled up by the reader's—here, the director's—culturally determined concerns?

Roy Ward Baker: *Dr. Jekyll & Sister Hyde* (1971)

Roy Ward Baker's *Dr. Jekyll & Sister Hyde* demonstrates how far the matrix stands configured not just by the reader but by the interpenetration of reader and text. In 1971, a year when the national and local branches of a British contractors' union warred over whether to admit one woman to their ranks, a year when a New York policeman hijacked a plane, threatened a stewardess with acid, and declared that he did so to recover his wife's love, Baker produced a movie that figures the ambitious woman as usurping both the male and his idealized female.[17] His film characterizes the Jekyll/Hyde split as male versus female and as feminine versus feminist—Dr. Jekyll/*Sister* Hyde.

By altering Hyde's sex, mustn't Baker change Stevenson's text beyond the point of recognition? Certainly this shift in a major character's gender has ramifications throughout the text. For instance, it allows an as yet unparalleled clarity in the division of characters. Baker's Dr. Jekyll stands above reproach—a luxury denied his predecessors. However innocent and attractive are the Jekylls of 1886, 1920, and 1941, each actively seeks to separate good and evil, and each thus stands implicated in Hyde. Moreover, their evil comes from within. Even Robertson's Hyde has only to be tempted to the surface. By contrast, Baker's Hyde is imposed on a young, attractive, and essentially good Henry Jekyll. Baker's Jekyll invents the dreaded potion for entirely noble reasons. Indeed, he conceives the drug in quite a new way. Afraid that in his short life he will not accomplish all the good he desires, that he will not discover a cure for typhoid and for cholera as well as for diphtheria, he invents an elixir of life. Thus his motivation excuses him when he countenances graverobbing and murder—even when he becomes a murderer himself to obtain the constituents necessary to his experiment. His aim also excuses him because it figures the drug's negative results not as sought but as side effects of a worthy cause. Further, this Jekyll's Hyde is visited upon him; it does not come from within. Jekyll's potion depends on female hormones, an imported factor. Consequently, whereas the earlier potions alter the balance of the individual, this one actually changes that individual. Hyde's evil, along with its gendered cognate, then, is imposed from outside, so much so that Baker's Jekyll is not obliged to sacrifice himself or to die for Hyde's sins. More precisely, unlike Stevenson's or Robertson's Jekyll, Baker's is not required to commit suicide to protect himself (whoever that might be) or his beloved. Unlike Mamoulian's and Fleming's Jekyll, strictly speaking he does not die at society's hand even as a participant in Hyde. Rather, this Jekyll dies because Sister Hyde insists on asserting herself while he is fleeing from the police. In a rooftop chase, Jekyll hangs spreadeagled across a window. As his face moves to reflect through the red glass, Sister Hyde erupts. Significantly, Jekyll's final gesture is to externalize and reject her as invasive and Other yet one more time. He cries, "No! No you'll kill me!" Then, as her weak fingers lose their grip, s/he plummets shrieking to the ground.

If Baker's Jekyll becomes preternaturally good, Sister Hyde constitutes a focus for reproach. First, the feminist spirit she represents actually appears responsible for Jekyll's experiments from their inception. How can this be? Jekyll's research requires the sexual organs of newly deceased young women because, unlike men, women enjoy an excess of life. Women's skin, Jekyll observes, stays soft; women don't go bald. It is thus the woman's excess of life that tempts the male to murder. In this context Jekyll's attempt to appropriate female excess and to modulate it to serve the male at the cost only of a few prostitutes, a few "professional" women, seems perfectly reasonable. Moreover, Sister Hyde's resistance, her usurpation of the male, seems not poetic justice but a negative assertion of precisely that female power that the male must seek to govern. Second, Baker overloads Sister Hyde with signs of an aggressive yet trivializingly kinky feminism. His Hyde is a sultry woman with black hair and a penchant for red dresses. But perhaps most important, she wears stiletto heels that are quite literally that. She stores her knife in her boot— one of a pair, one presumes, that are just waiting to "walk all over you."[18] Third, Baker endows only Sister Hyde with evil; Dr. Jekyll, who began the experiments and who committed murder himself, somehow retains his virtue. Sister Hyde even stands identified with Jack the Ripper. How, exactly, does Baker differentiate Sister Hyde's murders from Dr. Jekyll's? Sister Hyde outdoes Dr. Jekyll and Jack the Ripper; she attacks men, killing Jekyll's friend who might question his research or teach him a "proper," dominant attitude to women and thus save him. And she does not limit the attack on the female to an attack on prostitutes. She tries to kill the pure young thing Jekyll loves and in whom his identity significantly seems invested.

Even in Robertson's text, where Jekyll is led astray by his seniors, the evil that Hyde manifests comes from within. Although Hyde expresses it in absolute form, it is distributed across Jekyll as host and origin. In Baker's movie, however, good and evil, male and female, stand in exclusive opposition. The few moments when Sister Hyde usurps Dr. Jekyll in public, when the two occupy one body, only emphasize the point. Dr. Jekyll and Sister Hyde, respectively, admire the sister and the brother upstairs. On one occasion, in her female sexual excess, Sister Hyde makes advances to the object of her desires through the person of Dr. Jekyll. That is, the female expresses itself through the male body. At the moment of their death, too, male and female inhabit only one body; the face that turns to the gathered onlookers figures both Jekyll and Hyde. In the first instance, the brother, while perplexed, considers Dr. Jekyll amusingly kinky. But when Jekyll/Hyde turns his/her face on brother and sister, the man's man and man's woman seem frankly appalled. While "normal" people may flirt with deviance, within the social matrix male and female ultimately must exist only as exclusive, opposed categories.

Obviously, Baker's text arises from his cultural moment. In 1971, many Britons stood confused by feminism. They were both drawn to it and yet compelled to constitute it as the undifferentiated Other and to expel it. When Sister Hyde usurps Jekyll's body and declares, "It is I who exist . . . not you. It is I who will be rid of you," she manifests the feminist power that imposed a frisson of fear and desire on contemporary males—perhaps it was the tickle of her stiletto heels walking up their backs. When Dr. Jekyll writes, "This is the testament of Dr. Henry Jekyll, aged 30, male. Male. *Male*. I must set this down before it is too late," he asserts masculine hegemony in the face of growing feminist resistance. But while Baker's direction confirms that all readings are culturally determined, it suggests that the cultural determination of the reader's moment can swamp the text. Stevenson, after all, across his early drafts actually wrote any suggestion of sexual excess out of his text—and there is little hint of sexual indeterminacy in his Jekyll or Hyde.[19]

Is the text, then, entirely subject to the reader? Is the gesture of reading simply an imposition of current culture on a text? Does *Dr. Jekyll & Sister Hyde* indicate that through its readers a text stands infinitely and arbitrarily variable? In fact, for all Stevenson's efforts to write sexuality out of his text, Baker's sexual encoding of the novel enjoys a complex provenance that stretches back through generations of readers—many of them directors—to *Dr. Jekyll and Mr. Hyde* itself. Janice Doane and Devon Hodges have argued quite powerfully that in Stevenson's novel the female is a presence conspicuous by its absence, that in fact Jekyll constitutes himself against a distinctly gendered Hyde.[20] While Doane and Hodges's evidence stands open to interpretation, it is undeniable that almost since *Dr. Jekyll and Mr. Hyde*'s inception, readers have figured Hyde's otherness across gender. The stage versions of the novel swell their cast by introducing the pure and unattainable woman, and the movies specify her significance by adding the fallen woman as a focus for Jekyll's displaced desires.[21] For at least seventy years directors have located Jekyll's good and Hyde's evil in the pure woman and the prostitute. So, under pressure from his culture, Roy Ward Baker simply exaggerates and foregrounds a configuration for the Jekyll/Hyde relationship implicit in the text and articulated by generations of readers.

Baker's movie, then, suggests that while the reader responds according to his or her cultural complex, that complex itself stands to a degree determined by the reader's immediate reading context. For Baker, directing *Dr. Jekyll and Mr. Hyde* means viewing it through a lens ground by generations of readings now constituted as texts. Thus the text, when read, exists not merely as subject to the reader, nor yet in a one-to-one relationship with the reader, but through a tightly strung network of responses that each reading bends, stretches, twists, and alters.

If the reader, as culturally determined intertext, rewrites the text, if s/he rewrites it along the lines of his or her cultural divergences from and coincidences with the author's cultural complex, and if s/he writes it across generations of readings taken as texts, why does s/he do it? Does s/he simply channel the pressures of culture? And why does s/he do it so often? In particular, why do successive readers feel compelled to rewrite *Dr. Jekyll and Mr. Hyde* over and over again?

My research suggests that Stevenson's text carefully resists closure, actually inviting the reader to repeat and to supplement it. This appears suitably strange, for *Dr. Jekyll and Mr. Hyde* already epitomizes the overdetermined text. It appears replete with its own readers—Utterson, Jekyll's friend and lawyer, is only the most prominent. Does any space remain for the reader to write his or her concerns across the text? Indeed, Stevenson's text provides multiple significations for Hyde's evil. Can the reader add to them? In fact, the novel constructs gaps both for readers and for alternate readings through its very overdetermination. Although Stevenson provides a superfluity of readers, their readings prove inadequate. Even Utterson, despite all his detective work, despite all the documents he receives, ultimately provides no reading of Jekyll's strange case; all his reading ends in silence. So Stevenson projects reading as an unresolved dynamic, and he invites the reader to participate in that dynamic, appellating him or her even as he appellates his characters as readers of the Jekyll/Hyde text. Moreover, Hyde's multiple significations—his Darwinian, class, sexual, and generational manifestations—compete with one another, canceling one another out. Stevenson leaves the reader not with a meaning but with a process, one Jerrold Hogle has defined here as abjection.[22] Working cautiously through Kristeva's theories, Hogle defines this process as in part "an active 'throwing away' or 'casting off' of something. . . . [that implies] a knowledge of what is being cast down and a determination to throw it off because of what it is."[23] Such an abjective process, as inherently unstable, as an expression of insecurity attempting to secure itself through the suspect gesture of othering, pushes the reader to attempt its resolution.

But the reader does more than simply contribute to the text. While s/he accomplishes the task Kaja Silverman defines for the supplement in *The Subject of Semiotics,* "[compensating] through proliferation on the part of the signifier for a signified which can never be made fully present," s/he also receives a return.[24] The abjective structure, with its dynamic of othering, its tendency to distribute experience according to binary logic, provides a convenient locus for the reader to displace and disempower contemporary problems. While Robertson, Fleming, and Baker provide signification for the text, the text allows them to objectify their fears of the transformation threatened to the subject by alcohol, war, or female power. Indeed, not only can the reader fix a contemporary threat in one element of a localizing and disempowering binarism, in that distanced and diminished structure, s/he can tentatively work it through and yet bind it according to the trajectory determined by the text. Thus, whereas Stevenson studiously avoids hinting at whether his protagonist dies as Jekyll or as Hyde, in their final scenes successive directors focus on the body whose configuration constitutes the rewritten text's primary question: they all firmly fix the "source" of contemporary conflict within the abjected Other who is in the end ejected from life.

If, however, the abjective text allows the reader so successfully to lock contemporary culture's disruptive forces within diminishing and disempowering binary structures, why do we find generations of readers/directors not just rewriting the text but writing the same problem across the text? Why do successive directors similarly encode Stevenson's text with gendered anxieties, for instance? First, in that it cannot address the complex relations of self and Other, the abjective gesture is inherently false, falsifying, and thereby, in fact, destabilizing. Indeed, insofar as readers write complex problems across Stevenson's text, and insofar as they force these problems to the point of resolution through Jekyll/Hyde's death, they may short-circuit rather than facilitate resolution. They may displace the problem only momentarily and only to intensify it. So, for instance, despite its early encoding in Stevenson's text, female sexuality appears there again and again, and with greater urgency as time progresses. Second, as the readings performed by Robertson, Fleming, and Baker suggest, cultural expectations and anxieties are never singular; neither do they derive from one source. Consequently, whereas Robertson strives to play out contemporary anxieties about the transformative power of alcohol, these anxieties must compete for space in the novel's binary structure with fears of age and even of the alien Other— while his Hyde finds sex behind a speakeasy door, stereotypical Chinamen tend the brothel stocked with white women. Likewise, in Baker's reading, female sexuality and Irish nationality, to name but two contemporary fears, stand simultaneously othered through Sister Hyde and the newly introduced Burke and Hare. (In this early stage of the Northern Irish "troubles," it is perhaps no coincidence that Baker first displaces Jekyll's murderous tendencies into Irishmen famous for their attacks on British women.)[25] Such multiple anxieties playing across Stevenson's binary structure disrupt it no less than do Hyde's original Darwinian, class, sexual, and generational manifestations. Just as Stevenson's text, in its overdetermination, precludes meaning, so ultimately does the re-written text. Evidently each reading undermines itself, leaving a space for the next.

So, given our filmic data, what constitutes the act of reading? If, after and against the fact of the text, readers construct narratives according to their own cultural complex, and if narrative transmitted through text tantalizes culture with the notion of restructuring itself—again and again—then we need a culturally functional yet textually engaged definition for the interpenetration of reader and text. Still, the multiple remakes of *Dr. Jekyll and Mr. Hyde* suggest that the reader's response should be figured not as a phenomenon located in reader or in text, nor even as an interpretive operation. Rather, they indicate that we might most helpfully express response as a trajectory that simultaneously and paradoxically describes cultural circles in narrative form.

Notes

William Luhr and Peter Lehman, with their summaries of some *Dr. Jekyll and Mr. Hyde* movies in *Authorship and Narrative in the Cinema* (New York: Putnam, 1977), first piqued my interest in these texts and the theoretical problems/opportunities they raise. My thanks to the University of Wyoming's Alumni Association and Division of Basic Research for supporting my interest and funding, respectively, my searches for film and for theory.

1   Robert Louis Stevenson's *Strange Case of Dr. Jekyll and Mr. Hyde* was published in 1886. Page references are to the Authorized Edition (New York: Charles Scribner's Sons, 1886), and this text is referred to as *Dr. Jekyll and Mr. Hyde.*

2   See letter to F. W. H. Myers, dated March 1, 1886, from Skerryvore, in *The Letters of Robert Louis Stevenson,* 4 vols., ed. Sidney Colvin (New York: Charles Scribner's Sons, 1911), 2:325.

3   See "A Chapter on Dreams," in *The Works of Robert Louis Stevenson: The South Seas Edition,* 32 vols. (New York: Charles Scribner's Sons, 1925), 13:161–74, esp. 172–73.

4   See Margaret Mackay, *The Violent Friend: The Story of Mrs. Robert Louis Stevenson* (Garden City, N.Y.: Doubleday, 1968), 207–8.

5   Mackay, *Violent Friend,* 107.

6   See caption for photograph in article "Youth drug abuse explored in musical," *Laramie Daily Boomerang,* September 26, 1991, 2.

7   Harry M. Geduld lists movie versions of Stevenson's text up to 1976 in his edited volume, *The Definitive* Dr. Jekyll and Mr. Hyde *Companion* (New York: Garland, 1983). In the recent productions, Showtime put Anthony Andrews in the title role, and ABC opted for Michael Caine.

8   Norman Holland's *Five Readers Reading* exemplifies Reader Response's interest in the reader's individual psychology, and Michael Riffaterre's essay, "The Reader's Perception of Narrative: Balzac's *Paix du ménage,*" demonstrates its concern with the textual determination of reading. See Holland, *Five Readers Reading* (New Haven: Yale University Press, 1975); Riffaterre, "The Reader's Perception of Narrative: Balzac's *Paix du ménage,*" in *Interpretation of Narrative,* ed. Mario J. Valdés and Owen J. Miller (Toronto: University of Toronto Press, 1978), 28–37. Considering such examples as these, Jonathan Culler recognizes that in focusing on reader or on text, Reader Response critics have simply constructed two new texts for interpretation. See *The Pursuit of Signs: Semiotics, Literature, Deconstruction* (Ithaca: Cornell University Press, 1981), 52 and 98–99. Culler argues for a semiotic approach that would study not "literary works themselves but their intelligibility: the ways in which they make sense, the ways in which readers have made sense of them"; he privileges the interpenetration of reader and text (50). But even Culler cannot avoid the problem of data. He relies on critical readings of Blake's "London," thereby constraining his observations to those possible from responses that often are consciously constructed and that thus constitute comments on, more than readings of, a text. These readings may contribute to a theory of critical reading, but they cannot support a theory of reading in general.

9   For convenience and clarity in separating the text that is read from its readings, I will use the term *originary* to describe the text that is read. I choose *originary* because this text initiates reading, whether or not it determines reading's course. I make full obeisance here, however, to the fact that every text exists by virtue of its intertexts.

10   See Jerome Christensen, "Spike Lee, Corporate Populist," *Critical Inquiry* 17 (Spring 1991): 582–95, 589.

11   *Dr. Jekyll and Mr. Hyde,* dir. John Robertson, Famous Players-Lasky, 1920; *Dr. Jekyll and Mr. Hyde,* dir. Victor Fleming, Metro-Goldwyn-Mayer, 1941; *Dr. Jekyll & Sister Hyde,* dir. Roy Ward Baker, Hammer, 1971. These three are now available as videos through Viking, MGM/UA, and Thorn EMI, respectively.

12   Quotations from movies are transcribed.

13   *New York Times,* January 1, 1921, 1 and 2.

14   *Dr. Jekyll and Mr. Hyde,* dir. Rouben Mamoulian, Paramount, 1931. Virginia Wright Wexman analyzes Mamoulian's film at length in "Horrors of the Body: Hollywood's Discourse on Beauty and Rouben Mamoulian's *Dr. Jekyll and Mr. Hyde,*" in *Dr. Jekyll and Mr. Hyde after One Hundred Years,* ed. William Veeder and Gordon Hirsch (Chicago: University of Chicago Press, 1988), 283–307. (Book subsequently referred to as Veeder and Hirsch.)

15   Isaac Tepper, "Guns and Good Will: To Secure Our Way of Life," *Washington Post,* December 27, 1941, 7.

16   "Stand up, Stand up for Jesus," by G. Duffield. Verse 2, lines 5–8.

17 See "Executives' 'union' must expel woman," and "Hijacker wanted to recover his wife's love," *Times* (London), December 31, 1971, 3 and 5.

18 Nancy Sinatra's song "These Boots Are Made for Walkin'" was released in 1966.

19 See William Veeder's painstaking collation of *Jekyll and Hyde*'s manuscript remnants, "Collated Fractions of the Manuscript Drafts of *Strange Case of Dr. Jekyll and Mr. Hyde,*" along with his "The Texts in Question," in Veeder and Hirsch, 14–56 and 3–13, respectively.

20 While Doane and Hodges have argued that Hyde manifests the female Other, with much the same evidence Veeder has argued that the Jekyll/Hyde opposition manifests the larger categories of patriarchy and powerlessness. It seems to me that Stevenson's deliberate attempt to write out specificity for Hyde's aberrations suggests instead a principle of difference that can be read according to gender, race, class— or any system of othering. See Janice Doane and Devon Hodges, "Demonic Disturbances of Sexual Identity: The Strange Case of Dr. Jekyll and Mr/s Hyde," *Novel* 23 (1989–90): 63–74; and William Veeder, "Children of the Night: Stevenson and Patriarchy," in Veeder and Hirsch, 107–60.

21 In 1887, Richard Mansfield appeared in *Dr. Jekyll and Mr. Hyde,* which Thomas Russell Sullivan had scripted at his request. Sullivan adds the true and beautiful Agnes Carew to the tale as the object of Jekyll's noble impulses (see Geduld, *Definitive Companion,* 215). John Robertson, with screenwriter Clara S. Berenger, adds Gina, the Italian dancer, as the inverse to the newly named Millicent Carew, and Rouben Mamoulian makes the object of Hyde's evil impulses a prostitute.

22 See Jerrold Hogle, "The Struggle for Dichotomy: Abjection in Jekyll and His Interpreters," in Veeder and Hirsch, 161–207.

23 Hogle, "Struggle for Dichotomy," 171.

24 Silverman lucidly expresses Derrida's concept in *The Subject of Semiotics* (New York: Oxford University Press, 1983), 37.

25 Burke and Hare became famous for "assisting" Doctor Knox of Edinburgh first by body snatching and then by murdering potential experimental subjects. So notorious were they that they precipitated a new verb into English, *to burke,* meaning, originally, to make away with in the manner of Burke and Hare.

Mary Lou Emery

Sexological Plots: Primitivism and the Modern Woman in

Novels by May Sinclair and D. H. Lawrence

In the epigraph to a collection of essays titled *Love's Coming of Age* (1896), the socialist and sexologist Edward Carpenter predicts an evolutionary plot for "Love":

> The little god of Love is generally represented as a child; and rightly perhaps, considering the erratic character of his ways among the human race. There are signs however of a new order in the relations between the Sexes; and the following papers are, among other things, an attempt to indicate the inner laws which, rather than the outer, may guide Love when—some day—he shall have come to his full estate.

An ultimately revolutionary force, "Love" will progressively unfold according to his own "inner laws" until "he" grows into "his full estate." The gendering of Love as masculine rings oddly when we meet the hero of this progressive romantic plot: the free and "Modern Woman" of the future, who will transform society, according to Carpenter, rendering older sex and gender categories and class divisions obsolete. Already, "even in our midst," are women who "glance forth the features of a grander type—fearless and untamed—the primal merging into the future Woman; who . . . will help us to undo the bands of death which encircle the present society, and open the doors to a new and a wider life."[1]

As Emile Delavenay has thoroughly documented, Edward Carpenter's writings exerted a definite influence on D. H. Lawrence's fiction. Delavenay argues that Carpenter's narrative model of sequential unfolding toward ideal love in *Love's Coming of Age* guided the progression of Brangwen generations in Lawrence's *Rainbow* toward Ursula Brangwen's marriage to Rupert Birkin in *Women in Love*.[2] While Delavenay discusses Carpenter's descriptions of the "unevolved man" and the "free woman" in connection with Lawrence's novels, neither Delavenay nor other critics who comment on the influence have noted the tension between two oppositely gendered protagonists in Carpenter's plot. The turning in *Love's Coming of Age* from a masculinized Love to the Modern Woman as agent of transformation constitutes another Lawrencian plot, or counterplot—one that repeats in reverse the twist of genders in Carpenter's narrative social vision.

Lawrence's companion novels *The Rainbow* (completed in 1915) and *Women in Love* (completed in 1917) enact a reversal of the gender switch in Carpenter's essays, beginning with the Modern Woman as agent of social change and turning away from, even against, her toward the fulfillment of a masculinized Love. The novels draw upon sexological and fictional narratives, complex and conflicting in their attitudes toward women and heterosexual love, from the work of sexologist Havelock Ellis and the fiction of May Sinclair. Like Lawrence, Sinclair read widely in sexology and psychology, and her novel *The Three Sisters* (1914) offered Lawrence's two novels (originally conceived as one and titled *The Sisters*) tropes and characterizations through which to experiment with a "modern" portrayal of female subjectivity.[3] If we read these sexological and fictional texts alongside one another, we witness a trafficking in plots of female development that crosses and recrosses generic boundaries of popular "scientific" treatises and modern novels. Narratives of female subjectivity are stolen, turned around, and finally brought "home" in response to the question: Who shall be the hero—reformed, masculine Love or Modern Woman?

These sexological plots and questions are complicated by other texts, also progressive in the sense that they assume evolutionary development as a narrative pattern for the human race: the models of racial classification and hierarchy popularized in fiction of the late nineteenth and early twentieth centuries and reinforced by Victorian scientific theories.[4] In one evolutionary model, "savages" observed by ethnographers and explorers represented a previous stage in the evolution of "civilized man." Within this model of "primitive" peoples as "survivals" of earlier evolutionary stages competed two views of the savage: as inferior and ignoble, or as inferior in some ways but in others naturally noble (or nobly natural) and therefore possessing a quality missing in alienated, repressed, "civilized" people. But not all scholars of "primitive" peoples cast them as "survivals"; some, such as Charles Kingsley, believed they were inferior because they were degenerated forms of an earlier and higher civilization that had weakened morally, and hence had "evolved" in reverse toward their present "savagery."[5] Though opposed in their views of the origins of "savagery," each argument maintained the superiority of European civilization, albeit with some cautionary words to Europeans. Kingsley's degeneracy theory warned Europeans against moral dissolution, and the view of "primitive survivals" as nobly natural portrayed alienation and repression as the tragic but inevitable cost of European advancement.

Studies of "primitive" cultures often served, then, as critiques of "civilized" society and, simultaneously, as guarantees of its superiority, warnings of the fate perhaps awaiting it, and sometimes, as we shall see in Lawrence's novels, all these at once. These studies also provided data for sexological discussions of European women's sexuality. In *Studies in the Psychology of Sex* (1906), Havelock Ellis cites pages and pages of ethnographical studies in which explorers such as Captain Cook and adventuring anthropologists such as J. Stanley Gardiner describe their encounters with strange native customs. According to Ellis, none of these explorers and no scientists achieved more than "unreliable, slight or fragmentary" notes toward understanding the emotion of modesty, which, Ellis argues, is observed among all peoples of the globe. Placed alongside one another as they are in Ellis's study, the descriptions of sexual customs vary widely and contradict one another, but the sexologist is, in the end, able to make sense of them and to draw conclusions as to the universal characteristics of modesty.[6]

In the chapter titled "The Evolution of Modesty," Ellis begins by citing modesty as a secondary sexual characteristic in women. Many of the reports and studies that he proceeds to quote as evidence describe instances in which, for example, "we examined the tattoo-marks on the chest of one of the [Dinka] women, and she remained sad and irritable for two days afterward"; "It is very difficult to investigate the hairiness of Ainu women"; or "we surprised several of [the women of New Zealand] at this employment [lobstering with their lower garments removed]. . . . Some of them hid themselves among the rocks, and the rest crouched down in the sea till they had made themselves a girdle and apron of such weeds as they could find, and when they came out, even with this veil, we could see that their modesty suffered much pain by our presence."[7] It seems that everywhere the anthropologist or explorer went, infinitely various customs were found that all, ultimately, expressed or depended on female modesty. Furthermore, whenever an anthropologist viewed native women's bodies against their wills or came upon native women bathing (or lobstering), they showed signs of pained dismay. If, in some cases, women seemed immodest concerning the exposure to view of their bodies, the data do not conflict with Ellis's thesis. Rather, he attributes the differences to an evolutionary process whereby "physiological modesty takes precedence of anatomical modesty," and he explains that "the primary factors of modesty were certainly developed long before the discovery of either ornament or garments."[8]

Ellis concedes that the various forms of modesty may be taught, but he insists that its presence as an emotion is fundamental and natural to women. In a sequence of thought that connects modesty among women to practices of heterosexual courtship Ellis is able to claim also that women require, even desire, forceful coercion in lovemaking.[9] In the interests of "the natural ends of love," women must be pursued and overcome: "This essential element in courtship, this fundamental attitude of pursuer and pursued, is clearly to be seen even in animals and savages; it is equally pronounced in the most civilized men and women, manifesting itself in crude and subtle ways alike."[10] On the one hand, then, the European woman, like all women everywhere, is naturally modest and thus wishes to "be forced to do the things that she altogether desires."[11] On the other hand, only European women suffer the extremes of modesty in frigidity, so civilized have they become. Ellis states that 25 percent of "civilized women" suffer from "sexual frigidity."[12] Such an overly refined sensibility is a fault, a tragic result of repression, but one preferable to any overt, or "savage," expression of sexual desire.

I am interested here in charting the overlapping and often interlocking notions of "primitive" and "feminine" in the sexological plots of Sinclair's and Lawrence's novels.[13] The influences of sexology and ethnography also shape, I argue, their portrayals of a new female subjectivity that goes beyond the goals of feminism as the authors perceived them, a subjectivity that moves toward what both Sinclair and Lawrence considered a more spiritually vital reconstruction of the whole of society. In both cases, the reconstruction takes up sexological and primitivist notions of female sexuality only to find new barriers to the characterization of women. In a sometimes awkward textual scramble for new narrative and social visions, various culturally available plots are explored and traded. The sexological plot taken up only to be rejected by Sinclair in *The*

Three Sisters becomes, oddly, the solution to the narrative dilemma in Lawrence's *Women in Love*. The fulfillment of Love's estate in the latter begins when Rupert Birkin's increasing misogyny coincides with his encounter with modernist primitivism. He rejects modernist primitivism, not from the left-wing view that it is an expropriation of tribal art for Eurocentric purposes but from the perspective of older, high-colonialist ideologies. Furthermore, through his adoption of colonialist ideologies Birkin usurps Ursula Brangwen's role as Modern Woman. Sexological plots available from Ellis's work and Sinclair's *Three Sisters* enable Birkin to recast Ursula's wildness as sexual hysteria so that he may emerge as the new hero of Edward Carpenter's story of Love.

In *Women in Love* Rupert Birkin reflects on what he sees as two evolutionary possibilities for "the white races": one identified with masculine, northern European, "phallic investigation," and the other associated with feminine, mystical, sensual knowledge. Birkin rejects both the first, "Arctic," way and what he calls, in a conflation of the feminine and the primitive, "the long, long African process." He invents instead a third evolutionary possibility, which he describes as "the way of freedom," "a lovely state of free, proud, singleness."[14] This is a major turning point for Birkin's development as a character and for the novel's plot because realization of the third way prompts him to "run to follow it," and the direction in which he runs is to Ursula Brangwen: "He must go to her at once. He must ask her to marry him."[15] That "free, proud singleness" depends on immediate marriage does not seem contradictory to Birkin. What does occur to him, and what, I shall argue, resolves the contradiction before he can even become aware of it, has something to do with Ursula's complexion. To build his courage for making his proposal to Ursula, Birkin recalls "how sensitive and delicate she really was, her skin so over-fine, as if one skin were wanting."[16]

In running to Ursula for marriage, Birkin rejects more than two possible scenarios for the so-called white races; also, and most important, he rejects and reverses the plot, characterization, and epistemology of the novel—*The Rainbow*—to which *Women in Love* forms the sequel. Given the opposition he sets up in his reflection on the African process—between civilized, productive rationality and primitive, mystical sensualism—the narrative development of *The Rainbow* may be read in retrospect as an alternate "third way," already plotted. It is a third way in which Ursula Brangwen emerges as a woman who has gone through and beyond the ideals of the New Woman to become the representative of a newly envisioned society of self-realized, vital individuals. If we count *The Rainbow*'s plot as an alternate path, Birkin has actually opted for a "fourth" way, one in which he develops his freedom by depriving Ursula of her singleness, her pride, and her narrative agency.

In *The Rainbow* Ursula attempts to fulfill herself along both evolutionary paths charted by Birkin in *Women in Love*—as a sensually passionate woman *and* as a thinking, creative individual. Individuating herself from her foremothers while carrying forward the quests that they dropped or denied, Ursula pursues self-realization as the highest possible goal of her life—through heterosexuality and lesbian sexuality, through education and work in "the man's world," and through direct encounter with the "wild beasts" of her psyche. She is clearly a New Woman, yet one for whom academic knowledge, a public life, sexual and economic independence, and feminism are not enough.

Constituting female narrative subjectivity, *The Rainbow*'s plots and character types derive from and then supersede those outlined in Carpenter's *Love's Coming of Age*. Carpenter describes three types of women —the lady, the working wife, and the prostitute—which he claims a fourth type, the Modern Woman, will render obsolete. But Carpenter runs into difficulties when he tries to describe the Modern Woman:

> The women of the new movement are naturally drawn from those in whom the maternal instinct is not especially strong; also from those in whom the sexual instinct is not preponderant. Such women do not altogether represent their sex; some are rather mannish in temperament; some are "homogenic," that is inclined to attachments to their own, rather than to the opposite, sex; some are ultra-rationalizing and brain-cultured; to many, children are more or less a bore; to others, man's sex-passion is a mere impertinence, which they do not understand, and whose place they constantly misjudge.[17]

Viewing motherhood as "woman's great and incomparable work," Carpenter selects the New Woman's "deficiency in maternal instinct" as "the most serious imputation." However, he is willing to wait and see "what evolution is preparing."[18]

In *The Rainbow,* Ursula carries forward the plot of the "free woman," representing the generation that dissolves the dichotomy between lady and prostitute by enacting a nobility of the spirit at the same time that she engages in both lesbian and heterosexual love affairs. We can read *The Rainbow* as narrating a fall from the "natural" womanhood of Ursula's foremothers on the Marsh Farm into a freedom and emancipation that parallels an increasing alienation from nature. This fall seems analogous to Carpenter's dilemma over the New Woman, herald of a new age but alienated from the "natural" desire for maternity. And it parallels the evolutionary line of thinking that views the "savage" as nobly natural while "civilization" suffers from the price of alienation even as it progresses toward a future prize.

However, *The Rainbow* surpasses even Carpenter's progressive categories in characterizing a post–New Woman in Ursula. She is not at all deficient in passion, and she is granted a reprieve from maternity that does not imply a deficiency in maternal feelings. As he goes beyond Carpenter in envisioning the New Woman, Lawrence carries forward Carpenter's social evolutionary plot by making of Ursula the self-fulfilled individual whose freedom signals a new harmonious order. Ursula's character development also supersedes the opposition of alienated civilization and noble savagery. In her ecstatic communions with the moon—symbol of her longing for liberty, fulfillment, and the unknown—Ursula becomes a female, and therefore modernist, Tarzan: noble, savage, *and* English; heir to a large estate,[19] an estate promised and realized in her vision of the rainbow at the novel's conclusion.

The moon with its mystical yet physically urgent attraction represents Ursula's efforts to escape "the horrors of the machine" with which are associated her female and her male lovers, her job, and her education.[20] In a final scene with her lover, Anton Skrebensky, Ursula "seemed to melt into the glare, towards the moon. . . . [S]he went to meet the advance of the flashing, buoyant water. She gave her breast to the moon, her belly to the flashing, heaving water . . . 'I want to go,' she cried, in a strong, dominant voice. 'I want to go.'"[21] She insists on making love "full under the moonshine" and "lay motionless, with wide-open eyes looking at the moon."[22] Ursula's quest for something beyond what society offers even a New Woman becomes a search for pure sensation that culminates in the famous wild horse scene in which she achieves transcendent psychic freedom.

The one who quests and desires in a novel that extends Carpenter's sexological plot must be a woman because, according to Carpenter, "woman is the more primitive, the more intuitive, the more emotional," and will harmonize "all the faculties in the human being" sooner.[23] However, Ursula's passion expresses itself in association with the moon (and wild horses), not with men or women, and so the problem of her sexuality as a social relation remains. She is not Carpenter's asexual New Woman, but she still awaits a new man—in Lawrence's terms, one of "the sons of God."

In May Sinclair's *Three Sisters,* which directly influenced Lawrence's two novels, we find three women characters set up as distinctly different psychological "types," all waiting for a man, new or otherwise. The sister who becomes pivotal for the narrative development is the anemic and sexually indiscreet Alice. Everyone reveals his or her own character in response to Alice. Her hypocritical father, the vicar, claims that she is a sinful daughter who has "made a fool of herself" over men. Regarding her illness, "he knew what was the matter." What he "knows" is the projected image of his own destructive and lustful sexuality. Alice's sister Mary uses Alice's illness as a stage prop to enhance her contrasting but self-deceptive enactments of "virtue" and "goodness."

The narrative and dialogue are structured so that we perceive the only sister capable of any self-reflection to be Gwenda, who sees Alice as a "victim" and as "the fragile vehicle of an alien and overpowering impulse." The impulse is sexual, and the novel portrays Alice as an unaware sensualist. As Gwenda remarks to Mary, "Molly, it must be awful to be made like that." The point, however, is that Gwenda sees the awfulness as part of Alice's makeup, something she cannot help. Gwenda's opinion of Alice and the cause of her disabling anemia complements that of the only eligible man in town, for whose attentions the sisters compete. Steven Rowcliffe is a doctor who has read Pierre Janet on hysteria and thinks of Alice as "a poor parson's hysterical daughter."

However, in one scene, Steven throws away his copy of Janet in frustration, a gesture that suggests to one critic that he has rejected Janet's notions of hysteria as an inherited genetic trait.[24] In a later conversation with Gwenda, he declares that Alice "has been starved," alluding to the "sexual starvation" Havelock Ellis identified as the cause of hysteria in young women. Ellis believed that such hysteria and the anemia that accompanied it could be cured by marriage, the event that indeed, as Hrisey Zegger has pointed out, cures Alice. At the novel's conclusion, she has become heterosexually fulfilled in marriage and maternity with a rough but honest man who frightens her at first with his potential for violence.

As much as marriage, I would argue, the potential for heterosexual violence is crucial to Alice's cure. In Alice, the script for women's lives implicit in Ellis's *Studies in the Psychology of Sex* is played out in full.

Ellis's writings on heterosexuality broke with the Victorian description of women as feeling no sexual desire to declare that they do experience desire and, furthermore, that they have a right to sexual pleasure. Denial of sexual feelings might well create a hysterical and anemic young woman. However, she need no longer die or go mad, the alternative fates Steven Rowcliffe offers for Alice; her story might still end happily in a modern marriage with a husband who would instruct his naturally modest wife in the ways of sex, perhaps overcoming her necessary modesty with force since women feel pleasure, according to Ellis, in physical dominance and pain. Ellis noted "in woman a delight in experiencing physical pain when inflicted by a lover, and an eagerness to accept subjection to his will."[25] Furthermore, the natural outcome, one that served both the interests of the state and the healthy fulfillment of the woman, was maternity.

While Sinclair incorporates such a plot for her women characters, she gives it to one we are not meant to respect very much, a character portrayed from the beginning as an unself-reflexive sensualist—an "African," in Birkin's terms. The other less than admirable character, Mary, lives out a Victorian marriage plot, but one exposed as self-deceptive and unfulfilling. Leaving the more admirable Gwenda to a socially isolated fate, Sinclair seems to be throwing away Ellis, just as Rowcliffe tossed Janet aside. If Gwenda is a type, she is a social type—a New Woman constrained by Victorian *and* modern sexological marriage plots. Like Ursula in *The Rainbow,* Gwenda quests for self-realization and for a true and honest love between equals. Like Ursula, Gwenda leaves home to work and earn her own living; and though we do not know exactly what happens to her in London as the secretary of Lady Frances, we do know that such independence does not satisfy her spirit. Furthermore, Gwenda is given to very long walks across the moors at night under the moon's ecstatic pull: "'Oh, look at the moon!' she cried. 'All bowed forward with the cloud wrapped round her head. Something's calling her across the sky, but the mist holds her and the wind beats her back—look how she staggers and charges head-downward. She's fighting the wind. And she goes—she goes!'"[26] Reminiscent of and probably inspiring Ursula's "I want to go! I want to go!" Gwenda's communion with the moon expresses nobly and naturally her love of liberty. In a romantic primitivism coupled with Darwinian typologies that Sinclair passed on to Lawrence, Alice represents an undesirable savagery and Gwenda a noble one.

In *The Three Sisters* and *The Rainbow,* the moors and the moon become alternatives to domestic confinement, on the one hand, and work, financial independence, and public life, on the other. Romantic, primitivist, and maternalist tropes are refigured to represent a third way through and beyond the New Woman's goals of equality in a "man's world," for that world is perceived as lacking in spiritual and physical vitality. In both *The Rainbow* and *The Three Sisters,* the characters who remain true to these symbols of female self-fulfillment remain also outside heterosexual marriage and forgo any further sexual pleasure. Sinclair's later novels work out this apparent problem, which becomes a narrative limitation, through the concept of sublimation; she thereby avoids casting her independent women characters as "sexually frigid" or "homogenic." Lawrence, on the other hand, shapes a sequel in which Ursula finds her mate, and it is her mate who finds the new way to self-realization.

In this sequel, Lawrence returns to the plot that Sinclair, writing even before *The Rainbow,* suggests we throw away: Ellis's plot of the hysterical young woman cured by a psychologically, if not physically, coercive marriage. Following Birkin's dichotomizing the African and the Arctic ways and his decision to achieve his own free, proud singleness by marrying Ursula, a scene ensues in which Ursula's passion is recast as hysterical sexual jealousy. In the "Excurse" chapter, she raves under "the stress of her violent emotion":

> Yes, I am. I *am* a fool. And thank God for it. I'm too big a fool to swallow your cleverness. God be praised. You go to your women—go to them—they are your sort—you've always had a string of them trailing after you—and you always will. . . . Do you think I don't know the foulness of your sex life—and hers?—I do. And it's that foulness you want, you liar. . . . It *stinks,* your truth and your purity. It stinks of the offal you feed on, you scavenger dog, you eater of corpses.[27]

These are just the highlights of a fit that fills Birkin with "a wonderful tenderness" even as he responds, "coolly," that "this is a degrading exhibition."

Ursula inexplicably comes around, however, "hanging her head" modestly, abjectly. "Pursued and overcome," as Ellis prescribed, she now discovers a new source of passion—not the moon and *her* breasts and belly, but *Birkin's* flanks and loins, "the very stuff of being" in "one of the sons of God."[28] From a masculine "little god of Love," in Carpenter's words, she learns "at last to be still and perfect."[29] The lesson places Ursula in the vague but sexologically ideal space between overly civilized "sexual frigidity" and the "foul" sensualism of which she accuses Birkin. Her sexual relations with him and her "subjection to his will," in Ellis's words, immunize her against either extreme, save her from further "homogenic" attractions, and relieve her from the hysteria of her "violent emotions."

The text (through Birkin) tames Ursula's wild spirit by representing it as degrading, hysterical excess. The diagnosis becomes available only when Birkin rejects his own modernist appreciation for "primitive" art and adopts instead the colonialist evolutionary line of thought popularized by Charles Kingsley. For Birkin's dismissal of the "African process" and his decision to marry Ursula follow immediately a series of meditations on two carvings, one from the western Pacific and one from West Africa.[30] In an early scene, he defends the carving from the western Pacific, which depicts a woman in childbirth, as art and the result of "centuries of development." However, later he remembers an African statue as representative of all the "primitive" carvings he has seen. His emphasis then on Ursula's fine complexion and delicacy places her in contrast with both statues, with what he perceives as their "protruberant buttocks," a "face crushed tiny like a beetle's," and "the strange clutching posture" of a woman in labor. Ursula's exemption from the classes of women wholly given to sensuality in Birkin's theories suggests her potential as a companion on the new third way of Birkin's freedom. Still, he wonders if "this awful African process" remains for the Arctic races to fulfill.

Conceiving of the "primitive" condition as African, purely sensual, and degradingly feminine; conceiving of "the white races" and "the dark races" as possessing separate and opposed characteristics in which geography, physical appearance, and consciousness are all of a piece, Birkin follows typical late Victorian colonialist conventions of racial and sexual classifications. When he identifies the statues as representing a racial lapse in the desire for "creation and productive happiness" (a fall from a higher state), he holds with the degeneracy view of evolution expressed by Charles Kingsley. As Kingsley intended, the carvings become a warning to Birkin of what might befall the already lapsing "white races."

Turning in disgust from the "ultimate *physical* consciousness" he perceives in both statues, Birkin rejects the sexological celebration of maternity to legitimize his dismissal of *The Rainbow*'s alternate third way and to invent a new one. While *The Rainbow*'s plot grants Ursula a reprieve from maternity in her miscarriage, it portrays in other characters' experiences of pregnancy, labor, and motherhood a mysterious, mystical, and natural process. The process moves Ursula's mother, for instance, to dance naked and hugely pregnant under the full moon, so Ursula's ecstatic communions with the moon recall her mother's earlier dance. With Ursula, though, the meaning shifts to that of a combined longing for physical and spiritual fulfillment and liberty, a liberty that remains essentially female and powerful. Rejecting maternity as purely "savage" sensuality, Birkin claims this powerful liberty for men; the plot of the two connected novels gains a new protagonist and another trajectory.

Birkin's rejection of "savage" female sensuality and his new third way devolve on the rejection of one other plot event in the sexological narrative scripted by Carpenter. In the essay "Woman in Freedom," Carpenter predicts that in transforming the social order, the New Woman will " 'spank' or thump the middle-class man!" Her liberty becomes powerful, and her power is a physical threat to men. In *Women in Love,* Hermione Roddice, a "brain-cultured" and "ultra-rationalizing" New Woman, literally "thumps" Birkin on the head with a fine jeweled ball and sends him reeling, nearly unconcious, into a field of grass.

When he escapes Hermione's upper-class, emancipated, intellectual woman's society to a pastoral site, Birkin seems about to take refuge in the sensationalism he later rejects. Taking off all his clothes, he absorbs into his blood the sensation of grass, primroses, fir boughs, and hyacinths against his thighs, loins, and breast until the scene climaxes with the exclamation "how fulfilled he was, how happy." Here the narrative adopts implicitly the evolutionary theory of "primitive" peoples as "survivals" of earlier stages in the development of "civilization." In this scene Birkin usurps Ursula's role in *The Rainbow* as noble savage plunging into the dark field of pure sensation to retrieve an earlier, less alienated state of being.

But Birkin is hardly Tarzan; he is too modern and far too thin. We might read, as does Emile Delavenay, his slender frailty as a feminizing characteristic, especially in contrast with Gerald Crich, muscled but doomed symbol of Arctic masculinity. If Birkin is feminized, he is also revitalized through his noble and savage encounter with the primroses. Rather than contradicting Birkin's rejection of the African process, this encounter re-creates him as a male New Woman, taking up a New White Man's burden by taking over Ursula's quest. He shoulders his burden, not as what Carpenter called an "ungrown" or unevolved man but as a man who has grown by expropriating the "primitive" characteristics

Carpenter hailed in modern and free women. That he cannot fulfill himself in maternity no longer matters; rather, it becomes an added and even "natural" virtue.

Birkin feels himself capable of transforming, if not society, at least the old marriage pattern, and therefore he wishes to marry Ursula. Such a marriage is not at all incompatible with the "free proud, singleness" that is his new "way of freedom"; in fact, his freedom requires that he marry Ursula because only through marriage can her passion be domesticated and her place in the text become a perfect stillness. In this way the trading in plots of female subjectivity brings them all "home" to a (reformed) marriage plot, followed by a death plot.

Birkin's marriage is not enough closure for the narrative in which he now stars because, as Ursula repeatedly complains, she is not enough for him. Not only does Birkin also require intimacy with a man, he requires that all of his theories be proved correct. In the death of Gerald, Birkin finds his ideas confirmed: "He should have loved me. . . . I offered him."[31] The plotting of Gerald's death provides irrevocable (and untestable) evidence for Birkin's belief that intimate friendship between them would have saved Gerald from the fatal excesses of the Arctic path that Gerald followed in his relationship with Gudrun. Thus does Birkin, and not Ursula, hold the potential, in Carpenter's words, to "undo the bands of death which encircle the present society." If Birkin has been correct about Gerald and the masculine Arctic way, it may follow that he has also been correct about the "primitive" and "feminine" nature of an also doomed "African process." By extension, he may well have been right in persuading Ursula to seek liberty as his wife on his own third way. However, the marriage between Ursula and Birkin hardly achieves his ideal of "an equilibrium, a pure balance of two single beings:— as the stars balance each other."[32] He and Ursula remain "free" to disagree with one another in their marriage, but the disagreements portray Ursula, once again and finally, as the jealous woman. Her protestations— "Aren't I enough for you?"—remain those of a narrow-minded and envious woman who speaks no longer hysterically but "afraid, white, with mute lips."[33]

The plot given to hysterically anemic Alice in The Three Sisters resurfaces in Women in Love with one twist: while marriage may calm the bride's hysterics, it hardly cures—in fact, it requires—her increasingly anemic presence in the text. The early twentieth-century traffic in plots of female subjectivity and sexuality operates with violent coercion. The one who possesses narrative agency becomes not only the hero of a novel but also the governor of Love's "inner laws." In the social evolution toward "a new order in the relations between the Sexes," Love becomes territory to loot while its natives are subdued, their vital "primitive" traits stolen from them in a colonizing mission replete with contesting ideologies. Through exchanges, reversals, and retrievals of narrative possibilities for women characters, colonialist evolutionary plottings join sexological fictions to diagnose the New Woman's wildness as either ultrarationalizing and degenerate or hysterical but curable. Masculine Love does inherit his estate. Feminized and primitivized, he comes into his own as a nevertheless English and thoroughly modern husband.

Notes

I would like to thank Katherine Hayles, Huston Diehl, Rebecca Faery, Stephen Wootton, and Teresa Mangum for helpful comments on earlier drafts of this essay.

1   Edward Carpenter, *Love's Coming of Age* (London: Swan Sonnenschein, 1902), 71.

2   Emile Delavenay, *D. H. Lawrence and Edward Carpenter* (New York: Taplinger, 1971), 99–110.

3   Hrisey Dimitrakis Zegger offers substantial evidence to support his claim that *The Rainbow* and *Women in Love* borrow from Sinclair's *Three Sisters*. See Zegger, *May Sinclair* (Boston: Twayne, 1976), 73–78.

4   For discussions of these models, see Roger Ebbatson, "A Spark Beneath the Wheel: Lawrence and Evolutionary Thought," in *D. H. Lawrence: New Studies,* ed. Christopher Heywood (New York: Macmillan, 1987), 90–103; Sander Gilman, "Black Bodies, White Bodies: Toward an Iconography of Female Sexuality in Late Nineteenth-Century Art, Medicine, and Literature," in *"Race," Writing, and Difference,* ed. Henry Louis Gates, Jr. (Chicago: University of Chicago Press, 1986), 223–61; and Brian Street, *The Savage in Literature: Representations of Primitive Society in English Fiction, 1858–1920* (London: Routledge and Kegan Paul, 1975).

5   Street, *Savage in Literature,* 88.

6   For a discussion of Ellis's work in the context of feminism and the New Woman, see Margaret Jackson, "Sexual Liberation or Social Control?" *Women's Studies International Forum* 6 (1983): 1–17; and Carroll Smith-Rosenberg, "The New Woman as Androgyne: Social Disorder and Gender Crisis, 1870–1936," in *Disorderly Conduct: Visions of Gender in Victorian America* (New York: Oxford University Press, 1985), 245–96.

7   Havelock Ellis, *Studies in the Psychology of Sex,* 2 vols. (New York: Random House, 1942), vol. 1, pt. 1, 11–22.

8   Ellis, *Studies,* 58. Ellis seems to be making a distinction between modesty regarding physiological functions and modesty regarding the fact or sight of the body itself.

9   Margaret Jackson notes that this aspect of Ellis's work complements his better-known diagnoses of "sexual inversion" in women as efforts to "conscript women not only into

heterosexuality . . . , but into a form of heterosexuality which is both an expression of, and a means of maintaining, male power over women" ("Sexual Liberation," 6).

10   Ellis, *Studies,* vol. 1, pt. 1, 41.

11   Ellis, *Studies,* vol. 2, pt. 3, 549.

12   Ellis, *Studies,* vol. 2, pt. 3, 550. The implication of Ellis's argument here—that "primitive" women are more active in sexual expression than most European women—contradicts his assertion that "physiological" modesty precedes anatomical modesty in evolutionary development. Perhaps it is simply a matter of the degree of modesty that concerns Ellis in the implied comparison. Nevertheless, the arguments together catch European women in a double bind formed by accusations that, on the one hand, they are overly modest and that, on the other, as "civilized" women they must demonstrate an (inherent) modesty that justifies forceful sexual coercion.

13   For a related discussion of Lawrence's primitivism that offers readings and conclusions quite different from mine, see Marianna Torgovnick, *Gone Primitive: Savage Intellects, Modern Lives* (Chicago: University of Chicago Press, 1990), 159–74. Torgovnick offers a sympathetic reading of Lawrence's intentions in *The Plumed Serpent,* which she sees as portraying a masculine and regenerative primitivism.

14   Critics usually refer to this passage to explain the "Arctic" characters and fates of Gerald Crich and Gudrun Brangwen or to reflect on the portrayal of Minette and Gerald's relation to her. See, for instance, Gavriel Ben-Ephraim, *The Moon's Dominion: Narrative Dichotomy and Female Dominance in Lawrence's Later Novels* (Rutherford, N.J.: Fairleigh Dickinson University Press, 1981). It also figures in critical articulations of the tension in Lawrence's writing between dissolution and regeneration. See Cornelia Nixon, *Lawrence's Leadership Politics and the Turn Against Women* (Berkeley: University of California Press, 1986). All these concerns are somewhat related to mine here, which is the reversion, in Birkin's thinking, to colonialist hierarchies in the reconstitution of masculine subjectivity through the redomestication of female agency.

15   D. H. Lawrence, *Women in Love* (Middlesex, England: Penguin Books, 1979), 247.

16   Lawrence, *Women in Love,* 247.

17   Carpenter, *Love's Coming of Age,* 66–67.

18   Carpenter, *Love's Coming of Age,* 67.

19   Brian Street discusses the character of Tarzan as a hybrid figure in *The Savage in Literature.* Marianna Torgovnick criticizes the sexism in the Tarzan stories but also finds in them "more attractive forms of primitivism" (*Gone Primitive,* 71).

20   See Ben-Ephraim, *The Moon's Dominion,* for a comprehensive discussion of the moon in Lawrence's early novels as symbolizing an essential femininity.

21   D. H. Lawrence, *The Rainbow* (New York: Viking/Penguin, 1976), 479.

22   Lawrence, *The Rainbow,* 480.

23   Carpenter, *Love's Coming of Age,* 40.

24   Zegger, *May Sinclair,* 70–71.

25   Ellis, *Studies,* vol. 1, pt. 2, 89.

26   May Sinclair, *The Three Sisters* (New York: Macmillan, 1915), 159.

27   Lawrence, *Women in Love,* 298–99.

28   Lawrence, *Women in Love,* 305.

29   Lawrence, *Women in Love,* 307.

30   Marianna Torgovnick discusses Lawrence's meditations on these carvings in *The Visual Arts, Pictorialism, and the Novel: James, Lawrence, and Woolf* (Princeton: Princeton University Press, 1985). Here she is interested in narrative descriptions of visual art, and she describes the African sculpture as encoding for Birkin his fears of the two processes he defines as Arctic and African (197).

31   Lawrence, *Women in Love*, 471. For a feminist reading of Lawrence's changing conceptions of love between men and of his homophobia, see Cornelia Nixon's *Lawrence's Leadership Politics and the Turn Against Women*.

32   Lawrence, *Women in Love*, 139.

33   Lawrence, *Women in Love*, 471.

Marcel Cornis-Pope

Narrative Innovation and Cultural Rewriting: The
Pynchon-Morrison-Sukenick Connection

All good fiction today, in whatever form, is exploratory with regard to the medium
and highly conscious of it—even realistic narrative, given the context of the seven-
ties that it must take into account. . . . Fiction writers today are writing from a
point of view well anterior to the genres and subgenres of the novel. They begin by
questioning the medium itself, and their work involves an exploration of the idea of
fiction, not only in the novel, but in the culture at large.—Ronald Sukenick, *In Form*

I am valuable as a writer because I am a woman, because women, it seems to me,
have some special knowledge about certain things. [It comes from] the ways in
which they view the world, and from women's imagination. Once it is unruly and
let loose, it can bring things to the surface that men—trained to be men in a certain
way—have difficulty getting access to although I can think immediately of several
exceptions to that.—Toni Morrison

Postmodernism and the Critique of Narrative Articulation

Critics of postmodernism often identify narrative innovation with only
one component: a deconstructive, improvisational impulse usually regarded as devoid of cultural significance, reduced to slapdash invention and self-reflexive game playing. Three related criticisms are most
frequently heard: (1) the self-reflexive focus on the processes of writ-
ing/reading limits literature to narrow aesthetic concerns, preventing a
rigorous exploration of the conditions we live in; (2) the revisionistic
strategies of postmodernism have little sociocultural relevance outside
the world of fiction; and (3) postmodernism discourages serious articu-

lation, promoting a negative, self-ironic attitude that puts all categories of thought "under erasure." This "negativist vision," as John W. Aldridge has argued, "is not a response to, nor does it represent an attack on any specific social and political injustice. . . . In fact, a startling characteristic of such writing is that it expresses absolutely no discernible attitude of any kind toward society as a whole, no critical consciousness of the nature or quality of the milieu in which the characters carry out their insignificant lives."[1] By taking its politics of self-questioning to an extreme, postmodern experimentation weakens the critical edge of the novel, divorcing it from other sociocultural practices. Thus, in Brian McHale's characteristic description, postmodern fiction is an ontological rather than an epistemological or ideological genre because it has abandoned the "intractable problems of attaining to reliable knowledge of *our* world," resorting instead to "pure ontological improvisation."[2]

Underlying most of these critiques of the fractured, antiauthoritarian poetics of postmodernism is a nostalgic concept of narration as an effective totalizing machine. Within this model, compositional and epistemological concerns are either overlooked or willingly subordinated to the representational function of the novel, without much concern for the interconnectedness of these issues. What the contemporary novel needs, in Charles Newman's view, is a persuasive narrative mechanism that will reinforce "the positive socializing function of literature."[3] Novelists' awareness of the manipulative side of their craft should not prevent them from performing the comprehensive acts of assemblage and order making we expect of fiction: "What we finally want from literature is neither amusement, nor edification, but the demonstration of real authority which is not to be confused with sincerity, and of an understanding which is not gratuitous."[4] By endorsing such dubious, unexamined notions of narrative authority, critics of postmodernism reinstate the "phony duality," realism/formalism, that they elsewhere denounce. From their perspective, American fiction remains locked in a conflict between two irreconcilable traditions: a "self-taught" form of "iconoclastic realism" characterized by a "concentration on realistic detail so obsessive that it seems at times to border on the paranoid," and an off-centered, disaffected attempt to "push beyond the limits imposed by conventional realism into areas in which realistic details may become transformed into [cultural and ideological] metaphors."[5] What such critics cannot envision is the possibility of a radical form of postmodernism that would reformulate both mimetic narration and symbolic reflection. Instead of neutralizing "the oppositional extremes of realism and reflexity" into a bland form of "midfiction" that would "normalize" self-reflection, turning it into a mimetic mode,[6] postmodernism could critically implicate the processes of one in the activities of the other: regrounding sociocultural generalizations in a scrupulous analysis of experiential details and refocusing critical attention on the processes of realistic articulation.

Such a radically revisionistic orientation already exists in much innovative fiction: its role is to build awareness of the codes and assumptions that govern the production of narrative texts and to provide room for their transformation.[7] Experimental fiction is neither about "unanxious fictionalization," nor about narrative "self-erasure," but rather about the tension between innovation and constraint, the inclusive and the divisive impulses of a culture's narratives. The *self-reflexive* novels of Robert Coover, Joseph McElroy, and Thomas Pynchon simultaneously build and question systematic narration, carrying it to the point where its totalistic claims are undone by the underlying dialectic of articulation. In shifting from an earlier atomistic, causal, static model of narration to a new epistemology that emphasizes process, gestalt, and open dynamics,[8] these novels undermine the formal and axiological stability of society's "grand narratives." *Surfiction* and the new *feminist novel* upset the hermeneutic, libidinal economy of narration more profoundly, creating differential movements within it as a weapon against interpretive expropriations.[9] At the same time they pursue a more imaginative narrative dialectic that allows a re-creative rapport with reality to emerge.

What is foregrounded in each case is the process of fiction making as a whole, its conditions of articulation and mastery models. The self-reflexive focus on articulative and unifying devices allows these fictions to raise broader questions about the significant role that self-legitimizing narrative orders play in all types of cultural construction. Postmodern fiction provides, in Gayle L. Ormiston and Raphael Sassower's view, an ideal locus where claims of cultural authority are examined and reformulated.[10] The "construction and choice of one story over others" is shown to be governed less by a relation to truth than by "a will to power," "a desire *not* to hear certain other voices or stories."[11] Hence the need felt by most postmodern writers to "think in fragments," in "heterogeneous" modes of discourse; but also their critical awareness of the self-regulating "will to mastery" that informs all narrative structures, however innovative.

Narrative Disruption and Rearticulation
in "Systems Novels"

The question of narrative/cultural *mastery* and its critique is central to what Tom LeClair has called the "systems novel."[12] The richly layered, speculative works of Thomas Pynchon, Robert Coover, Ursula Le Guin, Joseph McElroy, and John Barth are directly concerned with social macrostructures and discursive systems, submitting the personal and local to a systemic evaluation. By taking such an integrative approach, the "systems novels" achieve a triple "mastery of the world in which they were written, mastery of narrative methods and mastery of the reader."[13] At the same time, they foreground the sources of their mastery by calling attention to the synthetic and structuring operations they perform. Instead of concealing the synecdochal mechanism of fiction, the "system novels" expose it with a vengeance, providing "discourse [that] represents other kinds and behaviors of discourse." The mastery they claim is finally revealed as a metaphor itself, a synecdochal illusion that allows the "parts . . . selected, structured, proportioned, and scaled" to "suggest, not exhaust, the whole of discourse." The result of this paradoxical dialectic of "excessive mastery" is a species of problematized process-text, a hybrid between systemic realism and postmodern deconstruction. This type of text both illustrates and violates our deep-seated need for order and axiological stability, deforming "the conventions of the realistic novel in order to defamiliarize the world, not only . . . the text."[14]

An immediate problem with this kind of systemic novel is that its insistent focus on global cultural systems affects its own narration, encouraging extensive patterning and narrative integration. LeClair argues, in fact, that the stability of cultural systems can be challenged only through confident acts of novelistic mastery, that in the presence of self-reproducing power institutions "only extraordinarily knowledgeable and skilled works of literature—masterworks—have the kind of power that asserts the efficacy of literature and leads readers to contest and possibly reformulate the mastering systems they live with."[15] I find this approach problematic not only because it compromises the postmodern critique of mastery by returning us to a nostalgic, integrative notion of literary "masterpiece" (according to this line of thought, *Gravity's Rainbow* is a more significant work than *The Color Purple* because it "masters a set of global conditions that *The Color Purple* does not address, conditions and systems in which all readers—black or white, female or male, old or young—are imbricated"),[16] but also because LeClair does not allow literary dissension to go far enough; he reduces it to such procedures as overloading, excess, and structural *complication*. The systems novels increase the entropy of the narrative process, creating an "informational density" that cannot be "naturalized" by the reader, but they do not significantly challenge "the power systems they exist within and are about." By LeClair's own admission, systems novels often arouse conventional expectations of plot, character, and setting, even though they deform and rescale them subsequently. The reader is temporarily disoriented but can still "reframe the text's materials within systemic conventions," recognizing a reassuring "correspondence between the novelistic system of information and systems of information in the world."[17]

A more significant systemic disruption can take place when fiction attacks, in Coover's phrase, "the supporting structures themselves, the homologous forms," making room for a "disruptive, eccentric, even inaccessible" narrative voice "peculiarly alert to the decay in the social forms that embrace it."[18] The best work of Coover and Pynchon moves in that direction, being concerned both with systems analysis and systems transgression, with mastery and its undoing. Their fiction challenges inherited modes of narrative representation in at least two ways: (1) by revising the referential system of traditional fiction, breaking down its norms of selectivity, unity, and verisimilitude; and (2) by exacerbating (and at the same time questioning) our need for self-explanatory orders. *Gravity's Rainbow* (1973) upsets these orders epistemologically and textually, denying the reader a controlling perspective. This book, according to Brian Stonehill, engages from the start two antithetical modes of reading: a "paranoid," systemic reading that finds everywhere support for the idea of a "massive conspiracy envelop[ing] Tyrone Slothrop and the other characters"; and a ludic-deconstructive reading, aware only of "perfect randomness, each point ideally independent of any other. . . . Like *Ulysses, Gravity's Rainbow* is both minutely mimetic, and egregiously ludic; it amalgamates literary realism with surreal fantasy."[19] This conflict of rhetorical-interpretive perspectives unsettles not only traditional realism but also master images of modern culture (the War, the Empire, Business, Science, Religion). In what amounts to a cosmographic rereading of modern Western history, Pynchon foregrounds the ubiquitous will to order that runs through it, detouring and redirecting it. His complex plots attempt, in Khachig Tölölyan's description, "to direct sexual desire, ballistic missiles, and interpretation (among others)" toward some "privileged structure of meaning."[20] By the same token, the plots prevent this cultural semiotic from reaching closure, recuperating some of its excluded areas (forgotten histories, disaffected professionals, victimized children and women).

This process of recuperation/rearticulation is more economically illustrated in *The Crying of Lot 49* (1966), where various disenfranchised groups participate in the arcane counterdiscourse of the "muted horn," a secret postal "network by which X number of Americans are truly communicating whilst reserving their lies, recitations of routine, arid betrayals of spiritual poverty, for the official government delivery system."[21] The history of "Trystero," the alternative postal organization that Oedipa investigates by accident, suggests that rearticulation/rewriting (in the form of textual insertions, forgeries, distortions of traditional icons, and garbled names) can play a subversive role in culture, enabling the marginalized to challenge the dominant discourse. In characteristic Pynchonesque fashion, this book leaves open the question of how successful Oedipa is at creating some room for women's experience in the incongruous, male-dominated society of Southern California in the 1960s. The W.A.S.T.E., or "muted horn," sign suggests both a breakdown in modern communication and a conspirative mutation of its discourse systems that allows the manifestation of dissonant, marginal voices such as Oedipa's. Oedipa herself remains an ambivalent figure to the very end: an excluded, paranoid overreader who vainly seeks to bring an existential and cultural void "into pulsing stelliferous Meaning"; but also a facilitator of intercommunication between disparate worlds, a "tryster" whose erratic drifting establishes tantalizing encounters between people and things.[22]

Dissonance (linguistic, cultural, symbolic) is an active principle of articulation in Pynchon's fiction. Rather than simply illustrate some form of cultural and textual anarchy, Pynchon seeks a provisional balance (creative dissonance) between the endlessly proliferating symbolic systems that his work evokes. Each microsystem is riddled by further discontinuity and dissonance between its signs, enhancing the semantic divisiveness of the novel. *Gravity's Rainbow* proliferates numerous series of antithetical images: gravity and rainbow, angels of God and angels of war, agents of order and "the Counterforce," "a good Rocket to take us to the stars, an evil Rocket for the World's suicide, the two perpetually in struggle."[23] These images function as system markers and structuring agents (selective decisions are left to "some angel stationed very high, watching us at our many perversities, crawling across black satin"), but also as semantic "excesses" in the text that suggest another, uncontainable side of reality (fictional, metaphysical, libidinal).[24]

Pynchon's work thus illustrates and enacts the idea of an "open system" that allows neither "ordered individuality" nor entropic disintegration to prevail. The complexity of Pynchon's novels demands continuous rereading, complex operations of interpretative restructuring. At the same time, as McHale has argued, we are "invited to become meta-readers, readers of our own (and others') readings—and, more to the point, of our *misreadings*"—in order to understand our desire for mastery of meaning.[25] (Mis)reading plays a crucial role in Pynchon's work, at once constraining and liberating, disrupting the linearity of a given system of "truths" and creating new, dissonant patterns of meaning within a culture's narratives. Oedipa Maas is perhaps the best example of this: in the course of her quest for "truth," she arrives gropingly at a performative notion of interpretation that turns her from a mere sifter of clues into an "executrix"-"projector" of worlds. By actively (mis)reading, "bringing something of herself—even if it was just her presence" to the world of business interests and androcentric texts,[26] she manages to alter partly the prescriptive "plots" that solicit her (the plot of male seduction, the Trystero plot, the historical narrative of cultural disenfranchising), infusing them with her own feminine desires and interests.

Prairie Wheeler, Oedipa's younger counterpart in *Vineland* (1990), undertakes a similar rereading of recent history (from the psychological revolution of the 1960s to the paranoid and benumbed 1980s), mainly to understand her immediate heritage. This rereading breaks up the smooth, flat reality she has been fed on computer videos, movie screens, and TV "tubes." At the same time, it manages to create, against the larger culture's inability to remember creatively, an imaginative bridge to the past. In the hyperreal, self-indulgent world of 1984, "cut into pieces" by the ubiquitous "Tubelight,"[27] Prairie embarks on a journey of self-discovery that inevitably centers on her missing mother, Frenesi. In her effort to piece together the incongruous fragments of her mother's biography (daughter of a labor activist and a Hollywood "revolutionary," herself a member of the radicalist "24fps" film collective, converted into a government informant in the Nixon years), Prairie triggers a process of narrative recollection in various characters who had been associated with Frenesi: Zoyd Wheeler, her former "hippie psychopath" husband, the former members of the 24fps collective, and federal prosecutor Brock

Vond, Frenesi's new lover and employer. These emotionally charged, private narratives create significant inroads into the "Tube-maddened" world of the 1980s, disturbing its easy, manipulative diegesis. Their role is thus twofold: psychologically, they purge Frenesi's generation of some of its guilty absorption in the past as "the enemy no one wanted to see, a mouth wide and dark as the grave";[28] they also give Prairie, the disinherited progeny of the Tubal Age, a sense of familial and cultural belonging. Politically, these oral retrospective narratives function as a collective form of anamnesis, providing a much-needed critical reexamination of the myths and failures of the postwar decades. Through them, the residents of "Vineland" can reconnect more freely with each other and with their shared past.

Two forms of order thus vie in *Vineland:* one is flat, soporific, controlled by digital technology and mass reproduction; the other is personal, interrogative, a form of re-creative storytelling in process of continual revision. As Jonathan Rosenbaum explains, "implicit throughout is the notion that thanks to the dominance, ideology, and druglike powers of the Tube (as Pynchon calls it), disseminating . . . 'the ruling ideas of epoch,' the recovery of even recent history has to be carried out through willful and sustained archaeological research into buried documents and testimonies; it is not automatically self-evident and available to everyone."[29] Zoyd's annual "dive through the window" routine at the beginning of the novel suggests metaphorically how storytelling works in this book: though Zoyd's dive is performed for the immediate benefit of TV cameras and "an ever more infantilized population" of "Tubeheads," it triggers a process of narrative recalling of "years and miles in the past" that breaks symbolically through the fake "mirror" to the truer, personal aspects of Zoyd's life.[30] The slow, plodding narratives of the various witnesses in Frenesi's life perform a similar function: they break through the deceptive surface of the plot-driven Tubal stories, revealing a deeper layer of truths. With their plethora of satiric-comic details and imaginative flights of phrase, these personal narratives resist a reductive reading back to situational and cultural stereotype.

But Zoyd's "transfenestration" adventure also points out the limitations of oral, personal narration in an age of electronic reproduction. Other significant events in Vineland's recent history are also submitted to mass media "rewriting" and absorbed back into the leveling "tubelight" that "finds no difference between the weirdness of life and the weirdness of death."[31] Rewriting itself becomes a dubious form of cultural reformulation in *Vineland,* fitting real-life stories to prescribed scenarios, forcing historical happenings to follow a retrogressive logic from "event" to pictures of pictures. As it is passed down from one generation to the next, Vineland's history becomes a Hollywood movie script "pounded flat," anybody's property, a "way-over-length, multitude-of-hands rewrite."[32] In her own effort to reconnect with her mother's history, Prairie has to settle for "watching" Frenesi on reels of film that are themselves the product of an ambiguous agenda: conceived initially as documentaries of a time of daring civil action, "liv[ing] out the metaphor of movie camera as weapon," these films become Frenesi's bargaining chips with the authorities. In them, Frenesi and other activists are "framed," dispossessed, turned into political tools. As she follows her "mother's ghost" through computer files, film footage, and newspaper clips, Prairie has great difficulty in extricating the human story behind the many framings meant to "conceal" rather than "illuminate . . . the deed."[33]

And yet, something does emerge from this "tale of dispossession and betrayal": a new sense of familial, female history.[34] The *Vineland* women challenge, more or less successfully, the male-dominated world of politics, reclaiming their right to articulate their own life stories. Through Prairie, the brave new child of the Tubal Age who can combine a rediscovered interest in oral narrative with a natural flair for reading images, Vineland's personal histories are restored to their original indeterminacy and open potentiality. At the end of the novel, Prairie is in possession of a truer, more tangible "mother story." Despite the strangeness of its plot, pitting well-meaning but faltering women like Frenesi against a world of paranoid anarchists, "Tube-crazed" federal agents, and shadowy international conglomerates, this story manages to recover the ignored, interpersonal aspects of culture.

Cultural Rewriting in Surfiction and the Innovative Feminist Novel

As long as they follow the two courses described by LeClair—excess of "mass-produced and institutionally controlled information" and the burrowing "into specialized and alternative sources for information that . . . undermines the dominant culture's legitimation"—the self-reflexive system novels remain trapped within the given power structures, transgressing them only superficially.[35] These parodic-reconstructive texts manage to focus attention on how cultural information is disseminated and governed through narrative channels, but they end by reinforcing synthesis, "showing how orders and forms in the world (and not just in the artistic text) can arise out of seeming chaos."[36] A more effective form of systemic disruption and cultural rewriting can be found in surfiction and in the innovative work of feminist writers. Both types of fiction make informational and systemic integration more difficult, denouncing its controlling mechanisms. They also seek to radicalize fiction's rapport with reality, using innovation and "framebreaking" to open, in Ronald Sukenick's words, the self-contained "system of language up to experience beyond language."[37] The disruptive strategies employed in surfiction have broader cultural and ideological consequences than the "quantitative deformations of conventions" practiced by the systems novelists. Their role is primarily to *denaturalize* and discredit the "perverse logorrhea" of realistic representation, exploiting its *errors* of focus, judgment, and interpretation. At the same time, these strategies allow alternative modes of narrative articulation and intelligibility—fluid, improvisational, multivoiced—to emerge. Though unsparingly critical of its own effort to enclose reality in a "fraudulent . . . edifice of words,"[38] surfiction does not give up articulation. Instead of simply parodying the "exhausted" conventions of realism like earlier metafiction, surfiction radically reformulates the novel's epistemological relation to reality and to its own rhetoric. By fracturing the discrete flow of narration into conflicting "voices" and diegetic roles, novelists such as Raymond Federman, Marianne Hauser, Gilbert Sorrentino, and Sukenick restore a performative dimension to the act of storytelling. Their fiction takes on a "platformatic" aspect in the sense both of a narrative mise-en-scène and of a polemical confrontation between teller and told, teller and listener, speech and writing.

Surfiction can therefore be described as a polemical, process-oriented form of narration that continually reformulates its modes of articulations, "push[ing] out to the edge of culture and of form" in order to "allow more reality into the work."[39] Through self-conscious disruption, improvisation, and rewriting, the surfictionist hopes to create an experiential text that can stand on its own in the world: "Rather than serving as a mirror or redoubling on itself, fiction adds itself to the world, creating a meaningful 'reality' that did not previously exist. Fiction is artifice but not artificial."[40] Disarticulation and re-creation are thus two related sides of the same surfictionist project. Ideally surfiction hopes to strike—in Federman's words—a "cunning," "irrational balance" between articulation and disarticulation, a substance-centered, phenomenalistic

narration and a language-centered, self-reflexive approach.[41] When sur-
fictionists break away from a controlling story, derailing narration with
digressions, self-reflexive glosses, or typographical inventions, they assert their imaginative need to *rewrite* their own life narratives. To take
one example of the many available, Raymond Federman's success at articulating a "real fictitious discourse" in his novels has depended on his
willingness to unwrite/rewrite the already existing stories of his life,
blocking their "masturbatory recitation," their "discourse system of recuperation."[42] The three major happenings in Federman's personal history (his survival of the Nazis' genocide; his "exilic" leap across the
Atlantic, from his native France to the New World; and his educational
wanderings through another "kind of void . . . America") are all dramatic and "tellable." But Federman has not been interested in pursuing
a conventional quest narrative or a Holocaust novel with a predictable
"catastrophic plot." Such story lines would have inevitably counterfeited
reality, misrepresenting the distinctive quality of these events with their
"fraudulent . . . edifice of words." Federman's problem, as I see it, has
not been in improvising a story, but rather in reformulating an already
existing autobiographical scenario, submitting it to a complex dialectic
of "destorifying" and retelling, repetition and revision.[43]

The task of unwriting a dominant narrative tradition, whose phallocentric orientation has been particularly binding for women, is central
also to innovative feminist fiction. Like its postmodern male counterpart, feminist fiction has been engaged in a critique of traditional narrative epistemologies, but its focus has fallen predictably on their systematic misrepresentation of women and privileging of the androcentric
viewpoint.[44] This critique has involved more than a deconstructive revision: rather than scrapping traditional epistemologies altogether, feminist theory and literature have contributed significantly to their reformulation, creating new structures of narrative intelligibility within which
female subjects may play liberated, imaginative roles. Feminist narra-
tology is currently divided between a critical task and an articulatory
task, between a desire to disrupt and expose totalizing narratives and
an equally compelling need to devise successful strategies for inscribing
female agency in cultural discourse.[45] This may explain the circumspect
position women writers have often taken on the question of experimentation: "Feminist fiction seldom is as self-conscious and artificial as are
male fictions, and experimentation usually serves the ultimate end of
realism. The conflict between representationalism and experimentalism

is resolved in this manner: it is women's real lives that defy the laws of the text; as women write their selves, so do they destroy the laws."[46] The narrative recuperation of women's real lives has undoubtedly radicalized the contents of the novel; but this epistemological and thematic orientation does not automatically radicalize the narrative practice itself and eliminate all androcentric vestiges of totalization. As long as it stays within the framework of conventional realism, feminist fiction risks repeating some of the traditional framings and exclusions. To use Linda J. Nicholson's example, in "try[ing] to identify unitary themes in the experiences or perspectives of women [this fiction] may require the suppression of voices different from our own."[47] Likewise, in attempting to write a coherent narrative of women's historical struggle against male domination, feminist fiction may relapse into a logocentric "search for ultimate causes or first principles."

Feminist fiction has therefore had to engage consistent revisionistic work at the level of narrative poetics: challenging the phallocentric symbolic order of realism, with its dream of mastery and penetration, and replacing it with more fluid, antiauthoritarian, collaborative discursive relations. Given their historical experience as controlled signifieds rather than configuring signifiers, women are perhaps in a better position to understand the need for such a radical shift in narrative semiotics, and they also know the many hurdles involved in such a transition. The best work of Marge Piercy, Toni Morrison, Joanna Russ, Grace Paley, and Marianne Hauser reflects on the problems women novelists encounter when they employ the available narrative forms for a new articulation: "I want to be better with words," Marge Piercy writes in *Small Changes*. "I want to be able to answer them back. But I don't believe that's how you do anything. I only want to use words as weapons because I'm tired of being beaten with them."[48] Feminist fiction must wrestle incessantly with the problem of narrative language, questioning its systems of conventions and symbolic truths and creating new expressive matrices in it for women's experience. As a consequence, women's position inside culture is rewritten and renegotiated continually: "We may live within patriarchy, but at different levels and in different ways the struggle to rearticulate locale continues."[49]

This process of ongoing articulation is best illustrated in Toni Morrison's *Sula* (1973), a novel that departs thematically and narratively from the conventional expectations of African-American literature. The "decidedly feminist slant" of this and other Morrison works disrupts—

according to Deborah E. McDowell—the male-centered canon of realism: "The narrative retreats from linearity privileged in the realist mode. Though dates entitle the novel's chapters, they relate only indirectly to its central concerns and do not permit the reader to use chronology in order to interpret its events in any cause/effect fashion."[50] Described by Morrison herself as a novel about black women's friendship, focused on "the other I" as confidante and companion, *Sula* struggles to "repossess, re-name, re-own" a space for women's experience within the androcentric traditions of fiction.[51] I would argue that the rebellious character of Sula, a woman who refuses to settle for the "extremely painful and unattractive" career of "mother and laborer,"[52] becomes possible precisely because of the revisionistic work going on at the level of the narrative and sociocultural models that the novel reexamines. After what looks like a false start (the narrative begins with a male character and a historicist framework that suggests a chronicle novel or a Bildungsroman), *Sula* gradually intensifies its focus on "femaleness" and a number of highly unorthodox attitudes and relationships among women. Room for this type of focus is created through a subtle process of narrative elimination/ restructuring. The few male figures that matter in the novel are bodily and mentally "amputated," accidentally drowned, upstaged by strong, sexually liberated women. The leading Peace women (Eva, her daughter Hannah, and her granddaughter Sula) gain increasing—if somewhat dubious—freedom through "amputation": giving up a leg, a son, marriage, sentimentality, or traditional domesticity, and replacing them with an unconventional enjoyment of their own sexuality. Sula's whole life becomes "experimental" by dint of its decenteredness and "dangerous" freedom from the normative: "She had no center, no speck around which to grow. . . . She was completely free of ambition, with no affection for money, property or things, no greed, no desire to command attention or compliments—no ego. For that reason she felt no compulsion to verify herself—be consistent with herself."[53]

A similar retrenchment goes on at the narrative level: *Sula* proliferates images that seem to reinforce known symbolic orders and explanatory frameworks (historical-causal, metaphysical, psychoethnic), but these orders appear "decapitated," emptied of their conventional content. At the same time they are refilled with the new, shifty reality of "femaleness." The motif of adolescent initiation, for example, is restructured around the experiences that the two young female protagonists, Sula

Peace and Nel Wright, share with each other: "In the safe harbor of each other's company they could afford to abandon the ways of other people and concentrate on their own perceptions of things."[54] In a succession of scenes that "dust off clichés," expropriating their meaning for female needs, the two girls are shown performing what looks like an ironic phallic ritual: "undressing" twigs, digging with them two separate holes in the ground until "they were one and the same," and finally burying their broken phallic tools together with other "small defiling things" in a common symbolic "grave." This is immediately followed by a dramatic scene in which Sula and Nel accidentally drown a little boy, *watching* the swift, dull water of the river close "peacefully over the turbulence of Chicken Little's" frail masculine body.[55] This incident cements their friendship around a complicity of guilt and power, but also around the exercise of what had previously been the prerogative of the male spectator: an *interested gaze*. Thus not only the coming-of-age plot but also the traditional specular economy of fiction are disturbed and restructured to make room for women as active focalizers and rewriters of traditional stories.[56]

To an even greater extent than Morrison's *Song of Solomon* (1978) or *Beloved* (1987), *Sula* disrupts genre and rewrites traditional stories and mythic-symbolic frameworks, providing an alternative representation of women.[57] But this process of restructuring is deliberately left open, prevented from reaching ideological closure. *Sula* disturbs the tight orders of patriarchy and heterosexuality, but it still resists a monological reading in the opposite direction. The divergent careers of the two female protagonists cannot be easily evaluated: Sula challenges the heterosexual, domestic paradigm, but she dies alone in her grandmother's sealed-up bedroom. Nel never really escapes patriarchy, but her cautious conformity is interrupted by moments of intellectual and emotional rebellion that seem surprisingly guilt-free. The intimate friendship between Sula and Nel enables both girls to "see old things with new eyes,"[58] but their fresh perspective, emphasizing female interactions and desires, is not allowed to entirely displace the patriarchal symbolic order. Femaleness itself (both in its nurturing and in its more defiant, self-assertive aspect) emerges as a powerful but ambiguous force.[59] No single narrative perspective or concept of selfhood is allowed to dominate: *Sula* remains an interesting example of a postmodernist text that engages strategies of disruption and rearticulation in order to create a space for a new, albeit "unfinished," concept of womanhood and narration. The whole novel works like a "deliberate hypothesis," a "discursive/imaginative project" that constructs, through an ironic rewriting of traditional narrative roles, a "character of possibility," a hypothetically free woman.[60]

Surfiction often works in similar ways, unfolding in a conditional, interrogative field where a number of conflicting stories and modes of articulation are tested and revised. In place of the end-stopped, teleological progress of traditional narration, surfiction involves us in a revisionistic, open-ended dynamic on several levels: *temporal*, since this type of process-oriented fiction is in permanent flux, provisional and self-corrective as time itself; *epistemological*, since the novel no longer allows a privileged position for evaluating its "reality," requiring instead an interactive hermeneutics that reformulates both reflecting consciousness and world; and *sociocultural*, engaging its various discursive agents in a radical form of experiential thinking that seeks to "undercut official versions of reality in favor of our individual sense experience."[61] The emphasis on the experiential dynamics of performance, as Sukenick has often insisted, enhances the percussive force of the novel: the self-generated structures of surfiction undermine fossilized representations, creating imaginative ruptures in established reality through which a transformative narrative consciousness can manifest itself. To interpret this project as narrowly self-reflexive is to miss its revisionistic orientation that seeks to reconnect fiction with "the mute world beyond language from which language above all separates us, and which, therefore, it has the power to restore."[62]

Sukenick's narratives characteristically move from *project* (narrative "notes," plot hypotheses, epigraphs that announce the leitmotifs of the ensuing narrative) to multiple *concretizations* and *revisions*. What emerges is a process-oriented narration that strives to capture (without directly imitating it) the "prosody of experience" with its "irreducible twists and possibilities" while also providing a re-creative response to it. "Stripped of inessentials and [the] historical trappings" of plot, character, and mimetic realism,[63] Sukenick's novels can pursue the "white noise of event[s]," trekking their "constantly erased and rewritten" course, "zig of inside through zag of out."[64] However, since their job "is not to record some preexisting reality but to contribute to the ongoing process of cultural building in and through the process of writing itself,"[65] these performative narratives also submit the superficial data of reality to a continuous process of (re)articulation that activates new connections in the flow of experience: "You see what's happening here you take a few things that interest you and you begin to make connections. The connections are the important thing they don't exist before you make them. This is THE ENDLESS SHORT STORY. It doesn't matter where you start. You must have faith. Life is whole and continuous whatever the appearances."[66]

Sukenick's experiential fiction thus balances a performative with a reformulative task. The novelist's effort "to get at the truth of experience beyond our fossilized formulas of discourse" begins with a deconstructive gesture, with a disruption of the "sanctioned descriptions of life" in order to make room for "a new and more inclusive 'reality.'"[67] But it is necessarily followed by an imaginative rewriting that converts the "petty iconography of the quotidian" into an ampler movement of "invention and even prophecy."[68] In response to Otis's conventional wisdom, "Well, that's what art is all about, right? The discovery of reality," the character-author of *Up* counters: "No. The invention of reality."[69] The privileging of narrative invention over traditional mimesis may have certain romantic connotations, recalling Wordsworth's treatment of art as a process of "self-creation." But whereas Wordsworth sought a transcendental connection with a preverbal world of organic feelings, Sukenick is more alert to the presence of "language as a coherent reality in itself, that both impedes and facilitates our description of experience."[70] For him the process of fictionalization is not escapist, illusionistic, but reformulative, engaging us in a creative dialogue with the extant cultural narratives. Improvisation and invention are used consistently to confer an experiential, proleptic dimension to fiction. Yet invention is rarely reduced to unchecked fantasizing, being more often put to work on preexisting personal and cultural stories, decomposing and recomposing them, opening them up to further experiential possibilities. Ideally, life and fiction collaborate under the aegis of a revised, radical epistemology. Fiction is promoted to the status of "an important experiential medium, no longer an imitation of life, but rather . . . an illuminating addition to its ongoing flow."[71]

Through imaginative rewriting, surfiction is expected to extricate experience from the straitjacket of preformulated stories; but its imaginative acts of rearticulation are constantly threatened by a cultural space of "negative hallucinations" and evasions. Finally, the task of formulating a new narrative epistemology in an age dominated by modes of cultural reproduction may prove to be as difficult for surfiction as it is for the feminist novel. Sukenick's books are acutely aware of the tension between two narrative approaches, two cultural styles: one is improvisational, transgressive, antimimetic; the other is largely representational, submitting to the inhibiting will to form of ordinary language. While the performative approach allows a certain degree of artistic intervention in reality, emphasizing the revisionistic process of articulation, the mimetic mode is reproductive and uncritical in Sukenick's view, reducing narration to a manipulative production of likenesses.

Like the personal, recollective narratives of *Vineland*, Sukenick's fictions strive to break through the discursive screens of traditional representation to the repressed, authentic data of experience. But they are also troubled by the realization that the two diegetic modes, one reproductive-manipulative, the other re-creative, are facets of the same process of narration; and that innovative fiction, no matter how liberated, cannot entirely escape the mastery system of representation.[72] The assault on traditional novelistic mirrors cannot do away with all reflection as long as surfiction wants to remain reflective in a sociocultural sense, articulating a significant self-critical discourse. The only other alternative is total deconstruction, the inspired inarticulateness of the "Bjorsk" lingo in *98.6*, a "stream-language" of emotional noises (growls, squeaks, farts, gargles, clicks, chuckles) that cannot communicate with the brain. Sukenick's narrators occasionally flirt with the notion of a visceral, nonrepresentational language, but their intention to "destroy the English language" as an instrument of (conventional) communication remains for the most part a theoretical project.[73] Sukenick's own characteristic pose is that of "a one man band playing all the instruments," "stitching together" his novel's "bungled fragments," rather than some dadaist demolisher smuggling around "word bombs."[74] Sukenick's fiction usually seeks a truce between an improvisational *stream-language*, "responsive to every nuance of mood" and yet "expressing" nothing definitive, and a revamped *representational language* that chooses to articulate without entirely giving up the experiential spontaneity of the improvisational mode.

The best illustration of this provisional balance between conflicting narrative modes is the technique of "psychosynthesis" in *98.6*. Following a performative, revisionistic hermeneutics that delays the incorporation of local details into a controlling metanarrative, this method first exposes and destabilizes the dominant images of contemporary culture (sexual violence, psychological stagnation, "negative hallucinations"); then it rearticulates the cultural scene around new, unforeseen connections that re-present reality in its differential possibility, in its hypothetical becoming. Based on "the law of mosaics [which is] a way of dealing with the parts in the absence of wholes,"[75] the technique of *psychosynthesis* replaces rigid cause-effect enchainments with an innovative, "anti-narrative mode of organization" that seeks a "luminous moment of coincidence" between history and invention: "A way of things happening without happening. A way of dreaming without dreaming. A way of going mad without going mad. We deny nothing. We incorporate the negation in the affirmation."[76]

Like the feminist novel, surfiction inhabits a stereophonic space, a "vast coincidence" of situations and discourses through which a "sideways" narrative imagination can trace infinite connections.[77] The success of both types of fiction depends on the right blend of "unwriting" and "rewriting" of our "cultural destiny." Improvising, retracting, projecting, revising—both surfiction and the innovative feminist novel manage to upset the fixed order of reality, repatriating it "from the realm of determinism to that of potential."[78] Narrative metamorphosis and reformulation replace plot teleology as the generative principle of fiction. But the novelist's faith in the constitutive powers of his or her imagination is by no means untroubled, oblivious to the manipulative side of narration. Both feminist narrative and surfiction are painfully aware of the inherent limitations of their medium, calling attention to their own acts of narrative appropriation and self-projection. Their "rewriting" violates not only the inscribed "order of fate" but also the traditional order of fiction, forcing a reevaluation of the novel's epistemological and cultural domain. Given their common interests and aspirations, a rapprochement between feminist fiction and innovative postmodernism (surfiction) is not only possible but desirable. The two forms of cultural rewriting could collaborate toward what Seyla Benhabib calls "an epistemology and politics which recognizes the lack of metanarratives and foundational guarantees but which nonetheless insists on formulating minimal criteria of validity for our discursive and cultural practices."[79]

Notes

The epigraphs are from Ronald Sukenick, *In Form: Digressions on the Act of Fiction* (Carbondale: Southern Illinois University Press, 1985), 47–48; and "An Interview with Toni Morrison," Hessian Radio Network, Frankfurt, West Germany, 1983, in

Critical Essays on Toni Morrison, ed. Nellie Y. McKay (Boston: G. K. Hall, 1988), 54.

1 John W. Aldridge, "The New American Assembly-Line Fiction: An Empty Blue Center," *American Scholar* 1 (Winter 1990): 34.

2 Brian McHale, *Postmodernist Fiction* (London: Methuen, 1987), 10.

3 Charles Newman, *The Post-Modern Aura: The Act of Fiction in an Age of Inflation* (Evanston: Northwestern University Press, 1985), 5–6.

4 Newman, *Post-Modern Aura,* 97, 173.

5 Aldridge, "The New American Assembly-Line Fiction," 26.

6 Alan Wilde, " 'Strange Displacements of the Ordinary': Apple, Elkin, Barthelme, and the Problem of the Excluded Middle," *boundary* 2 10 (Winter 1982): 192.

7 See especially "Postmodernism beyond Self-Reflection: Radical Mimesis in Recent Fiction," in *Mimesis in Contemporary Theory,* vol. 2, *Mimesis, Semiosis and Power,* ed. Ronald Bogue (Philadelphia: John Benjamins, 1991), 127–55.

8 See Anthony Wilden, *System and Structure: Essays in Communication and Exchange,* 2d ed. (New York: Tavistock, 1980), 241.

9 Introduced by Raymond Federman, *surfiction* designates a form of innovative fiction represented mainly by Steve Katz, Paul Metcalf, Ishmael Reed, Ronald Sukenick, Gilbert Sorrentino, and Federman himself. The "surfictionist" project involves two related tasks. The first is disruptive, a polemical denunciation of the mimetic, illusionistic traditions of fiction. Raymond Federman's own theoretical essays, beginning with "Surfiction—Four Propositions in Form of an Introduction," in *Surfiction: Fiction Now . . . and Tomorrow,* ed. Raymond Federman (Chicago: Swallow Press, 1975), 5–15, have pieced together a handbook of obligatory procedures for the "disruptive," antimimetic novelist. Displacement, cancellation, pulverization, repetition, revision, digression are the remedies most often prescribed against the fraudulent flow of conventional fiction.

    The second task is reconstructive, shifting focus from the "experience of life" to the writer's own effort to "reinvent" reality in a self-conscious process of narrative articulation. From a "pseudo-realistic document" of something preexisting it, fiction becomes an experiential reality in its own right, an imaginative object that can take its place in the world.

10 Gayle L. Ormiston and Raphael Sassower, *Narrative Experiments: The Discursive Authority of Science and Technology* (Minneapolis: University of Minnesota Press, 1989), 15, 16.

11 Jane Flax, *Thinking Fragments: Psychoanalysis, Feminism, & Postmodernism in the Contemporary West* (Berkeley: University of California Press, 1990), 195.

12 See Tom LeClair, *In the Loop: Don DeLillo and the Systems Novel* (Urbana: University of Illinois Press, 1987); LeClair, *The Art of Excess: Mastery in Contemporary American Fiction* (Urbana: University of Illinois Press, 1989).

13 LeClair, *The Art of Excess,* 5.

14 LeClair, *The Art of Excess,* 19, 18, 21.

15 LeClair, *The Art of Excess,* 1.

16 LeClair, *The Art of Excess,* 3.

17 LeClair, *The Art of Excess,* 6, 22.

18 Robert Coover, "On Reading 300 American Novels," *New York Times Book Review,* March 18, 1984, 37–38.

19 Brian Stonehill, *The Self-Conscious Novel: Artifice in Fiction from Joyce to Pynchon* (Philadelphia: University of Pennsylvania Press, 1988), 142.

20 Khachig Tölölyan, "Thomas Pynchon," in *Postmodern Fiction: A Bio-bibliographical Guide,* ed. Larry McCaffery (Westport, Conn.: Greenwood Press, 1986), 486.

21 Thomas Pynchon, *The Crying of Lot 49* (Philadelphia: Lippincott, 1966; New York: Harper and Row/Perennial Library, 1986), 170.

22 "Trystero" (also spelled "Tristero") triggers a number of interesting phonetic associations: "tryst," "tryster," "trist" (trust), "triste" (sorrowful), and "three-star." Juan Eduardo Cirlot notes that in the Tarot card system, from which Pynchon has drawn several of his symbolic references, the "Stars" card depicts "an allegorical image of a naked girl kneeling down beside a pool, as, from a golden jar, she pours a life-giving liquid into the still waters." Above this figure are a bright star and several lesser ones. Cirlot explains further that "the ultimate meaning of this symbol seems to be expressive of intercommunication of the different worlds, or of the vitalization by the celestial luminaries of . . . the purely material Elements, of earth and water." See Cirlot, *A Dictionary of Symbols* (New York: Philosophic Library, 2nd ed., 1971; rpt. 1974), 310. In ironic contrast, Oedipa Maas's name is one letter away not only from blind Oedipus but also from Maat, the perfidious Egyptian goddess of truth and righteousness who admits into the Afterlife only those who lie convincingly.

23 Thomas Pynchon, *Gravity's Rainbow* (New York: Viking Press, 1973), 727.

24 Pynchon, *Gravity's Rainbow,* 746.

25 Brian McHale, "You Used to Know What These Words Mean: Misreading *Gravity's Rainbow," Language and Style* 18 (Winter 1985): 113.

26 Pynchon, *The Crying of Lot 49,* 90.

27 Thomas Pynchon, *Vineland* (Boston: Little Brown, 1990), 38, 71.

28 Pynchon, *Vineland,* 71.

29 Jonathan Rosenbaum, "Pynchon's Prayer," *The Reader: Chicago's Free Weekly,* March 9, 1990, 29.

30 Pynchon, *Vineland,* 52, 27.

31 Pynchon, *Vineland,* 218.

32 Pynchon, *Vineland,* 81.

33 Pynchon, *Vineland,* 197, 114, 261.

34 Pynchon, *Vineland,* 172.

35 LeClair, *The Art of Excess,* 16.

36 LeClair, *The Art of Excess,* 21.

37 Sukenick, *In Form,* 11.

38 Raymond Federman, *The Voice in the Closet/La Voix dans le cabinet de débarras* (Madison: Coda Press, 1979), 6, 12.

39 Charlotte M. Meyer, "An Interview with Ronald Sukenick," *Contemporary Literature* 23 (Spring 1982): 129–44; reprinted in Sukenick, *In Form,* 135.

40 Sukenick, *In Form,* 31–32.

41 Raymond Federman, *Double or Nothing: A Real Fictitious Discourse* (Chicago: Swallow Press, 1971), 9.

42 Federman, *The Voice in the Closet,* 17.

43 For a more detailed discussion of Federman's narrative dialectic, see my article "Narrative (Dis)Articulation and the *Voice in the Closet* Complex in Raymond Federman's

Fiction," *Critique. Studies in Contemporary Fiction* 29 (Winter 1988): 77–94.

44 According to Jane Flax (*Thinking Fragments*, 210), postmodernism is as culpable as other previous literary trends of "the absence of any serious considerations of feminist discourses or of gender relations": "None of the metaphors for the postmodern (writing, the sublime, conversation, or aesthetic practices) seems congruent with the concerns of feminist discourses or practices."

45 See Nancy Fraser and Linda J. Nicholson, "Social Criticism Without Philosophy: An Encounter Between Feminism and Postmodernism," in *Feminism/Postmodernism*, ed. Nicholson (London: Routledge, 1990), 27.

46 Bonnie Zimmerman, "Feminist Fiction and the Postmodern Challenge," in *Postmodern Fiction. A Bio-bibliographical Guide*, ed. McCaffery, 177.

47 Nicholson, Introduction to *Feminism/Postmodernism*, ed. Nicholson, 6.

48 Marge Piercy, *Small Changes* (New York: Fawcett Crest, 1972), 267.

49 Elspeth Probyn, "Travels in the Postmodern: Making Sense of the Local," in *Feminism/Postmodernism*, ed. Nicholson, 182.

50 Deborah E. McDowell, " 'The Self and the Other': Reading Toni Morrison's *Sula* and the Black Female Text," in *Critical Essays on Toni Morrison*, ed. Nellie Y. McKay (Boston: G. K. Hall, 1988), 84–85. Robert Grant ("Absence into Presence: The Thematics of Memory and 'Missing' Subjects in Toni Morrison's *Sula*," in *Critical Essays on Toni Morrison*, ed. Grant, 90–102) also regards this novel as "anomalous" in relation to the traditions of black fiction, focusing "less on conventionally defined 'protest' than on a depiction of the black experience"—but an experience that is at once "rebellious" and "*anti*traditional . . . disputing the communalistic, socio-centric claims and 'verities' of much African-American literature."

51 Sandi Russell, "It's OK to Say OK," interview with Toni Morrison, *Women's Review*, March 5, 1986, 22–24; reprinted in *Critical Essays on Toni Morrison*, ed. McKay, 45, 46.

52 Rosemarie K. Lester, "An Interview with Toni Morrison," in *Critical Essays on Toni Morrison*, ed. McKay, 49.

53 Toni Morrison, *Sula* (New York: Knopf, 1973; New American Library/A Plume Book, 1987), 119.

54 Morrison, *Sula*, 55.

55 Morrison, *Sula*, 55, 58–59, 61, 170.

56 Cynthia Merrill persuasively argues this point in " 'Two Throats and One Eye': Visual and Narrative Dynamics in Toni Morrison's *Sula*" (Paper presented at the International Conference on Narrative, New Orleans, April 5–7, 1990; cited by permission).

57 Elizabeth J. Ordóñez similarly argues that *Sula* revisits/revises "a heretofore buried or subversively oral matrilineal tradition, either through inversion or compensation —of alternate mythical and even historical accounts of women: *Sula*'s Eva implicitly recalls her biblical foremother, then shifts our perspective away from the authority of the biblical text toward matrilineal autonomy and bonding"; see "Narrative Texts by Ethnic Women: Rereading the Past, Reshaping the Future," *Multi-Ethnic Literature of the United States* 9 (1982): 17, 19.

58 Morrison, *Sula*, 95.

59 As Karla F. C. Holloway notes, "Morrison has shown us the incredible potential invested in creative power by noting that the extreme of creativity is destruction. Eva

Peace is as much a part of her two children's death in *Sula* as she has been part of their living"; Holloway and Stephanie A. Demetrakopoulos, *New Dimensions of Spirituality: A Biracial and Bicultural Reading of the Novels of Toni Morrison* (Westport, Conn.: Greenwood Press, 1987), 24, 59.

60 Hortense Spillers, "A Hateful Passion, a Lost Love," in *Feminist Issues in Literary Scholarship*, ed. Shari Benstock (Bloomington: Indiana University Press, 1987), 184.

61 Sukenick, *In Form*, 67.

62 Sukenick, *In Form*, 39.

63 Sukenick, *In Form*, 243.

64 Ronald Sukenick, *The Endless Short Story* (New York: Fiction Collective, 1986), 47.

65 Sukenick, *In Form*, 78–80.

66 Sukenick, *Endless Short Story*, 7.

67 Ronald Sukenick, "Autogyro: My Life in Fiction," in *Contemporary Authors Autobiography Series*, 1.8, ed. Mark Zaderzny (Detroit: Gale Research, 1989) 8:294.

68 Ronald Sukenick, *Long Talking Bad Conditions Blues* (New York: Fiction Collective, 1979), 5, 6.

69 Ronald Sukenick, *Up* (New York: Dial Press, 1968), 217.

70 Sukenick, *In Form*, 72.

71 Sukenick, *In Form*, 31.

72 For an analysis of Sukenick's treatment of narrative mimesis as an "art of rape," see my article "Postmodernism beyond Self-Reflection: Radical Mimesis in Recent Fiction," 144–48.

73 Ronald Sukenick, *98.6* (New York: Fiction Collective, 1975), 75.

74 Sukenick, *98.6*, 187–88.

75 Sukenick, *98.6*, 122.

76 Sukenick, *In Form*, 14; *98.6*, 180.

77 Ronald Sukenick, *Blown Away* (Los Angeles: Sun and Moon Press, 1986), 20–21.

78 Sukenick, *Blown Away*, 114.

79 Seyla Benhabib, "Epistemologies of Postmodernism: A Rejoinder to Jean-François Lyotard," in *Feminism/Postmodernism*, ed. Nicholson, 125.

Carol Siegel

From Pact with the Devil to Masochist's Contract:

Dangerous Liaisons's Translation of the Erotics of Evil

Stirring up a flurry of poststructuralist questions about authorship and identity, John Malkovich purrs to Glenn Close, "I often wonder how you managed to invent yourself." And she, her magnificent head lifted proudly, replies, "I had no choice, did I? I'm a woman. . . . And I've succeeded because I've always known I was born to dominate your sex and avenge my own." Many associations place this scene from the film *Dangerous Liaisons* in the late 1980s. The characterizations seem to have grown naturally out of the actors' previous roles, especially Malkovich's as woman's subordinate dream man in *Making Mr. Right* (1987) and *Places in the Heart* (1984), and Close's as man's vengeful nightmare woman in *Fatal Attraction* (1987) and *The World According to Garp* (1982). Their pairing has the trendy topic of female-dominant sadomasochism written into it. The director, Stephen Frears, seems to have reached this theme through a natural progression from the defeat of male brutality by the feminine in *The Hit* (1984) and the aggressive male's guilty submission to a feminized partner in *My Beautiful Laundrette* (1985) and *Prick Up Your Ears* (1987), to the son's rejection of the bloodstained patriarch in favor of bitchy, capricious woman in *Sammy and Rosie Get Laid* (1987). Only the film's technical conservatism works against the sense that it could not have been made any earlier than it was. Yet it *is* a translation, not only from another language but from another time.

   If ever a film compelled its educated viewers to think about problems of translation, *Dangerous Liaisons* does. Since Choderlos de Laclos published *Les Liaisons dangereuses* in 1782, the story has undergone numerous retellings, the best known of which are probably Richard Aldington's translation of the novel into English; Roger Vadim's fluffy, jazzy *Les Liaisons dangereuses 1960;* Christopher Hampton's play, which was further adapted to make Frears's film; and Milos Forman's much less commercially and artistically successful film, *Valmont.* This most recent translation is successful not simply in terms of the film's popularity but, more important, in terms of its preservation of the novel's peculiar tone and energy, which seem to emanate from an erotics of evil.

Not all the sexual misbehavior in the novel can be understood in this way. *Les Liaisons dangereuses* often indulges in what seems to be merely a sophisticated naughtiness, as when the Marquise de Merteuil describes the "adventure with Prévan."[1] But the most powerfully charged erotic exchanges, those that make us understand Baudelaire's fascination with the novel, occur within its central games: the Vicomte de Valmont's seduction of Cécile de Volanges and the Présidente de Tourvel and the marquise's manipulation of Valmont. It is also here that the most formidable problem of translation appears because concepts of attractive sexual evil have changed considerably since the eighteenth century. Consequently, my discussion of the erotics of the film must begin with some attention to the erotics of its source.

Both film and novel concern themselves with sadism and masochism, but very differently, in ways that seem determined by era and medium. When Laclos wrote his novel, masochism had not yet been given a name, nor had the masochist been created in the Foucauldian sense, by the intersection of the discourses of Leopold von Sacher-Masoch, Richard von Krafft-Ebing, Havelock Ellis, and Sigmund Freud. Positions we now associate with masochism are assumed as disguises by Valmont, who obviously sees them simply as signifiers of romantic love. The perversity of the pleasure he takes in his comically exaggerated charade of self-abasement is suggested by Merteuil's contemptuous remark that in his letters, as in poorly written novels, "the author lashes his sides to warm himself up, and the reader remains cold" (79.33). The novel predetermines this alienated response to Valmont's letters by continually exposing his falseness and apparent emotional confusion. Since we have no way of distinguishing between what Valmont feels and what he pretends to feel, reader identification is precluded.

The novel's main source of erotic energy comes not from its masochism but from a sadism that closely follows Sade's in spirit, if not in practice, in that it is constituted largely in response to orthodox religious ideology. In 1782, sadism, too, was still nameless, but Sade was Laclos's contemporary, and if the two authors do not define themselves similarly in relation to theology, their cruelest protagonists do. In such texts as Sade's *Justine* and *Juliette,* God appears as a representation of the father in his most irrationally punitive aspect, not as superego but as destroyer, paradoxically authorizing opposition by smiting whoever upholds his laws. Thus, violent erotic impulses are freed from restraint not because their expression is not clearly prohibited but because such expression seems to allow man to appropriate divine power. In short, sadism is defined, by Sade, in deliberately blasphemous terms, as the ultimate male maturity and empowerment. *Les Liaisons dangereuses* engages with religion somewhat more conventionally. At the conclusion, vice receives a perfunctory punishment, and the dull, good Mme. de Rosemonde holds all the cards (and letters). Still, the dramas enacted in the vast majority of the letters are presented as deliberate campaigns against Heaven.

Merteuil means her manipulation of Cécile and Danceny to demonstrate, among other things, the worthlessness of the former's cloistered education and the latter's religious vows. When Merteuil's plot culminates in both young people hollowly professing religious vocation, as their last resort in a world in which they are too weak and foolish to survive otherwise, Merteuil has succeeded even beyond her intention in exposing the inapplicability of the doctrine of her time to heroic souls like herself.

Valmont's sacrilegious intentions seem, on the surface, more ambitious. Merteuil seeks to evade religious law, while Valmont would rewrite it. Like Satan, he sets out to rival God. In his eyes, Tourvel's religious faith is her greatest charm because of his desire to become "the God she has preferred" (34.6). Of her prayers, he boasts, "What God did she dare to invoke? . . . [I]t is I who control her fate" (64.23). In his efforts to redirect Tourvel's prayers to himself, Valmont even employs a priest, Father Anselme. It is finally Merteuil, however, who usurps the prerogatives of the divinity. First, she causes Tourvel, the apostate angel, to be cast out of her unlawful heaven of love. It seems worth noting that in the model letter Merteuil writes to structure Valmont's rejection of Tourvel, she is addressed consistently as "my angel" (325.141). Then, Merteuil demotes Valmont from devil to dupe and shows him that death is the price he has paid for his Faustian moment of omnipotence.

We might see Merteuil intertextually as the satanic figure of the traditional pact-with-the-devil tale, whose power is exercised only to reaffirm

God's, or, in Freudian terms, as the phallic mother in the masochist's fantasy whose cruelty is always implicitly in the service of a phallocentric concept of gender difference.[2] While she states her sadistic credo in anti-male language, Merteuil's sadistic desires are realized exclusively through masculine sexuality, and her power comes from its existence. She uses men like surrogate penises to sexually torture her enemies. In all her fierce resistance to male and divine power, she affirms both and suggests their oppositional interdependence. The attractiveness of the character depends on her figuration of male power as satanic. She mirrors man back to himself as a sexy devil.

Through the characters' role reversals, the erotics of the novel tease their era's sexual and religious ideologies, but these reversals do not deconstruct the patriarchal ideology that prescribes dominant-submissive gender roles as ordained by God. In fact, since a large part of the novel's surprising humor comes from Merteuil's and Valmont's mistake in believing that they can reverse the religious, social, and familial hierarchies on which cultural concepts of identity depend, it is doubtful that we are seeing any moments at all of what Barbara Babcock calls "symbolic inversion and cultural inversion."[3] While we may admire Merteuil's and Valmont's attempts to subvert a code that defines desire as weakness and sin, we may also find comic the abundant evidence that they have internalized that code. However, it is one thing for us, as readers, to enjoy the dual pleasures of identification with rebellion and detachment from its doomed excesses while both are safely contained within a novelistic "world" that is historicized for us by references to contemporary events and allusions to contemporary literature. Such a world is always elsewhere. It is another thing entirely for us, as audience, to smile at sadistic games played out by actors who are our contemporaries on a screen in front of us where images continually intrude from films set in eras other than the one in which the story ostensibly takes place.

As a primarily visual medium, film generally presents images into which probable narratives are intertextually coded. Male (hetero)sexual cruelty appears in such images, always predicting the punishment on behalf of woman that will follow. The torture, murder, or rape of an attractive woman, usually by a sneering sadist, at the beginning of the "action" film is as much a convention as the car chase at the end. Cinematic representation of heterosexual male sadism in the 1980s has increasingly seemed to entail contextualization within feminist or pseudo-feminist sensationalist narratives, in which it functions as the catalyst for a woman's "consciousness raising" and results in drawn-out acts of revenge. Some films that exemplify this genre are *Extremities, Shame, The Accused,* and *Sleeping with the Enemy.*

Conversely, during the same decade, women's enactment of sadistic roles has been more often represented not only in the tradition of ridiculous reversal, as belonging to the comic mode, but also as a wholesome or at least sensible response to a difficult world, as in *Eating Raoul, After Hours, Woman in Flames, Something Wild, Personal Services,* and *Track 29.* Consequently, for the frequent moviegoer, the image of a dominatrix is likely to be associated with characters who invite identification, and the image of a male sadist is likely to be associated with past evocations of anger. In addition, the politically sophisticated audience, at which Frears seems to have aimed at least his last three films, has been conditioned by a great many art house favorites to associate period costuming and sets with a condemnatory treatment of now repudiated social mores, perhaps especially those governing gender roles and behavior. Such otherwise different films as *The Devils, The Return of Martin Guerre, My Brilliant Career, Maurice,* and *Beatrice* project into an exoticized past—shown to be markedly other than the world the audience inhabits—the conflict between the individual libido and exterior authority, which psychoanalysis posits as eternal and which ordinary observation tells us is ongoing. To recapture the disturbing eroticism of *Les Liaisons dangereuses,* Frears works both within and, subversively, against these conventions.

Milos Forman's *Valmont* avoids the problem of translating the novel's erotics into modern terms by dismissing the question of evil entirely. The first scenes prepare us for the old story of the revenge of a woman scorned as Merteuil (Annette Bening) is depicted as sincerely—and pathetically, given his wooden unattractiveness—in love with Gercourt (Jeffry Jones), who rejects her in favor of marriage to Cécile (Fairuza Balk). The exposition suggests that Merteuil has been reduced by men's betrayals to a cackling hysteric. The victim of Valmont's violence in two scenes and the passive recipient of his declaration of war, she bears little resemblance to his demonic mistress in the novel. But Valmont (Colin Firth) seems more shallow and lazy than bad. He seduces Tourvel (Meg Tilly) with a minimum of effort (and screen time) and only briefly entertains the idea of falling in love with her. The shift in narrative focus away from the Valmont-Merteuil-Tourvel triangle to the love affair of Cécile and Danceny (Henry Thomas) shifts the emphasis from sexual power to sexual weakness. The moral background of the novel, which throws into stark relief the cruelties of Valmont and Merteuil, vanishes here. No one is religious, society metes out no punishments, and, most surprisingly, Mme. de Rosemonde (Fabia Drake) is a lascivious bawd who smirks and winks as a pregnant Cécile marries Gercourt. The result of these changes is a substitution of mild titillation for disturbing eroticism. Like a *Playboy* "bawdy tale," Forman's film evades the difficulty of attempting to recover the emotional content of a past text by reducing it to the schematic simplicity of a colorful backdrop for the display of entwined naked bodies.

Admirers of Laclos's novel may see the characters in Frears's *Dangerous Liaisons* in something like the form of nesting Russian dolls, each shaped and painted by a text or an intersection of texts. The outermost dolls are composed by Frears's direction, Christopher Hampton's screenplay, and the actors' interpretation. More central dolls are made by Laclos's published text(s). But where can we find the last doll? In prior texts? In the antifeminist cinematic theater of cruelty where crimes against women are enacted as farce, or the cinema of normative retribution in which Black Widows and Lady Eves turn to women in flames? In the text of society itself? If we think—even for a moment—about the source of the gorgeously compelling figures passing before our eyes, we may find ourselves looking into the dizzying mystery of identity. And it is exactly this antiessentialist vertigo that Frears evokes in the first images of the construction of those actors on the social stage, Merteuil and Valmont. Consequently, the fetishization of Close/Merteuil in star images, such as her golden descent from a carriage in front of Rosemonde's chateau, is problematized. Like the invented self of the novel's letters, the film's Merteuil is a self-representation, her own gaze in the mirror having endowed her with significant power before ours can.

The film's Merteuil, however, does not robe herself in the same satanic guise as the novel's Merteuil. How could she when satanic sacrilege in films mostly means slitting chickens' throats and wearing bright yellow contact lenses? Almost from the beginning, blasphemy and satanism in film have been relegated to the horror genre, where they function not to shock religious sensibilities but as motivational devices. In *Dangerous Liaisons,* the religious subtext almost disappears; Danceny is no longer a Knight of Malta, and neither he nor Cécile dedicates a life to the church. Tourvel's faith, which in the novel defines her seduction as blasphemy, appears in the film only visually and in highly compromised forms. We see her taking communion, but with her attention on Valmont, as is underscored by the camera's shift to her perspective just as the wafer dissolves in her sensuous mouth, and, later, giving him amorous glances during Mass. Her lack of appropriate religious response is emphasized by the auditorially confusing rapidity of the transition from Valmont's promising Cécile an obscene Latin lesson to the priest's disregarded droning. Even more suggestive of hypocrisy, before Tourvel's seduction she always wears dresses with transparent panels imperfectly closed over the tops of her breasts and a cross conspicuously gleaming at the beginning of her cleavage. Under these circumstances it would be comic for Valmont to aspire to replace God in her affections, and indeed, the scene in which he explains his intentions to Merteuil revises the original text to translate both his character and Merteuil's to accord with late twentieth-century concepts of sexy evil.

A series of cuts, from Cécile in the cloister to Merteuil describing her as "a rosebud" and Valmont protesting "she'd be on her back before you'd unwrapped the first bunch of flowers," to Tourvel picking roses in the Rosemonde garden, visually and verbally establishes the connection between flowers and sweet, pure women in their feminine seclusions as one that facilitates their commodification. In contrast, Merteuil appears unconsumable. A bow on her gown has risen up to conceal her breasts. The camera, like Valmont, leans toward her face, and her expression is cryptic and smug. Everything about her speaks self-containment. When Valmont tells her that he wants "the excitement of watching [Tourvel] betray" her own values, remarking, "Surely you understand that. I thought *betrayal* was your favorite word," she replies, "No, no, *cruelty*: I always think that has a nobler ring to it." This exchange, not in the novel, offers an interpretation of Merteuil's character: she is a sadist. But it also anticipates the much later revelation, which *is* in the novel, that Valmont is Merteuil's real quarry. For how can a rose betray itself or be abused? Cécile and Tourvel have been introduced as already objectified and appropriated. The viewer can be expected to understand this because films generally treat the sexual seduction of pretty women as inconsequential or comic, as if always already accomplished. Valmont, however, clearly does not understand that his plot is meaningless because he is distracted by the erotic value of Merteuil's self-revelation. At her words, his face is suffused with adoration, and for the rest of their scene he concerns himself with nothing but his desire for her. For the viewer, the film's plot is thus given meaning by Valmont's intensely dramatized masochism.

What follows, within the same scene, is an amazingly condensed version of the offering and acceptance of the contract between Merteuil and Valmont, which in the novel is not completed until letter 57. In the novel, as Peggy Kamuf points out, Valmont misreads Merteuil's dual intentions in offering the contract. She means both to set a limit to his affair with Tourvel and to defer forever his possession of herself, since her "project" is always to possess men "outside of an exchange in the public or symbolic register," which would define her as defeated.[4] The film suggests that he misreads the contract because of his preoccupation with his erotic subjection to Merteuil. It is through the circumstances of this misreading that Valmont is translated from an eighteenth-century sadist into a modern masochist.

As Gilles Deleuze shows in his discussion of Sacher-Masoch's *Venus in Furs,* the contract is an intrinsic element of masochism, as constituted by nineteenth-century erotic discourse. Valmont seems to understand his contract much as Deleuze understands Sacher-Masoch's—as a means of implying "not only the necessity of the victim's consent, but his ability to persuade, and his pedagogical and judicial efforts to train his torturer."[5] The contract creates the illusion that the man serves the woman, who now embodies law, while actually it exists only to authorize his desires. We see Valmont enjoying the complex irony of indulging himself by command, when, appearing to be melting with love, he rolls Tourvel on top of him in bed and startlingly asks, "When will you start writing to me again?" He does so again when, in an ecstasy of erotic misery, he beats and insults her, claiming to do so at the insistence of "a woman I adore." The Aldington translation correctly renders the "refrain" of this renunciation scene, "Ce n'est pas ma faute," as "it is not my fault" (325.141). The novel defines his cruelty in terms of morality. The irony comes from the reader's understanding that, as Merteuil insists, Valmont's sadism is the fatal fault that makes it impossible for him to be genuinely either "a woman's lover or her friend, but always her tyrant or her slave" (324.141). In the film, however, the words he reiterates are, "It's beyond my control." This reference to the contract suggests ironies, some obvious within the narrative, others playing on the social context of its translation.

The most obvious irony is that, at least superficially, Valmont has exercised far more control than he acknowledges. In the novel, Merteuil insists (in a renegotiation of the contract) on the "sacrifice" of Tourvel and provides Valmont with a model rejection letter, which he "simply" copies and sends (326.142). In the film, Valmont deliberately tempts Merteuil "to impose some new condition," and when she obliges, he invents the vicious wording of the rejection himself. Other readily apparent but contradictory ironies involve his belief that he can control his emotions, Merteuil, and their game. Bill Overton points out that the phrase —"It's beyond my control"—"also refers to what Valmont can recognize only later, that in betraying Tourvel he has surrendered control to Merteuil."[6] What seem to me to be the film's most interesting ironies, however, are generated not by Valmont's misunderstandings but by the confrontation that the film stages between different visions of sexual evil. These visions are historically determined.

E. Ann Kaplan asserts that "psychoanalysis and cinema are inextricably linked both to each other and to capitalism, because both are products of a particular stage of capitalist society."[7] In this sense, *Dangerous Liaisons* is self-referential. Like the novel, in which Merteuil repeatedly compares herself to an author or playwright, the film defines her as a director, most explicitly in her use of theatrical performances as backgrounds for manipulations of the other characters. The opening and concluding images of her creating herself as both the object of the gaze and its source seem constructed to subvert the usual relationship of female film characters to director and audience. Consequently, the film's knowing treatment of psychoanalytic and Marxist theories is presented as if from within Merteuil's consciousness. This is made obvious when, seeming to speak from outside the character and historical setting, Merteuil gives a conventional modern interpretation of Valmont's obsession with sexual pursuit, calling it "immaturity." The film's construction of masochism is informed by psychoanalysis. That Valmont's attraction to Merteuil comes from an unresolved Oedipus complex is suggested by his obsessive rivalry with the childlike Danceny and his reference to sex with Merteuil as "coming home." The film's insistent visual association of mirrors with Merteuil suggests her role as narcissistic mother, and it also suggests, because Valmont is seen receiving only fragmented images of himself in her realm, her blockage of his individuation. However, the film's representation of masochism owes much more to sociology than to psychoanalysis. We are shown symbolic practices and objects that continually return us to questions about objectification and commodification, questions about masochism's relation to capitalism that seem related to Merteuil's enormously attractive resistance to being consumed.

Throughout the film, flesh means vulnerability to commodification. First, the nakedness of Tourvel's maid, Julie, allows Valmont to buy her. Then, Emilie's nakedness is the sign of her prostitution and objectifica-

tion, as Valmont names her his "desk." This scene and a later one in which
Cécile takes dictation on Valmont's bare back are equally tainted with
implications of masochistic subjection, both because they comically reify
cultural inscription on the body as sex play and because they suggest the
physical marking so important to sadomasochistic ritual. The early, ob-
jectifying images we have of Cécile and Tourvel also suggest their status
as victims within a sadomasochistic drama. Cécile appears behind bars
in the Gothic setting of the convent; Tourvel bends across a cane.

If the bodies of other characters become signifiers of their enslave-
ment, Merteuil's provides a space for the display of fetishes of her dominance. When she arrives to instruct Cécile in the harsh facts of sex
her black leather gloves stand out with almost surreal intensity against
her gold traveling suit. When Valmont, trying the same trick he used
on Julie, surprises Merteuil in bed with Danceny, they are both neatly
clothed, as if to emphasize the protection that she extends even beyond
the boundaries of her person. But, through this usage, Merteuil's body
also becomes the site of a powerful validation of capitalism. She buys
her own physical integrity in the form of objects that cover the body and
onto which its incipient objectification is displaced.

Dangerous Liaisons is by no means unique in linking sadism and consumerism. Beyond the obvious fact that both can more easily be indulged
in by the affluent, sadism has an intrinsic affinity with purchasing goods.
The ritual sadomasochistic drama offers what may be the most "commercial form of sex," as Barbara Ehrenreich, Elizabeth Hess, and Gloria
Jacobs observe, because its enactment depends on the use of costumes
and equipment that are not generally available free and also because its
articulation as fantasy "contains its own narrative" and so lends itself
particularly well to commercial publication.[8] As fiction and metafiction,
as telling and as selling, as highly appealing, commercial envisioning
of sadomasochistic drama, and as a self-referential commentary on its
own erotics, *Dangerous Liaisons* shows us that "from a strictly capitalis-
tic viewpoint, [sadomasochism] is the ideal sexual practice."[9]

However, the film also makes us aware that, as Deleuze claims, sadomasochism is a misleading term, for in the novels of Masoch and Sade
neither the sadist nor the masochist desires or could even survive intact
an encounter with another subject.[10] It is through a complexly ritualized
objectification of the object of desire that each hopes to obtain subject-
hood. Walter Benn Michaels argues that all masochists' contracts express
a capitalist desire for ownership; the masochist "wants to own the right

to sell himself."[11] By the end of the film, Valmont twice conflates offering documents to support his upholding of the contract with offering up himself, once when he brings Tourvel's letter to Merteuil's bedroom, and again when, having impaled himself on Danceny's sword, he gives the youth his confession and Merteuil's letters. Merteuil miraculously seems to own herself without having to sell herself because she successfully presents a disguise to the world as self. Fools like Belleroche and Danceny who fall into love with her mask of kindness are given a costume to make love to. Valmont falls in love with her cruelty, but her sadomasochism is a closed system. She sticks a fork into her hand under the table and smiles. There is no place for Valmont within her system. So she denies the contract that would authorize the fulfillment of his desires and paradoxically, through his subjugation, create him as a subject. Where he wants affirmation of his right to own under the law, she exposes law as a fiction to contain desire and laughs at the very idea. Within a capitalist system, what could be more nefarious?

Perhaps to liberal audiences Merteuil's greatest evil is in rejecting the erotics of political correctness characteristic of the last two decades. Like an exemplary feminist, she attacks the "rose world" where, according to Rosemonde's doctrine of sexual relations, male desire is always primary: "Men enjoy the happiness they feel; we can only enjoy the happiness we give." Like the heroines of classic Hollywood comedy as Naomi Scheman persuasively describes them,[12] Cécile and Tourvel are good Freudian daughters whose desire exists only in response to a man's. In a late 1980s film by a director known for his critiques of gender politics, their downfall must have a didactic overtone. After Merteuil accelerates their romances to their inevitably tragic conclusions, however, she then rejects the properly modern substitute for traditional romance: monogamous, egalitarian love. In its place she demands unequal relations with a weaker, subservient partner. And unlike the Joe Orton character, who chooses similarly in *Prick Up Your Ears,* or her own literary model, Merteuil eliminates her self-proclaimed mate, refuses to be limited even by her own writing of herself, and returns to the mirror to create herself anew. The final image urges us to see her not as she has invented herself previously, but as she sees herself now.

Through Merteuil's and Valmont's sexual transgressions, both the novel and the film eroticize resistance to the moral discourses that empower society. Both locate that resistance within a contract. However, while *Les Liaisons dangereuses* finds the contract itself excitingly evil, the greatest charge of excitement in *Dangerous Liaisons* comes from the violation of the contract. Around this central and profound difference in erotics, what often seems to be a faithful translation is built; and despite its many departures and changes from the original text, the translation is faithful: like its original, the film allows us the subversive pleasure of a thorough enjoyment of what our society calls evil and what, in all rationality, we hardly know how to call otherwise.

Notes

1   Choderlos de Laclos, *Les Liaisons dangereuses,* trans. Richard Aldington (New York: Signet/New American Library, 1981), 642.113. References are to page number and letter number. All subsequent citations are to this edition, unless otherwise noted.

2   Parveen Adams, "Of Female Bondage," in *Between Feminism and Psychoanalysis,* ed. Teresa Brennan (New York: Routledge, 1989), 260–61.

3   Barbara Babcock, *The Reversible World: Symbolic Inversion in Art and Society* (Ithaca: Cornell University Press, 1978), 14.

4   Peggy Kamuf, *Fictions of Feminine Desire: Disclosures of Heloise* (Lincoln: University of Nebraska Press, 1982), 135–36.

5   Gilles Deleuze, *Masochism: An Interpretation of Coldness and Cruelty,* trans. Jean McNeil (New York: Braziller, 1971), 66–67.

6   Bill Overton, "The Play of Letters: *Les Liaisons dangereuses* on the Stage," *Theatre Research International* 13 (Autumn 1988): 269.

7   E. Ann Kaplan, "Is the Gaze Male?" in *Powers of Desire: The Politics of Sexuality,* ed. Ann Snitow, Christine Stansell, and Sharon Thompson (New York: Monthly Review Press, 1983), 315.

8   Barbara Ehrenreich, Elizabeth Hess, and Gloria Jacobs, *Re-Making Love: The Feminization of Sex* (New York: Anchor-Doubleday, 1986), 123.

9   Ehrenreich, Hess, and Jacobs, *Re-Making Love,* 124.

10   Deleuze, *Masochism,* 36–39.

11   Walter Benn Michaels, *The Gold Standard and the Logic of Naturalism: American Literature at the Turn of the Century* (Berkeley: University of California Press, 1987), 133.

12   Naomi Scheman, "Missing Mothers/Desiring Daughters: Framing the Sight of Women," *Critical Inquiry* 15 (Autumn 1988): 70.

Vera Mark

Cultural Pastiches: Intertextualities in the

Moncrabeau Liars' Festival Narratives

Modernity enters into a cyclical process of change, where all the forms of the past (archaic, folkloric, rustic, traditional) are dredged up, drained of their substance, but idealized as signs in a code where tradition and *neo,* ancient and modern, become equivalent and function as alternates. Modernity no longer has the value of rupture at all: it nourishes itself on the vestiges of all cultures in the same way that it does from its technical gadgets or from the ambiguity of all values.—Jean Baudrillard, "Modernity"

Baudrillard's conception of modernity frames this discussion of a "traditional" folkloric event, the Moncrabeau Liars' Festival of southwestern France. Like the idea of rural community, the Liars' Festival is predominantly residual as it presents a fantasy and an escape from modern urban life during prime French vacation time.[1] The Liars' Festival draws upon identification with previous cultural forms such as the village fête and its accompanying patterns of sociability, and upon earlier genres such as tall tales, lies, and ethnic *blasons populaires,* even as it is grounded in a fragmented present. This identification with a "past" of the archaic, the folkloric, the rustic, and the traditional occurs both at the level of the staging of the fête and in the content of the narratives performed in the liars' competition. The particular representations of the contemporary worlds of advertising, television, and cinema, and of rewritten History found in the narratives, make the Moncrabeau Liars' Festival a specifically postmodern celebration.[2]

The festival is held on the first Sunday in August in Moncrabeau, a village of nine hundred people in the Lot-et-Garonne department of southwestern France. The celebration begins in the morning with folk-dances performed by a local, mostly female group and a display of local food and craft products. After a noon buffet of regional foods, the festival continues in the afternoon liars' competition and ends in an evening dance on the village square.[3] The liars' competition typically involves fifteen to twenty participants, mostly men, from surrounding towns and villages. They compete to tell the "saltiest" and/or biggest lie before a largely adult audience of local residents and vacationing tourists.[4] The winner is crowned king or queen of the liars and holds this title for a year before passing it on to a successor the following August. In 1984 and 1987 several women participated in this male-dominated event, and a woman first won the title in 1979.[5]

The saltiness of the tales ties in with their potential for excess in the obscene and the scatological. These qualities are ethnically marked with respect to the Gascons as famous liars, and with respect to the village and festival totem, a goat, an animal associated with excessive sexuality in many folk narrative traditions. The requirement to tell a salty tale leads many, both men and women, to focus on the consequences of excessive human or animal sexuality in their recitations.

The fête, which has historical roots in the nineteenth and perhaps even the eighteenth centuries, was revived in the early 1970s, a time when a number of fêtes were revived or reactivated in rural France. Although many were based in earlier celebrations such as village patron saints' days, their reemergence was a consequence of the political decentralization and regionalist movements of the late 1960s in France. Pride in local and ethnic identity is a central theme in these fêtes. At the Moncrabeau Liars' Festival, the food stands full of local foie gras, wines, and *pastis gascon,* a regional apple tart, reinforce an initial impression of the event as a celebration of local Gascon culture. Such an impression is paralleled textually by certain narratives that give accounts of the Gascons' superiority over other groups. The importance of the local is further underscored when the members of a Belgian delegation from a corresponding liars' festival in Namur, who attend the festival every four years, attempt to incorporate themselves into Gascon culture. One strategy favored by these "outside" narrators is to propose that the origin of a Gascon food item is in fact Belgian. In this way the inhabitants of a country that adjoins France are incorporated into textual space. The subject matter of other narratives concerns relations between local Gascons and various groups such as the North Africans and East Asians, whose status has figured prominently in the French political scene in recent years, although the narratives reveal different images in the aggressive and violent terms that typify ethnic joking.[6]

Finally, another series of narratives focuses on the transformations brought about by the new technologies associated with agriculture, which continues to form the basis of the region's economy. These technologies range from artificial insemination to techniques to improve the size of goose liver or increase crop production. As the narratives reflect demographic changes that transform the image of the region's Gascon identity and technologies that are altering its rural economy and earlier orally based culture, the Moncrabeau Liars' Festival is more than a mere celebration of tradition; it is deeply concerned with the consequences of modernity.

Indeed, other genres of folk and popular literatures reveal a concern with the consequences of modernity. This is the case in the folktales that appeared in the Gascon language almanacs published between the late nineteenth and early twentieth centuries in southwestern France.[7] Thus, during the interwar period of the 1920s, concerns focused on the linguistic consequences of passing from Gascon, the regional language, to French, the national language; on the cultural and economic consequences of peasants leaving the land for nearby towns and cities to form a new working class; and on the conflicts between traditional folk remedies and modern medicine in resolving health problems. In these earlier narratives, the destruction of customs and traditional culture that accompanies the continual progress of science and technology is ever present. However, the narratives of the Moncrabeau Liars' Festival are not merely a 1990s version of the conflicts between tradition and modernity that have systematically appeared at critical points throughout history.[8]

To use the terms of Fredric Jameson and Margaret A. Rose, the narratives form a postmodern series of cultural pastiches. *Pastiche* has several meanings. A general definition given in dictionaries and glossaries of literary terms refers to the copy of an original and to the imitation of a particular artist, composer, or author, past or present. Jameson's writings on postmodernism have focused on the effects of pastiche in the contemporary postindustrial capitalist world dominated by mass media. In this case, pastiche includes a mixture of styles, or a pluralism, that opens up former divisions between expressive culture according to social class.[9]

In the context of the Moncrabeau Liars' Festival, this mixture of styles sees the juxtaposition of ethnic groups from France with groups from the rest of Europe and more distant places, as well as the interweaving of elements from folk and popular culture, and mass and elite culture.

Pastiche necessarily involves a turn toward the past in its borrowing of earlier forms, which, however, are decontextualized and thus can be seen only in the present. In the case at hand, this involves drawing upon an older folkloric genre such as the tall tale, upon the idea of the village fête in a nostalgia for things lost, and upon History. The focus on the tall tale evokes a past in which orality and storytelling were central features of rural life. The velvet costumes of the Moncrabeau Liars' Club jurors, vaguely Renaissance in style, contrast with the styrofoam hats sold as souvenirs to the audience. The hats evoke music hall and cabaret entertainers of the 1930s. The use of historical names such as Joan of Arc, Charles VII, and various Habsburgs serves to focus the audience's attention on the knowledge of the narrator, although this "knowledge" usually subverts conventional images. Finally, central to pastiche is an intertextuality of expressive forms, which refers to other texts and to previous versions, such that both become constitutive and essential parts of the narratives' structure. Multiple encodings of postmodern texts result in certain ambiguities.[10] In the case of the Moncrabeau narratives, ambiguities are grounded in verbal puns, whose emphasis on the sexual and the scatological situates the listeners in the Bakhtinian laughter of the carnival but at the same time encodes messages of gender and racial domination.

The following discussion considers four narratives from the 1984 and 1987 festivals, where a total of thirty stories were told. One of the narratives won its teller the title of king in 1987; the other three were ranked highly by the judges and the audience. The success of the narratives is due, I will argue, to their postmodern character.

In the postmodern world of consumerism, advertising invades the street, the scene, and the festival.[11] The Moncrabeau recitations reflect earlier generic forms in their emphasis on the etiological as they explain the ethnic-historic "origin" of items ranging from the festival itself to Joan of Arc to, of course, goose livers.[12] After having established the origins of these items, the narratives proceed to detail their appropriation and/or commercialization by ethnic outsiders. Food products—regional comestibles of *magret de canard* (duck breast) or foie gras (fatted goose or duck liver), or, at the national and international levels, Dannon yogurt—remain popular subjects. Since advertising is a paradigmatic form of mass culture shared across national boundaries,[13] it functions as a common point of reference to unite a diverse audience. In the case of Moncrabeau, the audience consists not only of local inhabitants but also of tourists from northern Europe, Belgium, and Holland and the occasional anthropologist. Thus a significant aspect of the narratives' entertainment value derives from the audience's ability to decode speakers' complex references to advertising and the media.

Yet, if the advertising world appears frequently in the narratives, it is taboo in the performers' self-representations. At the conclusion of the 1987 fête, in which I participated, two of my male competitors criticized me for unjustly using the Liars' Festival stage to promote the restaurant that I had described in my recitation. I explained that in truth I did not run a restaurant at all—this had merely been part of my lie. One of my critics, who was crowned king that year, is the manager of a very successful paint company. However, he was careful never to reveal this identity during the fête. The apparent contradiction between framing the narratives through advertising while refraining from framing oneself in this fashion emerges from the dominant function of the fête. To adopt Mukařovský's terminology, the fête's dominant function is perceived as aesthetic and ludic.[14] To sell oneself or one's product would make the festival stage too much like real life, in which one pays for the publicity that helps to sell a product.

A Russian Wet Nurse Produces Dannon Yogurt after Dancing the Viennese Waltz

In the Liars' Festival narratives the world of advertising merges with representation. The crisis in representation, announced by marginal or repressed discourses, including feminism, finds expression in the representation of difference and otherness within mass culture, for which the main vehicle is woman and/or people of color.[15] Thus a narrative from the 1984 festival reveals that French Dannon yogurt originated in the breast milk of a young Russian wet nurse as she danced the waltz one evening at the nineteenth-century Habsburg court in Vienna. This practice was taken up by the other Austrian court ladies. At a critical point in the process their husbands could no longer dance with them, and the ladies had to turn elsewhere for partners to finish the job. The courtiers did "what the French do when need arises . . . turn to immigrant workers." The call was sent out to a group of Bulgarian dancers, who waltzed backward, resulting in a slightly different product, aptly named "yogurt with a Bulgarian taste" (a play on the actual French *yaourt bulghare,* yogurt made from a rich base of whole milk). The audience held its breath as the narrator announced the need to turn to immigrant workers' labor, but it visibly relaxed and laughed when he mentioned their nationality as Bulgarian rather than Algerian, Moroccan, Senegalese, or some other non-European population, about whose real presence there is considerable xenophobia in contemporary French society.

The reference to advertising is clear when the narrator goes on to explain that the person who discovered how to produce this Dannon yogurt on a large scale was a certain Swiss gentleman, Mr. Gervais de Chambourcy.[16] His yogurt maker was a yoke with wicker baskets that hung from the ladies' shoulders as they danced the waltz. This same gentleman was the great-grandfather of Mamie Nova, a dignified matron in a current television ad who dutifully serves dairy products of the same name, such as yogurts, custards, and puddings, to her grandchildren for their four o'clock after-school snack. The narrator adds that this Mamie, or Grandma Nova, dropped Grandpa Brossard—a kindly figure who advertises a brand of cookies—to run away with Mr. Clean.[17]

In this narrative, immediate outsiders are incorporated into the textual space of the plot to help resolve the problem of how to produce yogurt on a commercial scale. The Russian wet nurse produces the breast milk that the Austrian court ladies and their Bulgarian partners transform into yogurt by waltzing, an upper-class leisure form. Woman's body is represented in a Bakhtinian image of sustenance and nurturing as the natural, breast milk, is made into the cultural in more ways than one. The tracing of European cultural genealogies of contemporary food products takes place against a backdrop of the recent past—the nineteenth century—and incorporates the older cultural practice whereby poor women hired themselves out to nurse rich women's babies, even as it refers to contemporary French economic relations, which depend on North African immigrant labor.

The Japanese Invade Moncrabeau and Buy up Its Foie Gras to Fight Their Constipation

In a narrative from the 1984 festival, the Japanese, a more distant Other, are the center of attention. A Belgian narrator from the Namur Liars'

Festival delegation explains how the Japanese invaded the village and bought every gram of its foie gras. According to the narrator, the Japanese desperately sought Moncrabeau foie gras after they discovered it could cure the constipation they had developed from eating their typical foodstuff, rice.[18] The Belgian contestant also noted that their constipation had caused their eyes to slant. Here the otherness of the Japanese is associated with their native food habits, which inscribe irregularities upon their bodies, both internally and externally. Only when the Japanese replace their rice with a Gascon-Belgian food can they become "normal": the constipation passes, their tightened eyes relax, and they become "Western" looking. The local makes the distant more familiar.

The depletion of local supplies of foie gras left the Moncrabelais in an economic crisis. The Belgian residents of Namur decided to help their Gascon friends in their hour of need. The Belgians proposed combining Namurois snails with foie gras to produce a sufficient supply of the highly sought product for the Japanese clients. The two groups— the residents of the Gascon village of Moncrabeau and the Molons (the members of a festive society in Namur, Belgium)—decided to produce this hybrid snail-liver food item on a commercial scale by setting up a food cooperative. The Japanese, who in recent years have begun to produce foie gras and consequently are seen as economic competitors by certain regional newspapers, will thus become unwitting consumers of a culinary hoax.

At present, many of the products that have made French cuisine famous no longer come from France, as Patricia Wells has shown. "That *foie gras* you rave about in Michelin-starred restaurants? There's a 75 per cent chance it came from Hungary, or Poland, or Israel. Those luscious *escargots?* Probably from Hungary. The frog's legs? From Yugoslavia. The *brochet* in your *quenelles?* Canada. The mustard grain in your Dijon mustard? From Kansas." The economic cooperation brought about through the Common Market indisputably raised living standards throughout western Europe. But the European Community's agricultural policy is leading to a steady, irreversible industrialization of farm practices.[19] At the same time it is leading to increased protectionism and cultural chauvinism about the distinctly French or regional origins of some foods.

In a critique of local economic practices, the narrator suggests that the village's major industry, tourism, be transformed into international cooperation and the industrial-scale production of food on a former site of leisure, the village campground. The potential threat of evil, evidenced in an invasion and alimentary appropriation, is controlled by the united front between southwestern France and southern Belgium, which turns the threat into economic profit. The French and Belgians maintain cultural and alimentary superiority when faced by an economically superior racial Other. This outcome brings to mind Fredric Jameson's discussion of the concept of good and evil within romance as a positional one that coincides with categories of Otherness. Other is evil constituted as alien, different, strange, unclean, and unfamiliar. Of course, as Jameson notes, the conflict between good and evil appears elsewhere—in the medieval *chanson de geste* from which the romance emerged and in the American western. The Liars' Festival narratives are also structured by this conflict. Finally, the juxtaposition within textual space of the near and the far—in this case, the Japanese versus the Belgians and the Gascons— corresponds to Jameson's concept of pastiche, which sees a mixture of many "styles" in the consumer culture of advanced capitalism.[20]

A Chinese Ancestor of the Reverend Moon Is the True Ancestor of Moncrabeau and Its Festival

The winning tale from the 1987 competition epitomizes the postmodern as it collapses performance and narrative frames and juxtaposes the representations of distant Others with traditional and mass cultures in a series of verbal puns. The ultimate origin myth, it purports to explain the origin of the village of Moncrabeau and of the Liars' Festival as Chinese rather than Gascon. A Chinese ancestor of the Reverend Moon (who in reality is Korean) left China in mythical times in order to study French cooking. The festival's emphasis on the sexual and scatological is evoked in the preamble when the male narrator explains that the inventor of *l'engrenage* (gear wheel) and *la tyrolienne* (the yodel) was a Chinese man. Due to his lack of knowledge in making the gear wheels function, this fellow got his testicles caught in the gears. His pained yell from the accident became a yodel. In a verbal pun that reinforces this image, the audience hears that the man got himself into a jam (in French, *être pris dans un engrenage* refers to a combination of circumstances that mutually reinforce each other), both literally and figuratively. The body and sexuality are aligned with a machine that makes the Chinese man impotent.

The narrator goes on to situate the tale in traditional cultural time. He notes that after having arrived in France, the hero, another Chinese man named Moon, did his culinary *tour de France* accompanied by several goats and the totem of the village. The *tour de France* refers to the traditional crafts system in which apprentice artisans journeyed or worked their way around the country along more or less fixed routes, knowing that they would find a welcome among colleagues of their craft wherever they found them.[21] But this expression may also refer to the annual bicycle race through France and neighboring countries that takes place every June and is avidly followed by Europeans at key *étape* points or on television; or, in the most general sense, *tour* may refer to a journey around the country. The story continues that after completing his trip around France, Moon ended up at the village that would eventually take his name. Having settled there, he put his goats out to graze in the nearby plains of mint grass. After eating this grass, the goats gave forth a delicious milk, which was made into mint milk cheese well before modern flavored cheeses became popular. The narrator refers here to soft, rich cheeses with special flavors such as *Boursin à l'ail et aux fines herbes* or *au poivre* that have gained popularity in recent years. These cheeses contrast with the older artisanally produced types, which are exclusively milk-based and do not have spices added to them.

In a series of verbal puns that combine the alimentary with the scatological, the narrator describes how the hero, Moon, continued culinary innovations in his speciality, rice dishes. In contrast to his travels, from the distant and international to the national and the local, Moon's culinary innovations work in reverse fashion as they move from the regional to the national, the international, and only then return to the local. These innovations are expressed in a series of verbal puns, which, depending on syllabic stress and liaison, may have two meanings. The audience learns first that Moon did not "*servir du riz noir/servir d' urinoir*" (serve black rice/use a urinal). Black rice, made with squid ink, is a Mediterranean dish prepared in the towns and villages of nearby Spanish Catalonia. Thus Moon maintained Gascon cultural authenticity by not serving a regional Catalan dish. At the same time his rejection of the civilizing object of the urinal aligned him with nature. In a move from the regional to the national, his serving of "*lotte-au-riz/loterie*" (monkfish with rice/lottery) became a national dish, a common event in mass culture. A move from the national to the truly universal was marked by his dish consisting of "*jambon de Laconne-riz/la connerie*" (Laconne ham and rice/stupid action). In a return to the scatological, Moon's combination of the pope's nose from the turkey and rice became "*cul-riz/cari*" (ass-rice/curry). And in a final return back to the local, Moon's best and simplest dish, a mix of rice and chopped mint, became "*menthe-riz/men-terie*" (mint rice/lie). Moon's best dish was a lie, like the very genre in which the narrator performs.

In addition to modifying traditional rice dishes, Moon adapted another native practice by his use of fresh mint leaves to brew tea, which resulted in "*thé-menteur/t'es menteur*" (tea with mint/you're a liar). Here the narrator draws upon the audience's knowledge that mint tea is associated with the North African cultures of Algeria, Morocco, and Tunisia.[22] Thus one distant Other, the Chinese man, who has become incorporated into cultural and alimentary space, appropriates the food of a different distant Other, the North Africans. The blame of appropriation, however, is placed on the latter when the narrator informs the audience that the Arabs stole two of these "Gascon" dishes in the course of their return southward after having been defeated by Martel in 732.[23] He goes on to note that they now sell back to French people Moon's "*thé-menteur*" as "*thé à la menthe*" (mint tea) and "*magret de canard*" (duck's breast), which through their linguistic reappropriation has become "*canard du Maghreb,*" or North African duck. The Arabs steal one item that is ethnically associated with them both now and historically—mint tea—and through verbal play appropriate another. By reselling stolen goods, they commit the ultimate moral travesty. However, at the same time there is a dig at postcolonial relations between the French and the North Africans. Through double entendre the Arabs can sell back "you're a liar" to the French as "mint tea."

Later, in another complex blending, this time of ethnicity and gender, the narrator explains that Moon married a local Gascon woman. Her name was Mi-Moon, a verbal pun that means "half" (as in a husband's other half, or wife) but also refers to the Algerian Olympic champion long-distance runner Alain Mimoun, who ran for France in the 1950s. So a Chinese man, who in reality is ethnically Korean, marries a Gascon woman, who in reality is an Algerian man. In partnership with this "wife," Moon opened a restaurant and tearoom and named it after the products that he used so often—Chinese tea, goats' milk, fresh mint, Camarguais rice—and the resulting "*Thé-lait menthe-riz/Télémenteries*" (tea-milk-mint-rice/lies on television) continues to this day. In the still-unspecified mythical past time of the tale, the hero, like Coluche, a popular French comedian of the 1970s and 1980s, opened up his restaurant to the poor.[24] In return for this hospitality, the poor were obliged, as were the travelers of days past, to tell a lie as part of getting a meal of mint rice, the main dish. The telling of lies in Moon's restaurant explains the origin of the Liars' Festival.

Although this narrative takes place in mythical and traditional cultural times, it constantly breaks with the past and refers to the present. In addition to temporal discontinuities, cultural ones—of the carnival and the village fête; of the mass media world of television and radio personalities; of local, national, and international groups and/or nations—find themselves juxtaposed in ludicrous ways within this and other Liars' Festival tales. The particular success of this narrative lies in its multiple pastiches: (1) the double meanings of the verbal puns; (2) the collapsing of performance and narrative boundaries as the teller exhorts his audience to fill in words or to cheer; (3) the disintegration of ethnic and genealogical boundaries so that a Chinese man can be the mythic ancestor of an entire Gascon village; (4) the imitation of two texts: the comic style and images of the comedian Coluche along with the kinds of verbal puns that lace France's most satirical newspaper, *Le Canard Enchaîné;* and (5) the appropriation of the festival's textual symbols of the goat and the lie, highly charged icons of Gascon identity.

In addition to the presence of advertising and mass media and the representation of various Others, a third element of postmodernism, the "schizophrenic" representation of time,[25] typifies many of the Moncrabeau Liars' Festival narratives. The schizophrenic refers to a breakdown in temporal continuity so that attention is focused on an ahistorical present while other time periods are juxtaposed in incongruous ways. In the Liars' Festival temporal anachronisms abound. The joining of two disparate elements from different times leads to humorous effect, as is common in other genres of popular literature such as folk recitations, and folk drama such as the puppet theater.[26] However, in the case of Moncrabeau, temporal anachronisms do not merely provide comic relief. The juxtaposition of various time periods also communicates complex ideological messages.

Joan of Arc Helps to Sell Firewood from Burgundy by Pretending to Burn at the Stake

One of the most telling narratives centers on a rewriting of Joan of Arc, a sacred French heroine from the distant fifteenth century. A national emblem, Joan of Arc is doubly displaced in the opening lines of the narrative. First, she is displaced spatially from her true region of origin,

Lorraine, to the Lot-et-Garonne, where the Liars' Festival is located, when the narrator observes that she really was from the Lot-et-Garonne. The second, temporal, displacement collapses time periods, sexuality, and technologies when the narrator identifies her as Jeanne d'Arc, known under the *"pseudo[nym]-minitel"* (pseudonym/a computerized data bank connected with the telephone and developed in France in the 1980s) as "Jeanne la Pucelle d'Orléans," or Joan the Virgin of Orléans. French history books frequently use the latter term; and in this instance such a characterization allows the male narrator to repeatedly frame the heroine in terms of her sexuality.[27]

In this narrative the figure of woman appears against the backdrop of national and regional conflict. Nationally, the conflict was between France and England during the Hundred Years' War when England attempted to extend its domain over an as-yet-ununified France. Regionally, the same conflict pitted the counts of Burgundy of eastern France against the counts of Armagnac of southwestern France. The former sided with the king of England, and the latter supported the king of France during the Hundred Years' War. The audience is told that Joan went to see the French king, Charles VII, to ask for a loan to expand her hog business—not to ask for an army to deliver the French from the English, as history tells us. With a loan at 20 percent interest in hand, she stopped off in Burgundy on her way back home. There she met up with some Burgundian businessmen who wanted to settle in Lot-et-Garonne in order to invest in the region and create a wood business. History gets rewritten here through the postmodern mechanism of "colonization"; the threat of military conquest and domination is transformed into a mere business transaction. The narrator continues by noting that a severe drought in 1430 (the year before Joan of Arc burned at the stake in true history), comparable to that of 1976, resulted in no crops and therefore no way of feeding the hogs. Joan, parenthetically referred to as "still a virgin" by the narrator, had to turn to something or someone else to save her business and keep up her loan payments. This situation evokes the possibility of prostitution. An outsider and a lone woman traveling without roots or family, Joan must overcome financial and emotional depression.

Rather than selling herself, however, Joan sold the image of herself. A national figure and canonized saint is rewritten here as a contemporary woman who sells things in a society of media and spectacle in which gender and sexuality are aligned with political economy. Joan collaborated with the historical enemy, the Burgundians, in a scheme: she agreed to sell her image in order to help sell the latter's product, firewood. In a broadcast spectacle, she would prove that a strong-willed and dynamic woman could resist the flames of the Burgundians' burning logs. The Burgundians sponsored the burning at the stake with the slogan "With Burgundian wood, you can smoke hogs." The subtexts read that woman (an insider who in historical reality is an outsider, albeit a national heroine) resists the flames of passion (from other outsiders, the Burgundians, historical enemies), and that Joan of Arc's body can be consumed and destroyed by the same fire that makes her animals' meat edible as smoked ham. The female heroine and the casting of fire and wood in sexual terms evoke two verses from Leonard Cohen's song "Joan of Arc."

> "well then fire, make your body cold
> I'm going to give you mine to hold"
> and saying this, she climbed inside
> to be his one, to be his only bride
>
> it was deep into his fiery heart
> he took the dust of Joan of Arc
> and then she clearly understood
> if he was fire, oh she must be wood.[28]

In the Cohen song, if fire is male and can consume his cold bride, then she is wood. In the narrative, however, both the fire (termed Satan's flames) and the wood (of Burgundian businessmen) are male. The song and the narrative reverse the mythic-folkloric image of man consumed by woman's devouring vagina and show woman consumed by man. Historical accounts portray Joan of Arc as an androgynous character, a woman who donned men's clothing not only for battle but also in prison as a means of signifying her spiritual resistance. Joan's refusal to disavow her perceived heretical stance was accompanied by her refusal to wear women's clothing.[29] This aspect is ignored by the narrator, who concentrates on the sexual identity of the presumed virgin.

In a further sexual desacralization of this national heroine, the speaker concludes for the first time that Jeanne la Pucelle, Joan the Virgin, was not what she appeared to be: realizing that she could not "resist the flames of Satan" when first put at the stake, Joan called on her friend Merlin, who replaced her with the latest model rubber latex dummy.[30] In a second sleight of hand, also effected by Merlin, she was placed back onto the stake after the dummy had burned. In his concluding remarks, the narrator comments that although she was a businesswoman, Jeanne was above all a woman, as she noted in her diary after these dramatic events: "I'm not what you think." By this double entendre, the narrator completes a second and final recasting on a sexual plane, with several ambiguous possibilities: "I'm not what you think" reads "I am a virgin" (despite the flames of passion)/"I'm not a virgin" (despite the repeated references to Joan as Jeanne la Pucelle throughout the narrative), or "I did burn at the stake" (historical "truth")/"I didn't burn at the stake" (instead, the female doll/dildo got screwed by male Burgundian fire).

The narrative draws upon the audience's familiarity with this historical figure. Central to its reception is the audience's profound identification with already acquired knowledge—which lends the text an extraordinary sense of déjà-vu and a peculiar familiarity—rather than involving any historiographic formation on the listeners' part.[31] Joan's burning at the stake is first recast as feigned resistance to intercourse, whereas recorded history tells a different version of a disfigured body, reminiscent of the tortured bodies of accused heretics depicted in medieval *diableries*. In a carnival-like spirit, where the highest are debased and the lowest are elevated,[32] Joan's holy image is desanctified as her whole body is consumed, literally by the fire and visually by the spectators' eyes. What is serious is made ludicrous, although in this case the audience knows the historical "truth," and so the tale can only be a lie.

In the preceding discussion I have focused on the complex kinds of ideological messages about ethnicity, gender, race, and the body that underscore many of the Moncrabeau Liars' Festival narratives. Following Jameson, we may note:

> In its emergent, strong form a genre is essentially a socio-symbolic message, or in other terms, that form is immanently and intrinsically an ideology in its own right. When such forms are reappropriated and refashioned in quite different social and cultural contexts, this message persists and must be functionally reckoned into the new form. . . . Folk dances are transformed into aristocratic forms like the minuet . . . [and] reappropriated for new ideological (and nationalizing) purposes in romantic music. . . . The ideology of the form itself, thus sedimented, persists into the later, more com-

plex structure as a generic message which coexists—either as a contradiction, or on the other hand, as a mediatory or harmonizing medium—with elements from later stages.[33]

In the Moncrabeau Liars' Festival, the genre of the tall tale and the presence of motifs of outrageous exaggeration or extraordinary occurrences indicate to the public that an "old" literary form is being used in a contemporary setting. The opposition between the forces of good and evil, reflected in ethnic pride and superiority over non-Gascon groups, provides a contemporary reframing as the narratives comment on cultural and economic relations with the near and the far. In this respect they appear as a variant of what Jean Franco qualifies as a master narrative of nationalism, which appeals to rootedness, place, and community, but which finds itself expressed here at the level of the region.[34]

The residual nature of the genre—the use of the tall tale to reflect messages of cultural, racial, or sexual domination—makes it appear even more anachronistic in the 1990s. Is this merely a reflection of the process described by Franco, whereby residual genres possess a contradictoriness of old and new discursive formations, old and new plots, and old and new proverbial wisdom? In the late twentieth century, amidst the loss of the regional language and other overtly regional emblems in southwestern France, a turn is effected toward national emblems or products such as Joan of Arc and Dannon Yogurt. Displaced back into the region, these figures maintain foreigners' and women's subordination within the narratives of the Liars' Festival.

By way of comparison, we may turn to Rayna Rapp's analysis of a summer fête held in Montagnac, a village in Haute Provence in southeastern France. The annual Montagnac fête pits the "outsiders," newcomers to the village and summer tourists, against "insiders," older residents and returned native children. The latter group, youth who have left the area to live and work elsewhere, continues to identify strongly with the village morally and culturally. These young people therefore communicate their renewed identity with the village by attempting to reactivate the traditional practice of the *quête,* or quest.[35] However, either because the young people do this outside the festive space and the communal solidarity generated by the fête, or because this archaic cultural practice has no meaning in the contemporary world, they go empty-handed. Yet, even if the *quête* fails, the "insiders" maintain their dominance in other ways: by progressively moving from contemporary music to older regional forms during the evening dances; by charging the temporary residents higher fees for game licenses, and by forcing new businesspeople, such as the café owners, to subsidize their excessive food consumption at the fête. In the Montagnac fête, conflicts of social class prevail, in contrast with the conflicts of ethnicity and gender that characterize the Moncrabeau Liars' Festival.

As communal events, both fêtes provide an arena in which to express and maintain difference. In the narratives of the Moncrabeau Liars' Festival, the themes of foreign commodification, xenophobia, sexuality, new technologies, and marginal histories insistently appear and reappear. Local experience is allegorized through pastiches and schizophrenic time in these telling and hilarious tales, which show how the "imagined community" of the nation is reimag(in)ed in accordance with the transnational realities of the postmodern era.[36]

Notes

The fieldwork on which this essay is based was supported in summer 1987 by a grant from the Pennsylvania State University's Institute for the Arts and Humanistic Studies. Nathalie Chevrin and Anne-Marie Barrère provided valuable cultural decoding and transcriptions of the 1984 and 1987 performances. I am grateful to Mary M. Crain for a wide-ranging preliminary discussion of this essay, which helped to frame it with respect to the literature on postmodernism. Pauline Greenhill, Joan Gross, Kristin Koptiuch, and Janet Roesler gave critical readings of later drafts. Monique Oyallon offered further insights into the role of Coluche in contemporary French popular culture and into the French puns. I also thank Diane Zabel and Lynne Stuart of the Reference Division of Pattee Library at Penn State, Joan Gilroy of the Dannon Company, and Janet Tauxe of Nestlé S.A. for information about the history of Dannon and Chambourcy yogurts.

1 Jean Baudrillard, "Modernity," *Canadian Journal of Political and Social Theory* 11 (1987): 69. On rural community, see Raymond Williams, "Dominant, Residual and Emergent," in *Marxism and Literature* (Oxford: Oxford University Press, 1977), 122.

2 Baudrillard, "Modernity"; Fredric Jameson, "Postmodernism and Consumer Society," in *The Anti-Aesthetic: Essays on Postmodern Culture,* ed. Hal Foster (Port Townsend, Wash.: Bay Press, 1983); and Jameson, "Postmodernism, or the Cultural Logic of Late Capitalism," *New Left Review* 146 (1984): 53–92.

3 Historically, like many other village votive fêtes, the Moncrabeau Liars' Festival was largely a celebration for the community itself. However, changes in the cultural and economic bases of these fêtes have shifted their calendar to the summer months in a move to cater to vacationing tourists. Like its counterparts throughout rural France, the Moncrabeau Liars' Festival appeals to both local people and outsiders (Daniel Fabre, *La Fête en Languedoc: Regards sur le Carnaval aujourd'hui* [Toulouse: Privat,

1980]). This is particularly evident in the displays of food items for sale. No resident from the village or nearby towns would ever buy from such stands because there is ample opportunity to obtain these local products from larger and more economical regional distribution points. The food stands are intended for the casual passer-by to the fête and to the region. For a discussion of the consequences of change in the economic and cultural base of a summer village fête, see Rayna Rapp's account for the village of Montagnac in Haute Provence, "Ritual of Reversion: On Fieldwork and Festivity in Haute Provence," *Critique of Anthropology* 6.2 (1986): 35–48.

4   In French, *une histoire salée* (salty story) refers to a dirty joke or narrative with licentious and scatological elements. It may also be termed *une histoire verte* (a green story) or *une histoire gauloise* (a story with Gaulish wit). This last term, the metonymical—the Gauls are the ancestors of the French—is displaced into the regional, as the Gascons are said to be experts at these stories. The Gascons inhabit southwestern France, in what was originally the province of Gascony. The term *histoire salée* is situated even more precisely in the village of Moncrabeau, which translates from Gascon as "Mountain of goats" into French. It is well known that goats like salt. The Moncrabeau Liars' Festival brochure therefore depicts a billy goat seated in the Liars' Armchair, licking the "salty" stone of truth, dated 1748, the presumed beginning of the festival. The literary representation of the Gascons as liars, as part of a larger series of stereotypes concerning people from the South of France, has yet to be systematically studied.

5   For an analysis of women's performances, see Vera Mark, "Women and Text in Gascon Tall Tales," *Journal of American Folklore* 398, 100 (1987): 504–27.

6   Mahadev L. Apte, *Humor and Laughter: An Anthropological Approach* (Ithaca: Cornell University Press, 1985); Sigmund Freud, *Jokes and Their Relation to the Unconscious,* trans. J. Strachey (London: Routledge, Kegan and Paul, 1960). The power of jokes to accomplish social ends is noted by Freud: "On a psychological plane, jokes and hostile aggressiveness exploit something ridiculous in our enemy which we could not bring forward openly or consciously" (103). Furthermore, jokes that denigrate are told most frequently in the *physical absence* of the individual/group under attack; see Gary Alan Fine, "Sociological Approaches to the Study of Humor," in *Handbook of Humor Research,* ed. Paul E. McGhee and Jeffrey H. Goldstein (New York: Springer-Verlag, 1983), 2:166. Although North Africans and East Asians form part of the contemporary French population and figure in the narratives as protagonists, they do not attend the Liars' Festival.

7   Colette Barbé, "La Littérature Populaire Gasconne dans les Almanachs Gersois de la fin du XIXe Siècle à 1940," 2 vols. (Ph.D. diss., Ecole des Hautes Etudes en Sciences Sociales, Paris, 1983); Dominique Blanc, "Lecture, écriture et identité locale: Les almanachs 'patois' en pays d'oc (1870–1940)," *Terrain* 5 (1985): 16–28.

8   Baudrillard, "Modernity," 64–65; Fredric Jameson, "Magical Narratives: On the Dialectical Use of Genre Criticism," in *The Political Unconscious: Narrative as a Socially Symbolic Act* (Ithaca: Cornell University Press, 1981), 103–50.

9   Jameson, "Postmodernism"; Margaret A. Rose, "Parody/Post-Modernism," *Poetics: International Review for the Theory of Literature* 17.1–2 (1988): 49–56. See also Charles Jencks, *Post-Modernism: The New Classicism in Art and Architecture* (New

York: Rizzoli, 1987), 13, 21; Tania Modleski, ed., *Studies in Entertainment: Critical Approaches to Mass Culture* (Bloomington: Indiana University Press, 1986).

10 Jameson, "Postmodernism," 67; Jencks, *Post-Modernism,* 338–40.

11 Baudrillard, "The Ecstasy of Communication," in *The Anti-Aesthetic: Essays on Post-modern Culture,* ed. Foster, 129.

12 Stith Thompson defines the genre of the *explanatory tale* as concerned with explaining the existence of some highly localized feature of a particular landscape. Also termed an etiological tale, Natursage, or *pourquoi* story, the genre focuses on the origins and characteristics of various elements of the natural world such as animals, plants, and the stars, and on people and their social institutions. Frequently this explanation seems to be the entire reason for the existence of the story, but more often than is usually recognized these explanations are merely added to a story to give an interesting ending; see Thompson, *The Folktale* (New York: Harper, Row and Winston, 1946), 19. In the context of the Moncrabeau Liars' Festival, the explanatory tale, a subgenre within the larger category of "lies," permits social comment on ethnic origins and/or on the new technologies and products of contemporary mass culture.

13 Jean Franco, "The Incorporation of Women: A Comparison of North American and Mexican Popular Narrative," in *Studies in Entertainment,* ed. Modleski, 119–38.

14 Jan Mukařovský, *Aesthetic Function: Norm and Value as Social Facts,* trans. M. E. Suino, Michigan Slavic Contributions, no. 3 (Ann Arbor: Michigan Slavic Publications, 1970), 21–22.

15 Craig Owens, "The Discourse of Others: Feminists and Postmodernism," in *The Anti-Aesthetic,* ed. Foster, 57–82; Judith Williamson, "Woman Is an Island: Femininity and Colonization," in *Studies in Entertainment,* ed. Modleski, 99.

16 The Danone yogurt company was founded by Isaac Carasso in Spain in 1917. He named the company after his son, Daniel, who later founded a related yogurt company in France. In 1942 Daniel Carasso emigrated to the United States, where he once again started his own yogurt company. Gervais is part of the French Danone yogurt company, and Chambourcy belongs to the Nestlé S.A. company headquartered in Vevey, Switzerland. Chambourcy is the name of a small market town in Normandy, France, which gave its name to the product and the company. Initially a regional company, Chambourcy was partially acquired by the brothers Jacques and André Benoît in the early 1960s, and next acquired partially by Nestlé in 1968. By 1978 Chambourcy was predominantly owned by Nestlé.

17 The Brossard cookie line, of Gringoire-Brossard, a French company, was recently acquired by Pillsbury, which is in turn part of Grand Metropolitan, a British company. Thus the locations and owners of these lines and companies change hands in multinational capitalism.

18 The irony is that foie gras is high in animal fat and very rich. A luxury item, it is consumed in small amounts at Christmas and New Year's meals and on festive occasions such as communion and wedding meals. It is a totally incongruous choice to aid digestion. *Avoir mal au foie,* or liver troubles, is a French expression used to account for malaises ranging from indigestion to depression.

19 Patricia Wells, *The Food Lover's Guide to France* (New York: Workman, 1987), 14–15.

20 Jameson, "Postmodernism," 64.

21 Peter Burke, *Popular Culture in Early Modern Europe* (New York: Harper Torchbooks, 1978), 40.

22 Ironically, in France and in North Africa, *thé à la menthe,* or mint tea, is made by first brewing *Chinese* green tea, heavily sugaring it, and then adding thick bunches of fresh mint leaves to steep in the infusion.

23 The year 732 is commonly referred to in French textbooks as a critical date in which European forces turned back the tide of the "Arab invasion" of western Europe, which got only as far north as southern Spain.

24 Coluche (stage name of Michel Colucci) was a comedian and an ascerbic commentator of contemporary political life on daily prime-time television and radio programs. He even campaigned for president in 1981. Coluche was particularly well known for his *histoires belges,* or Belgian stories, the French equivalent of American Polish jokes. In these narratives the slow-witted Belgians always lose out to the French or other nationalities. Other targets of his biting humor included politicians, the pope, the British royal family, the police, and the French themselves, particularly (but not exclusively) those in authority; see Richard Bernstein, "French Comedian with Political Bite," *New York Times,* January 16, 1986, 22. Coluche became even more famous when he opened a series of soup kitchens, named *les restaurants du coeur,* that offered free meals to unemployed people. The narrator refers to this fact in his recitation. Coluche's soup kitchens have continued to operate, with financial support from many French entertainment personalities, since the comedian's tragic death in a motorcycle accident in 1986.

25 Baudrillard, "The Ecstasy of Communication"; Jameson, "Postmodernism and Consumer Society."

26 Roger Renwick, " 'Till Apples Grow on an Orange Tree': Time in English Folk Poetry" (Paper presented at the panel on Time and History in Folk Poetry, American Folklore Society, Philadelphia, 1989); Joan E. Gross, "The Form and Function of Humor in the Liège Puppet Theater," in *Humor and Comedy in Puppetry,* ed. Dina Sherzer and Joel Sherzer (Bowling Green, Ohio: Bowling Green State University Popular Press, 1987).

27 The alignment of sexuality and technology present in the preceding narrative about the gear wheels and their Chinese inventor appears here in the image of the Minitel. A national videotex system created and operated by the French PTT (Postes, Téléphones et Télécommunications) and launched in 1981, the Minitel has transformed business and culture. In addition to providing information about cultural events and the current financial world, its Minitel rose is a personal ads service (like 900 numbers in the U.S., both for voice messages and for actually meeting people). The irony of being known through the Minitel, where people may indeed choose pseudonyms to meet partners, is underscored by Joan of Arc's code name, Joan the Virgin.

28 Leonard Cohen, "Joan of Arc," Columbia Records, 1970. My thanks go to Janet Roesler for bringing the Leonard Cohen song to my attention. A preliminary overview of Cohen's poetry and lyrics reveals a frequent use of the image of fire and of woman as lost lover. While it is not clear that the narrator of this tale is familiar with Cohen's "Joan of Arc," the ambivalent image of woman as virgin/harlot appears regularly in male narrators' jokes and narratives.

29 Marina Warner, *Joan of Arc: The Image of Female Heroism* (New York: Knopf, 1981), 117–58.

30   The rubber doll is an ambiguous object. It can be either a dildo or, following Gillo
     Dorfles's example of advertising kitsch, indeed a life-size doll and the object of male
     desire; see Dorfles, *Kitsch: The World of Bad Taste* (New York: Bell, 1968), 189. The ad-
     vertisement that Dorfles reproduces shows a leopard-skin bikini–clad woman with
     an hourglass figure and eyes demurely cast down, grasped at her left elbow by a
     tuxedo-clad man in top hat with a ready smile who positions her hand toward her
     left breast. Next to this picture the caption reads:
       A Sensation . : . at every fun-occasion! Life Size INSTANT PARTY DOLL SHE'S THE
       LIFE OF EVERY PARTY! . . . stands 5'5" tall, measures 40-20-40 . . . is instantly in-
       flatable and molded of sturdy flesh-like vinyl with lovely soft-skin finish. You'll
       think of a thousand uses for her at: the office—beach or pool—club—parties—
       conventions—parades—advertising displays—mannequin (plastic stand $10.00
       extra) guaranteed as advertised $69.95 includes postage and mailing anywhere in
       U.S.A. or A.P.O. address.
     In his discussion of the role of kitsch in advertising, Dorfles underscores "the impor-
     tance of the subliminal factor, linked to representations of a symbolic, crypto-sexual
     nature, often allied with evident kitsch connotations . . . in showing how certain as-
     pects of detached sexuality slip easily into bad taste; as in a verbal sense the same
     thing happens with double meanings, and lewd, more or less disguised words" (191).
31   Jameson, "Postmodernism," 70.
32   Mikhail Bakhtin, *Rabelais and His World,* trans. Helene Iswolsky (Bloomington: Indi-
     ana University Press, 1984), 347, 383.
33   Jameson, *The Political Unconscious,* 141.
34   Franco, "The Incorporation of Women," 134–35.
35   Rapp, "Ritual of Reversion."
36   Kristin Koptiuch provided this formulation.

Contributors

Nina Auerbach, author of such studies as *Woman and the Demon* (1982) and *Romantic Imprisonment* (1985), is John Welsh Centennial Professor at the University of Pennsylvania. Her books about Victorian theatricality include *Ellen Terry, Player in her Time* (1987) and *Private Theatricals: The Lives of the Victorians* (1990).

Thomas B. Byers is professor of English at the University of Louisville, where he teaches American literature, film, and interpretive theory. He is author of *What I Cannot Say: Self, Work, and World in Whitman, Stevens, and Merwin* (1989) as well as numerous essays on literature and culture.

Janice Carlisle is professor of English at Tulane University. She is the author of *John Stuart Mill and the Writing of Character* (Georgia, 1991) and has published articles on Victorian fiction and autobiography.

Jay Clayton is professor of English at Vanderbilt University. He is author of *Romantic Vision and the Novel* (1987) and *The Pleasures of Babel: Contemporary American Literature and Theory* (1993). He is coeditor of *Influence and Intertextuality in Literary History* (1991).

Marcel Cornis-Pope is professor of English at Virginia Commonwealth University. His publications include *Anatomy of the White Whale: A Poetics of the American Symbolic Romance* (1982), *Hermeneutic Desire and Critical Rewriting: Narrative Interpretation in the Wake of Poststructuralism* (1991, 1992), and numerous essays on contemporary literature and critical theory.

Mary Lou Emery is associate professor of English at the University of Iowa, where she teaches courses in the literature of the anglophone Caribbean and in modernist studies. Her book, *Jean Rhys at "World's End": Novels of Colonial and Sexual Exile,* appeared in 1990. She has also published essays on Wilson Harris and on Virginia Woolf.

Colleen Kennedy is assistant professor of English at the College of William and Mary. Her interests include feminist theory and contemporary fiction, and she has published articles on Kathy Acker and Maxine Hong Kingston.

Caroline McCracken-Flesher is assistant professor of English at the University of Wyoming; her research interests include the literary formulations of cultural marginalization, particularly in nineteenth-century Scotland, and cinematic renarrations of the novel. She has edited *Why the Novel Matters: A Postmodern Perplex* with Mark Spilka (1990) and published essays on, among others, Scott and Stevenson.

Vera Mark, an anthropologist, is assistant professor of French at Pennsylvania State University. She is interested in folklore and culture and has published articles on social identity, folk poetry, and folk narrative in a variety of journals.

Paul Morrison is associate professor of English at Brandeis University. He is the author of *Sexual Subjects,* forthcoming from Oxford University Press.

Ingeborg Majer O'Sickey is assistant professor of German at the State University of New York, Binghamton; her area of specialization is contemporary German literature, feminist theory, and film. She has published articles on German women's literature and popular culture.

John Carlos Rowe, professor of English at the University of California, Irvine, teaches the cultures of the United States and critical theory. He is the author of *Henry Adams and Henry James* (1976), *Through the Custom House* (1982), and *The Theoretical Dimensions of Henry James* (1984). *At Emerson's Tomb: The Politics of Literary Modernism in the United States* is forthcoming from Columbia University Press.

Daniel R. Schwarz is professor of English at Cornell University. He has published eight books, including *The Case for a Humanistic Poetics* (1991), *Reading Joyce's "Ulysses"* (1987, 1991), and *Narrative and Representation in the Poetry of Wallace Stevens* (1993). He has lectured widely and in 1992–93 held the Visiting Citizen's Chair at the University of Hawaii.

Carol Siegel is assistant professor of English at Washington State University, Vancouver. She is the author of *Lawrence among the Women: Wavering Boundaries in Women's Literary Traditions* (1991) and has published articles on Woolf, Mansfield, and Lawrence.

Felipe Smith is assistant professor of English at Tulane University, where he teaches African-American and American literature. He has written on John Dos Passos, F. Scott Fitzgerald, and Alice Walker.

Index